How My Mind Has Changed (or not)

A Theological Memoir

Nigel G. Wright

Copyright © Nigel G. Wright 2024

All Rights Reserved

No part of this publication may be reproduced, distributed, or transmitted in any form or by any means, including photocopying, recording, or other electronic or mechanical methods, without the author's prior written permission, except in the case of brief quotations embodied in critical reviews and certain other non-commercial uses permitted by copyright law. For permission requests, please get in touch with the author.

The Scripture quotations contained herein are from the New Revised Standard Version Bible, copyright © 1989, by the Division of Christian Education of the National Council of the Churches of Christ in the U.S.A., and are used by permission. All rights reserved.

Contents

Dedication i
Prelude 1
Post One: A Brief History of a Changing Mind 13
Post Two: The Bible as both Indispensable and Disreputable 36
Post Three: Interpretation – a Crucial Challenge 52
Post Four: Election and Predestination 61
Post Five: Universalism and the Human Condition 80
Post Six: Grace, Merit, and Atonement 95
Post Seven: The Resurrection and its Narratives 128
Post Eight. The Nature of 'Finality' 140
Post Nine: Hell and Damnation 158
Post Ten: God's Good Creation 166
Post Eleven: Christ and Incarnation 185
Post Twelve: Jesus, the Spirit, and the Church 206
Post Thirteen: Church – An 'Impossible Possibility' 225
Post Fourteen: Church, State, and Politics 235
Post Fifteen: Divine Judgement 255
Post Sixteen: World, Flesh, Devil 275
Post Seventeen: Wrestling with Demons 298
Post Eighteen: Realising the End 312
Post Nineteen: The God of Jesus Christ 322
Post Twenty: Faith, The Faith, and Other Faiths 340
Post Twenty-One: The Obedience of Faith 354
Post Twenty-Two: The Moral Vision 363
Post Twenty-Three: The Holy Spirit and Charismatic Renewal 391
Post Twenty-Four: Returning to Holy Scripture 409
Postlude 446
Publications 449

Dedication

In loving memory of

Judith Mary Wright

1st October 1949 – 5th January 2024

And with thanksgiving for our family

Jonathan and Louise, Charis, Miriam and Joel

Hannah and Ritchie

Asma and Anya

Prelude

Partway through his career, Karl Barth, arguably the foremost theologian of the twentieth century, wrote a book entitled *How I Changed My Mind.*[1] In it, he charted his theological development and the shifts in approach that he had considered necessary. Because of his stature and the increasing attention being given to his work, the book attracted considerable interest, so much so that it, in effect, created a new genre of theological literature, a disposition of other theologians to give an account of their own theological pilgrimage in a parallel fashion. Without in any way believing myself to be on the same level of sophistication as Professor Barth (to whom I owe much), in what follows, I intend to give a modest account of my own theological journey. I do so primarily to set in some kind of order the many disparate reflections that have come my way in the course of time, which I have yet failed to explore to my own satisfaction and which, by writing, I hope to advance to a state of greater (though certainly not final) clarity. Over several decades of teaching theology, it has been my practice to tackle subjects from several points of view, seeking to be fair to different positions. Fairly often, after what I have thought might be a balanced presentation, I have then been asked, 'But what do you think?'. It's a great question and has often required me to 'land' my own thoughts somewhere. In the

---

[1] ET edited by John D. Godsey (Edinburgh: St Andrew's Press, 1969).

present work, that is what I seek to do, to land my thoughts as best I can for my own satisfaction and perhaps that of others.

At this point, I have no great sense of an order in which thoughts will emerge nor of how long it might take to complete the task, if indeed it can ever be completed. Neither can I judge whether it will prove of interest to others than myself or whether it would ever evolve into a publication. I write without any greater motivation than the desire to understand where I have come to at the present advanced stage of my life, a stage at which, in various ways, I have sought to tie up loose ends. The words '(or not)' in the title are important to me as I consider myself a convergent rather than a divergent thinker. There is a certain genre of religious writing that intends to explain or describe the loss of faith, or at least the loss of a certain kind of faith. It also seems that the watching world tends to make more of those who depart from orthodox belief than those who stay the course, almost taking a perverse pleasure in disillusionment. I think of the immense interest shown in the 1960s in Bishop John Robinson's book *Honest to God*[2] in which he was thought to proclaim that 'our image of God must go'. I have also enjoyed reading the autobiographies of John Hick[3] and Richard Holloway,[4] even though feeling saddened in each case by their

---

[2] (London: SCM Press, 1963).
[3] *John Hick: An Autobiography* (Oxford: One World, 2002).
[4] *Leaving Alexandria, A Memoir of Faith and Doubt* (Edinburgh: Canongate Books Ltd, 2012).

inability to stay true to the faith with which they began. I firmly believe that I can empathise with and understand their urge to diverge, and by no means would I deny them their place in the kingdom of heaven. Persuaded as I am by the doctrine of justification by faith, I suspect that humility and honesty should be placed alongside it in importance. However, what follows is not of the loss of faith variety. It is a record of a continuing journey into faith rather than away from it, an arriving back at the place where I first began to know it, so to speak, for the first time. Although I may, from time to time, have been tempted to let go of the truth that is in Christ, that truth has never let go of me. So, though my mind has indeed changed, I would argue that I embraced a fuller and better understanding of the reality of God and of God's Christ into which I entered as a young person and fully intend to maintain until the end. It does not diverge from but converges on the goal of knowing Christ in whom the whole fullness of God was pleased to dwell.

The fact of change and development is a necessary part of any person's life. The one who does not grow and expand remains within a narrow and limiting perspective. This is true of everyone and of every branch of human understanding. *Fides quaerens intellectum*, faith-seeking understanding, is a standard theological posture. We search for an understanding of a faith into which we have already entered. To wait for a full understanding of anything before we commit ourselves is a recipe for an unliveable life. If we were to speak only of those things of which we have full understanding, the world would indeed be full of long, majestic silences. Again, this is true across the board: we live life before we come to understand it. We swim in the ocean of human existence before we find the words and concepts to define that existence and this is a lifelong, open-ended, and never-fully achieved enterprise. In philosophical or theological terms, the ontological will precede the epistemological; we will live within the reality of God before we gather the concepts and doctrines that we use to conceptualise the divine. Although the experience of divine realities is initially mediated through words and ideas, through proclamation if you will, these serve as an invitation and an introduction to an encounter with God, a fuller understanding of which can only unfold once it is embraced. There is that which must be known, however partially, to embrace faith, but thereafter, there is that which can only be known once faith has been embraced. Perhaps the clearest example of this is the fact of reconciliation with God. The Christian experiences what it means to be made one with God through Christ, his atoning death and resurrection mediated through the word proclaimed and sacraments enacted. Yet both Christ's death and resurrection remain profound mysteries, which means that things are not incomprehensible but so dense, meaning that they can never be exhausted by human thought. We will be contemplating their meaning for all time. Once they are reduced to a formula, as sometimes they regrettably are, our understanding becomes sterile and immature. The upshot of these things is that when we are first drawn to faith, we are, to use a phrase borrowed from a colleague, 'converted on a scrap', that is, attracted by some aspect of Christian faith that makes its appeal to us but yet remains only one part of an immense whole. It is only in further development that we begin to embrace the vast whole of the Christian vision. Though we may bemoan the limitations of our understanding at all points, we may celebrate the adventure of growing in faith and understanding.

To begin at the beginning then, while still a teenager, my life underwent a re-orientation when I experienced an undramatic but nonetheless enduring conversion. I could say that the light of Christ began to shine into my life and has gone on doing so ever since. Standard stories of Christian conversion, such as, for instance, in Puritan biography, often describe a protracted period of existential angst over one's inability to live a good life, of suffering under the 'law' that one proves unable to fulfil, followed by a marvellous relief in discovering Christ as the one who can save me from myself and has indeed done so in his life, death, and resurrection. In this way, assurance of salvation is obtained. I have immense respect for this narrative and, of course, recognise it in part and in whole. It does not, however, reflect my own initial experience. It is fully comprehensible against the background of a Christianised culture within which ideas of a divine moral law and a widely embraced image of God instilled by years of Christian tradition were taken for granted. British culture of the 1960s was well beyond such thoughts, although they were certainly in the background, probably unconsciously so for many. Mark Twain is reported to have said that the two most important days in a person's life are the day they were born and the day they realised why they were born. This was my experience. Conversion for me represented finding not just a purpose in life but also the purpose of life, a purpose that I could now articulate as knowing and loving God. The purpose of life then became *my* purpose in life, and this has made all the difference. It is interesting how some small moments in life can define all that is to follow – a small step becomes a giant leap. The 'scrap' that seemed to draw me was the promise of eternal life. This had little to do in my case with what might happen after death, less still just than with the idea of 'going to heaven'. It had everything to do with the promise of something bigger, of entry into the spiritual reality that is the knowledge of God, of becoming truly alive and more fully human. Although hesitant and uncertain to a degree, its impact on my life was marked. I became aware of a spiritual and moral change, of being 'born again'. It happened at a stage of my life where other decisive changes were also taking place – entry into the world of part-time work, a first student exchange to Germany that was to be highly influential academically and culturally, the beginning of A-level study and so on. I was at that point in transition into adulthood with a growing sense of personal identity, rootedness, and confidence. Yet the idea of 'picking up scraps' still rings true. We piece our understanding of faith together fragment by fragment until some coherent whole or worldview emerges.

Having been brought up in a family that had lost the habit of churchgoing, I was in a state of ignorance about the Bible or its meaning. I started to read from the beginning in order to fill the gap. I knew nothing. The Baptist congregation into which I was converted, baptised and received into membership was essentially in steady decline. Its members were God-fearing and kind but typical of many Baptist churches of the era in not holding to any clear doctrinal framework. This was not true of the recently appointed pastor, Rev Fred E. Finch, who leaned in the opposite direction. In time, this was to create tensions and to lead to a short pastorate. In my case, however, I was quickly introduced to some significant and formative doctrines that undoubtedly shaped the faith I was discovering. I try here to identify some of these. Foremost was a conservative evangelical approach to the Bible that, without being fundamentalist, prized the authority of the Bible and of teaching and preaching based firmly upon it. This was a mood and an approach rather than a set of formulations about the Bible, but it carried with it a defensive approach to some of the critical theories about authorship, composition, and the dating of various books. Fred was a mid-range Calvinist, which is to say that whereas the doctrine of election by grace through faith was a strong theme, there was no obvious mention that I can recall of the concepts of reprobation or double predestination (as I later learnt to call them). Along with this was a firm commitment to the concept of the wrath of God expressed not in a vengeful way but in an insistence that the doctrine of the love of God should not be limply expressed so as to subvert the reality that 'our God is a consuming fire' (Hebrews 12:29). God's love is holy love and resists as well as accepts sinners. Not surprisingly, this was associated with an understanding of atonement as both penal and substitutionary. I shall have things to say about these approaches in due time.

One of the things I appreciate about Fred in retrospect, and by which I believe myself to have been shaped, is that he was independent-minded. That is to say that although he certainly understood himself as a loyal conservative evangelical, he was not someone who simply toed the line. He had thought through his positions and expected others to do the same. He would have claimed that he was forced to do this when studying at Northern Baptist College, which was certainly more 'liberal' in its theological stance than he was (I am inclined to think it was less 'liberal' than he himself thought, but this requires some clearer understanding of what 'liberal' means). However, his doctrinal position was not unreflective, so I was encouraged to think things through for myself. Where he demonstrated this was in his espousal of the concept of 'conditional immortality', a rejection of the traditional understanding of the immortality of the soul and of hell as everlasting torment. These doctrines are staples of Protestant Reformed orthodoxy. He was bold to reject them primarily because neither was clearly attested in scripture, according to his reading of it, and a strong doctrine of normative biblical authority rakes priority over tradition, whether that tradition is Catholic or Protestant. I shall return to some of these early themes and shall, in time, set out how they re-emerge in my own thinking, albeit with some differences. However, I find a helpful illustration of how I have lived with them in some comments by T. H. L. Parker on Karl Barth's modified, 'neo-orthodox' doctrine of predestination and election. He likens Barth to a landscape gardener: 'We can now see that in his landscape gardening, Barth has transformed the scene from severity and even gloom into a place of joyfulness and light. He has brought about a miracle that even Capability Brown could not achieve – he has made the sun shine on the scene'.[5] This is how I regard my own changes of mind – by no means a rejection of the tradition but a reimagining of its major themes such that the continuity is maintained, but the goodness of the good news is accentuated.

I am not trying to be particularly systematic in this work, though it would be surprising if some kind of order in what follows fails to emerge.[6] Rather, the coming pages might more resemble an extended conversation, more with myself than with others, and so could seem somewhat erratic. To be fair, as I write, there will be different voices speaking in my mind and representing alternative

---

[5] Article 'Predestination' in Alan Richardson, editor, *A Dictionary of Christian Theology* (London: SCM Press, 1969), pp. 264-72, p. 272.

[6] I have attempted more systematic approaches in *The Radical Evangelical: Seeking a place to stand* (London: SPCK, 1996 and Eugene, Oregon: Wipf and Stock, 2016), and *Vital Truth: The Convictions of the Christian Community* (Eugene, Oregon: Wipf and Stock, 2015 and Cambridge: The Lutterworth Press, 2016).)

views that need to be engaged. Another way of expressing this is to say that what follows is 'associative' in that thoughts lead to others in a way that might not be rationally clear but could be emotionally connected. Alternatively, it may still resemble a blog, with the attendant untidiness, even though I have never gone in for blogging nor taken much interest in those who do. I am among those unfortunate people who are 'cursed' with the ability to see different points of view, and so I am sometimes unable to plough on regardless but need to pause. This could make me lack confidence in my own perceptions, but my hope is that I can be a person of firm conviction who, at the same time, retains an openness to other points of view. I once heard Bishop Lesslie Newbigin say, 'It is good to have an open mind, but not open at both ends at the same time'. Progress is made in intellectual development by sifting the things of which one is not sure by means of those of which one is confident. Like any life form, my intention has been to draw from the environment, intellectual or otherwise, that which enables me to be more truly what I am, and what I am, or seek to be, is a faithful Christ-centred Christian. To my mind, it is inevitable that any enterprise dealing with the divine mystery will have to contend with paradox, the clash of ideas in which the truth is not in one end or the other but somewhere in the tension between diverse thoughts. In Christian theology, this is certainly the case. It is accurate to call it 'dialectical' in a Hegelian kind of way, allowing ideas to sharpen ideas. Constantly, I find myself shifting from one leg to another when encountering colliding truths to find an appropriate balance. However, at times, the tension goes beyond even this and approaches 'cognitive dissonance', not making sense at all, putting the whole enterprise in crisis. How, for instance, do we reconcile belief in an infinitely good God with the sheer wretchedness of human experience? The wonder is that we persist in faith at all, like the concentration camp rabbinic court that, having found God criminally guilty of injustice, immediately adjourned to say evening prayers. Lest we think this is a solely religious problem, the same may be true of the convinced secular humanist who has to reconcile humanism with anti-humanism, the depravity of human actions with any belief in the 'basic goodness' of human beings.[7] That too, takes a leap of faith. The wonder is, on both counts that faith in the goodness of God, or of the goodness of humanity, insists on persisting against the apparent evidence. Something extraordinary is going on here.

As a guiding principle in setting out my theological stall, I wish to go beyond the quite proper concerns any thinker must have with the coherence of thought and with correspondence to reality to address the question of what it means to be a good person. What kind of person does my theology require me to be? And given that 'religion' is often implicated in the world's dehumanising tendencies, do some forms of theology achieve the opposite of what

---

[7] Sarah Bakewell, *Humanly Possible: Seven hundred years of humanist freethinking, enquiry and hope* (London: Chatto and Windus, 2023), p.21. '

they intend? Religion, apparently, is a perennial and integral human activity, universally present wherever human beings abound. This suggests, to the chagrin of the atheists, that it is not possible to be fully human without a religious dimension. But religion can be bad as well as good. So how do those of us who wish to be on the side of the angels ensure that we hold fast to that course? In the next section, I will give a brief overview of my own progressive attempts to stay true.

My last contribution to this prelude comes as I am preparing the final text for publication. Two things strike me. The first is the amount of space I have devoted to questions of salvation, personal and cosmic. This does not surprise me, given that I have spent most of my life as a minister of the Gospel seeking to see people reconciled to God. The second I find embarrassing, and that is the amount of repetition I engage in when discussing those themes. This is not good style, and I believe it to derive from the fact that what I have written has been over a number of years. I have thought of removing some of that material, Post Nine in particular, but have also been concerned not to lose other material in the process. I can only say that I am not a perfectionist and so leave things as they are. I hope however that readers will prove patient.

Post One: A Brief History of a Changing Mind

Let it be said that in teaching theology, I have often observed a certain kind of pilgrimage that proceeds from *absolutism* through *relativism* to *conviction*. I view this as a necessary journey, but some sadly get stuck along the way. Students often begin with the kind of clarity and certainty characteristic of youthful discovery or of the new convert, even a form of cockiness. This is undermined as they encounter new patterns of thought, some of which are felt to be threatening to the assumptions with which they have begun. This can lead to relativism, in which people are not certain which to believe in the variety of options open to them. Yet beyond this is a place of conviction where having cut through the undergrowth, they achieve not a new *certainty* but a new *confidence* in the convictions with which they emerge. They may feel those convictions are not absolute; after all, they are shot through with fallibilism, which is the human lot. But they may be securely held and joyfully proclaimed. I rather like the word 'probably'! I suggest this journey of understanding is not unique to theology but to all branches of knowledge, each in its own way. Humility is entirely appropriate.

Concepts have always been important to me, and I am attracted to the study of the 'history of ideas'. Theology fits well within this milieu since it is both entangled with the wider currents of human thought and in turn influences them. From the beginning of my theological journey, I have shown an interest in finding 'a place to stand', which is an overall perspective from which to view the theological landscape, interpret the scriptures, and engage in strategic action. I have detailed the fact that *conservative evangelicalism* is the context within which I came to faith. Although often seen as an alternative term for 'fundamentalism', I deny that this is the case. To be fair, this latter term as an '-ism' has gathered a meaning to itself for inflexible, literalist and frozen categories of belief and has also come to be applied to ideological belief systems beyond the religious that lack self-criticism and nuance, including fundamentalist atheism; this is fair enough to my mind. Yet, in so far as the term includes those who are committed to certain fundamental beliefs, I can embrace the term since I most certainly am. The point is sometimes made that this, rather than literalism, was the original intention of those who, in reaction to 'modernism' published early in the twentieth century the pamphlets known as *The Fundamentals,* some of whom were by no means fundamentalist in the newer sense. I have never been a self-defining fundamentalist and have never been entirely comfortable with conservative evangelicalism, though I acknowledge a debt to it, even if this is in distinguishing myself from it. One of its strengths is its power to convert, a power that is conspicuously lacking in more liberal forms of the faith, and to my mind, this is significant since I harbour the prejudice that theologies that lack the power to convert are parasitic on those that achieve it. Early on, my preferred designation came to be *radical evangelicalism*,[8] and the streams that fed into it included the theology of Karl Barth, the charismatic movement and Anabaptism. Barth remained a thoroughly orthodox theologian but managed to refashion the tradition in ways I found entirely credible. He upheld the authority of the Word of God but had no time for the theory of inerrancy. His rejection of the latter led to a long-time suspicion of his work from conservatives for whom the doctrine was a supposed touchstone of orthodoxy and still is. As the essential content of his theology became more obvious, the trend to regard him as a powerful friend rather than an enemy gathered pace. For me, the Christo-centrism and trinitarian shape of this theology were and are crucial. My embracing of charismatic renewal, though never uncritical, offered new perspectives on the place of the New Testament as the guiding norm for the life of the church and opened my eyes to the fact that whatever the claims of conservative evangelicalism, it did in effect value a tradition of interpretation above the authority of scripture itself. It blunted the freedom of scripture to speak afresh to our situation. And, very importantly, my discovery of historic Anabaptism opened a source of renewal and pointed to an alternative way of being evangelical, one that had the potential for how the church is the church and how such a church relates to the powers that govern society and that we may in brief call 'the state'. I think my written theological output carries the imprint of these ideas relatively consistently. The confluence of

---

[8] *The Radical Evangelical: Seeking a Place to Stand* (London: SPCK, 1986).

Barthian theology and Anabaptism, though undoubtedly counter-intuitive and one that might puzzle him, was most resonant in the Christ-centredness of both. In Barth, this was carried out most conspicuously, with the insistence that all theological thinking must pass through Christ. The greatest fruit of this was the reconfiguring of the doctrine of election that transformed it into good news rather than bad. The emphasis in Anabaptism on *Nachfolge Christi*, following Christ in life, seemed to me a healthful complement to this, and one that refocussed biblical interpretation on the Gospels rather than Paul (not that I regard Paul as in any way a departure from the Gospels). Whereas conservative evangelicalism concerned itself with 'boundary issues' such as doctrines of penal substitution and eternal conscious torment and found importance in questions such as the authorship of the Pentateuch, the unity of Isaiah, the historicity of Jonah and an early date for Daniel, I could happily sit loose to these and accommodate much of critical scholarship. I defined myself, therefore, as a 'radical evangelical' and still do, notwithstanding some tensions that derive from this when ministering in churches and in a denomination in which many have been conservative evangelicals and some even fundamentalists, consciously or otherwise. Since I hold firmly to the heart of the gospel, and this is evident to all, I hope this has not been so great a problem as might first appear.

Having defined myself as a 'convergent' rather than 'divergent' thinker, I have no great difficulty in adding to the 'radical' category that of *catholic evangelical*, notably with a small 'c'. This might seem odd if one assumes that those in the radical mode are somehow obliged to reject or diverge from the 'Great Tradition' of mainstream Christianity. Perhaps those who see themselves in some radical camp or other can be separated into those who desire to distance themselves from the mainstream on the one hand and those who want to maintain as much continuity with it as possible on the other. When it comes to church-state issues, I am in the first of the tendencies, but when it comes to fundamental doctrine, I remain firmly in the mainstream. I very much welcome the notion of 'generous orthodoxy' in which the fundamental and catholic doctrines, indeed dogmas, of the faith are confidently affirmed whilst being presented in their most affirming and inclusive light. In my first theological studies, I gave myself (I don't remember being formally instructed by others) a firm grounding in early Christian doctrine and specifically in the intellectual struggles that led to the formulations of the divinity of Christ, the 'consubstantiality' or 'homoousion' of the Spirit with the Father and the Son, and so the doctrine of the Holy Trinity. While I recognised that to bring these realities to expression required the adaptation of language not found as such in the New Testament, it was clear to me that such language was the helpful servant of the structure of the New Testament, indeed biblical thought, in being faithful to God's self-revelation. Christians experience and know God as Father, Son and Spirit and believe that God's self-revelation in time is true to God's own being in eternity. My thinking followed that of the early church in concluding that in God's own being, there is an inescapable Threeness. Precisely because this vision of God is deeply radical, it harmonised with my placing of myself in the radical tradition of church life, one that is sometimes described as 'Orthodox Dissent', as distinct from the heterodox dissent of Unitarianism. I have more to say about this below, but a primary outcome for me is an ecumenical one: whatever the alternative ways of 'being church', I am content to recognise the church as church wherever there is the essential core of Christian experience and belief that is set out in the doctrine of the Trinity. If one of the roles of doctrine is to safeguard the authentic content of Christian faith, the Trinity provides that protection. And to confess that God in Christ came among us and continues so to be through the Spirit can be described as 'dogma'; in other words, these are the beliefs without which the church would cease to be the church. Whichever Christian beliefs may be thought of as 'negotiable' that is debated and disagreed over without forfeiting the status either of 'Christian' or 'church', these core doctrines are not; although fair enough, their exact formulation might be a matter of continuing discussion.

So, I come, not illogically, I think, to a place to stand that occupies my current attention. I confess that this has become clearer to me as I have worked on this present project. It is further to define myself as an *evangelical humanist*. The 'h' word might seem risky as, like other words, what it is taken to mean depends on whose mouth it has been in previously. As it happens, the word has an honourable list of associations. Its concerns are usually traced to the Renaissance, though it could go back to the Greeks, at which point a flood of literature from the ancient world, largely preserved in Islamic culture and language, entered the Western mainstream and prompted a new interest in the study of humankind as distinct from the study of religion (not that the two can ultimately be separated). It would be a mistake to see this as an anti-religious impulse, more a broadening of the fields of human inquiry. In that spirit, the Renaissance was a preparation for the Reformation in that the early Reformers, such as Calvin and Zwingli, count as humanists whose instincts and scholarship were to reach beyond the authoritative dictates of the Roman church and to test them against the sources of the Christian faith in the scriptures and the early church. This return to the sources was the impulse for reformation, as invariably proves the case. I have long thought that there is a need for a renewal of Christian humanism to counteract what I can only describe as the misanthropic tendencies of *some* formulations of Christian doctrine. As this is an outrageous statement I do need to justify it, not least to myself. In addition, I further need to elaborate on the concept of 'evangelical humanism'.

Christians have the most pronounced reasons for affirming the value of human beings, both male and female. The idea that together they are made 'in the image of God' is set out at the beginning of the Hebrew Bible in Genesis 1. Whereas this concept is clearly related to the origins of human beings and is a statement of what humans were and are, it should also be read in an eschatological light as, to my mind, should be the case with the whole of that chapter: it is concerned with what we are to become as well as what we intrinsically are. We are to become the image of God in truth, and the fact that we are repeatedly being diverted from this is the tragedy and catastrophe of the human story. Intrinsically, there is a dignity to being human and the recognition of this is one of the great gifts of the Christian faith and of Judaism to the world. For Christians, this can only be intensified beyond measure by the belief that God was in Christ, that the Word became flesh, that God in the person of his own Son has been among us, living our life, sharing our mortality, and triumphantly negotiating on our behalf what it means to be human. Christ is both the divine way of being human and the human way of being divine; as such, he is not only a real human being but also the true human being, the 'last Adam', or Ultimate Human Being, and embodies the hope that we may be 'conformed to his image'. This surely is the ultimate humanism and casts its light on the whole of our existence, both revealing what we can be and exposing what we, in fact, are. Doctrinally, it is the ground for proper theological anthropology, which is a massive but realistic estimation of human value.

This perspective is under attack both externally and internally. External attacks come when the image of God, human value and importance are caricatured as a kind of licence to exploit rather than nurture creation as if only human beings count, and everything else is bent to serve their interests. I reject this as an irresponsible slur on a noble doctrine. Yet internally, the churches subvert their own doctrine by failing to do it justice. It is absolutely the case that any doctrine of human goodness is immediately qualified by the assertion of radical fallenness. This is a clear case of the kind of 'cognitive dissonance' to which I have referred and the need to shift from one leg to the other in seeking the truth. In doing so, there is a severe risk of misanthropy and swallowing up the positive in the negative. It has been pointed out that in the development of theology, a contrast, perhaps even a contest, emerged between affirming God's fatherly mercy or God's majesty as judge and that at the head of Western theology, Augustine chose to pursue the latter course. In one of the (to me) more luminous passages of Paul Tillich, he argues the tension between understanding God as Lord and God as Father. The first indicates God as 'holy power' and the second as 'holy love': the two have to be understood together if the distortion of God as destroyer is not to prevail on the one hand or as a 'friendly' father who gives what men want him to give on the other.[9] I find truth in this and fear that theology can fall unhelpfully on one side or the other, with 'conservatives' stressing one and 'liberals' the other, the balance not being easy to maintain. Yet, for my current purposes, much theology, both in the Catholic and Protestant

---

[9] Tillich, *Systematic Theology, Volume 1* (Welwyn, Herts: James Nesbit and Co. Ltd, 19??), pp.318-20.

traditions may have majored on fear and negation of our humanity. Augustine's assertion that human beings are 'worthless lumps of perdition' surely begets a form of self-loathing and self-hatred – and possibly mutual loathing that is hard to welcome. It gives rise to doctrines that are excessively negative and can be found in both Catholic and Protestant formulations, not least where they take their cue from Augustine. Here, I state my reservations about some of them, though bearing in mind that it is particular formulations of those doctrines to which I object rather than what I consider their essential truths.

I begin with the doctrine of original sin, which raises large objections both inside and outside the church. I shall set out in due course what I consider to be the proper place of such a doctrine. However, the formulation to which I object runs along the following lines: When Adam and Eve first sinned, the whole of subsequent humanity was involved in their actions, as if they were in the 'loins' of both. They not only represent humanity, therefore, but *are* humanity in the sense that we have all sinned in them: in Adam, all die. We are born spiritually dead and inherit their guilt since it is also our guilt. Before a righteous God, we do not stand a chance but are helpless sinners who are, by nature, children of wrath destined for hell unless this course is somehow interrupted. In Catholic tradition, this situation is alleviated, with some echoes in some forms of Protestantism, by infant baptism that is deemed to wash away the taint of original sin and so secure an infant's salvation.

Unbaptised infants, however, cannot be granted this assurance since they die guilty. The sheer severity of such a judgement has not gone unnoticed and has been catered for by inventing the category of 'limbo' by which otherwise innocent though unbaptised infants pass into a state of suspension that is neither heaven nor hell. It should be noted that this doctrine, for which there is no warrant in scripture, has now been officially rejected. It is hard to square with the ways in which Jesus welcomed little children and blessed them, passages in which there is no implication that he also baptised them, and in which God's accepting kindness is plainly revealed in the Son of God. Protestants generally replace infant baptism in this scheme of thought with the role of faith as the means of salvation but then have the question about how small children, billions of whom have died before attaining maturity or faith, stand before God. Suffice it to say that whatever truths are concealed here, the doctrines as described above are unnecessarily dark. They give rise to a religion of fear rather than of hopeful benevolence and can fairly be described as cruel. They portray God not as one who loves creation, wills to save it and will indeed do so, but who is repelled by it and takes no pleasure in the works of his hands. In contrast, my firm belief is that there is a wideness in God's mercy. Jesus took pleasure in welcoming children, insisting that they should come to him, laying his hands on them, and blessing them. This is God at work.

Yet, can we genuinely say that God takes pleasure in humanity, given the depravity that cannot be denied? Do we still have dignity despite it all? Instinctively, I want to say yes, but there are hurdles to overcome. How about, 'And without faith, it is impossible to please God' (Hebrews 11:6) or Genesis 6:5: 'The LORD saw that the wickedness of humankind was great in the earth and that every inclination of the thoughts of their hearts was only evil continually. And the LORD was sorry that he had made humankind on the earth, and it grieved him to his heart. There's not much to go on here and other verses could be added. There's another side, of course: 'For the LORD takes pleasure in his people; he adorns the humble with victory (Psalm 149:4). But even here, it is not clear that this can be said about humanity as a whole or simply those who count as 'his people'. In short, it may be the case that God loves us, but is there anything about us that God likes? We are back to cognitive dissonance and the tension between a God who is Lord and at the same time, a kind and merciful Father.

Let me say here that though a religion of fear is not a good basis for a wholesome faith, there is that which is to be feared. If it is a 'fearful thing to fall into the hands of the living God' (Hebrews 10:31), it is infinitely more fearful to fall out of those hands. I certainly fear this and suggest others should do the same, as I would fear forfeiting the love and acceptance of those I most care for. Some fears are entirely reasonable, and we all have them. However, the best and the highest virtues and realities are only achieved through love and are the responses to the kindness and compassion that come to us from beyond ourselves. For the Christian faith to be presented as supremely a manifestation of God's grace and goodness into which we can be drawn should be the intent of all theology and preaching. Even so, love is not complacent about the sin and evil that are its contradiction, and it does not pretend that they do not exist. But it is of supreme importance that the recognition of a dark side to human beings and their history, 'anti-humanism', and the despair that all of us sometimes feel about the world they create should not lead us into misanthropy. This is not only a temptation for serious Christians who have a high view of the human vocation. I find it also in those who turn away in disgust from humanity to embrace the animal creation that is so often victimised by humans. It is not only believers who find other human beings more problematic than other creatures.

Alongside human depravity, an evangelical humanist will set human dignity. There is that about us that is worthy of praise. This is to be seen in the magnificent achievements of the race in so many parts of our cultural existence. Surely, these things are not destined to perish, but in the new Jerusalem, 'People will bring into it the glory and the honour of the nations' (Revelation 21:26). Yet it is not only the elite achievements that I find inspiring in my fellow humans. Every day, I am confronted by acts of kindness and sympathy, of cooperation and mutual service that restore my respect for people. I find it in the interactions between children and parents, the tenderness that is on display towards those advanced in life, and the care that is shown by parents, most of all, to children who are born into the world damaged and disadvantaged. These are intimations of the continuing goodness of people. We may be fallen, but we are fallen human beings, not devils. I cannot believe that God is indifferent towards these things. There is a school of thought that suggests God be so utterly different from us that it is useless to ascribe typical notions of right and wrong to God. God alone knows where this might lead us. I take comfort from the fact that this was not the way of Christ: 'If you then, who are evil, know how to give good gifts to your children, how much more will your Father in heaven give good things to those who ask him! (Matthew 7:11). Here, Jesus employs a characteristic Jewish argument 'from the lesser to the greater'. He indicates that there are limited but real human emotions that may be magnified beyond measure to describe God's own self. Whatever inklings of goodness are found in us may be increased beyond measure in the heart of God. God loves us, feels for us, and celebrates the good in us while lamenting the wrong. This is not a doctrine of human merit but a confidence that despite our demerits, there is something in us worth redeeming. Believing firmly in the priority of God's grace and that all good things come from God, I go on to say that the love of God not only recognises this *but has created it in the first place*. God has not abandoned us. Life is graced. Human life is graced. This is evangelical humanism.

I continue this section by suggesting that there are two ways we might think about this redeeming work of God. One way is to focus on humanity in its lostness and self-destruction and to hope for the salvation of as many as possible. This is sometimes expressed in the idea of a 'brand plucked from the fire' (the language, though not necessarily the meaning, is from Zechariah 3:2). Here is the idea that the house is burning and so will soon be destroyed, though some (few) may be snatched from it. All is lost, but some of us may be extracted by God's grace. An alternative view is that the world has already been saved. Christ has done what is necessary for the cross, resurrection and ascension to bring about a new creation (2 Corinthians 5:16): the old has gone and the new has come with universal impact. 'From now on, therefore, we regard no one from a human point of view'. We see people differently when Christ becomes our horizon. In the first perspective, everything is lost until it is saved. In the second, all are saved until they exclude themselves from salvation. All are Christians 'in hope'; so, the world is not divided into Christians and non-Christians but Christians and not-yet-Christians. At the least, this is quite a helpful, perhaps less gloomy way of looking at things. Christians are those who know what has happened, who have been enlightened as to the salvation that Christ has come into the world and have entered the new creation. But all may enter in. Even those who resist may yet have a great future before them in Christ. The duality of thought I suggest here might be reflected in a further consideration: A typical evangelical and Protestant anthropology places a primary stress on 'Man in Revolt' (Emil Brunner) and so characterises sin as active rebellion against God, a shaking of the fist at the Creator. The primacy of this image is already under criticism from feminist perspectives when it is objected that for women, it is not revolt but lack of assertiveness that is the sin, the internalisation of subservience with consequent loss of humanity. To take this further, I am deeply aware that for multitudes of human beings, there is little room for revolt. Much as I hate to revert to 'victimology', so many are, in fact, victims and not just of political or cultural oppression. Children who are born disadvantaged by reason of cruel disabilities or who are mistreated, abused, and even killed by those who should have the care of them. And those who don't stand a chance in life surely cry out for divine compassion rather than judgment. Within any 'scheme' of salvation, there must be a place for vindication, compensation, or divine restoration to set aside the condign punishment of the perpetrators of their sufferings. Judgement is not only to do with accountability but reversal, putting right life's inequities, healing the broken and the broken-hearted. I am not sure my own tradition has maintained this balance consistently.

I draw a connection here between what are reputed to be the distinctive differences between Eastern and Western traditions of theology when it comes to salvation. The claim is that the West has focussed on legal categories of guilt and accountability, of retribution and punishment. This is confirmed to my mind when much evangelistic preaching first tries to persuade 'sinners' of guilt, especially in transgressing law, so that it may then offer forgiveness and acceptance through the atonement. By contrast, in the East, the stress has been on 'deification' or 'be-godding', that is, restoration of the divine image by enabling communion with God's participation in the divine nature. Christ participates in our lives so that we may participate in God's and be healed of our sins and lostness. I have no wish to choose between these emphases, but I have come to find more potential in the latter. All of God's work is directed at healing a wounded creation. I find beauty and humanity in this.

While continuing to be a radical and catholic evangelical, I find value in also naming myself an evangelical humanist. The humanism here is not free-standing or self-originating but derives from the 'evangel', the good news of God's salvation in Jesus Christ, the 'last Adam' (1 Corinthians 15:45), the 'ultimate human being'. This enhances my ability to appreciate not only the dignity of humankind but also the winsomeness and decency I find among ordinary, 'bog-standard' people, among whom I gladly count myself one. There will be those who find the 'humanist' term problematic because 'secular humanism' is often set up as the enemy we need to oppose. I would sooner subvert it. Secular humanists who see religious faith as their enemy seem to imagine that if only we could eradicate religion, we would automatically be left with an obvious secular humanist residue. This is to neglect the fact that secular humanism itself is the product of many centuries of Christian intellectual and moral formation. Both the words 'secular' and 'humanism' have Christian pedigrees and putting the words together only accentuates their indebtedness to the Christian tradition.[10] I see both delusion and opportunity here: delusion in imagining that once a Christian doctrinal basis is rejected humane values can still be upheld and opportunity in that nurturing a common humanism across the spectrum of Christian, other-religious and non-religious ideologies might provide coherence for our pluralistic and diverse society, a place where we might meet and agree.

Having expatiated on 'a place to stand' and ascribed to myself various labels, I am inclined here to identify a label I do not wish to claim, and that is 'liberal evangelical'. I have read some suggestions that this may be where I am heading, but I do not see this. The adjective 'liberal' is a bit too problematic. I would gladly embrace some of its shades of meaning. When it is taken to mean 'generous' or 'willing to give freely', I gladly embrace it. Equally, I aspire to be liberal in the sense of being 'open-minded', 'willing to respect opinions different from my own', and 'favourable to or respectful of individual rights and freedoms'. These are all standard understandings and I regard them as positive qualities. I also cannot avoid their usage as comparatives since all of us are relatively more liberal or more conservative on certain issues or preferences, and why not? But in my mind, there is 'good liberalism' and 'bad liberalism'. As a nonconformist or dissenting Christian, I certainly embrace the former when it comes to freedom of conscience and

---

[10] Note the case for this in Theo Hobson, *God Created Humanism: The Christian basis of secular values* (London: SPCK, 2017).

belief since I regard compulsory religion or coerced acts as being insincere and defective, not a manifestation of true devotion. But I do not endorse an absolute rather than relative use of the term when it denotes a set of doctrines that deviate from orthodox Christian belief, such as rejection of the Trinity, or the atonement, or the divinity of Christ in the manner of 'Liberal Protestantism'. To my mind, this is 'bad liberalism', the reduction of Christian faith to a form of religious humanism that has neither the power to convert nor to transform. I am too 'evangelical' to be 'liberal' in this sense and so while embracing some of the word's possible meanings and certainly celebrating God's overwhelming generosity (Romans 8:32, 2 Corinthians 9:15), I decisively reject others. I view with suspicion the tendency in my own denomination to celebrate the values of 'good liberalism' while neglecting the prior theological doctrines out of which they have emerged. Unlike previous generations, the tendency now is not to reject or openly decry those doctrines (as did Liberal Protestantism) but simply to neglect them. To my mind, you cannot have the entailments without the theological convictions that precede them.

Some aspects of secular humanism are also distasteful to me. It is a common trope in such circles to caricature religious faith as holding to a defective morality. So, the religiously minded have a morality based upon the fear of going to hell or on unreflective obedience to commands rather than a love of goodness for its own sake and beauty. It is a noticeable feature of popular literature that the religious are often presented as shrunken, constricted individuals, whereas those who are without such convictions are morally superior and unprejudiced precisely because they lack them. Similarly, the secular like to think of themselves as 'freethinkers' because they are untrammelled by 'dogma' or tradition and rely solely on autonomous 'reason'. Whatever the past may have held, my contention would be that in the face of the 'illiberal liberalism' of much contemporary culture, it is people holding to a transcendent faith who are more truly free to critique that culture and where necessary, stand apart from it. The price for this is undoubtedly to be labelled 'controversial' and to be thought strange. To my mind, this is good, yet it is a subversive vocation that is to be pursued intelligently and graciously and not as a bid for dominance and power over others. To do otherwise is not to pursue *Christianity* but *Christianism*.

This next section serves as a bridge into what follows and might be considered a keynote.

Perhaps the largest shift in my own thinking compared with the evangelical culture into which I was (not unwillingly) incorporated in my youth concerns the scope of salvation. To say it again, there is a wideness in God's mercy. In short, 'salvation' in much evangelical religion has been largely concerned with 'going to heaven when you die'. In retrospect, I regard this restricted vision as surprising since the biblical perspective is so much broader and evangelicals consider themselves bound to scripture. Now, when I die, I certainly hope to share in the life of the age to come or, in Paul's words, to be present with the Lord once I am absent from the body (2 Corinthians 5:8). Yet I have come to see, precisely by studying the Bible supposedly so concerned with the salvation of the soul, that salvation is far more than this. In fact, the term 'going to heaven' is markedly absent from the New Testament. Somehow, however, it has come to be a primary focus of popular evangelical thinking such that the burning issue when discussing the fate of others, say in discussions of the 'unsaved' or children who die in infancy or those who have never heard the gospel, is whether they will 'go to heaven' when they die. Frankly, it is assumed that they will not unless they make a conscious commitment to Christ within their own lifetime and that death is the point of finality beyond which hope must be abandoned. For all that I fully believe that outside Christ, people are in some sense of the word 'lost' and need, as did I, to turn to Christ and confess him as Lord to be 'found' the questions abound. There is an inherent dualism involved in the assumption that 'going to heaven' means an escape from our embodied existence into a heavenly realm, and this, in turn, depends upon the idea that our present world and everything in it is fated to pass away and to be destroyed. Granted, there are biblical texts that seem (on first and superficial reading) to imply this. Yet it leads to the assumption that all that really matters to God in our present world with its mineral, animal, human and communal levels of existence is the disembodied human soul. The rest of creation is the waste product of our salvation. Despite this story being deeply ingrained in the popular evangelical imagination, a proper reading of scripture offers a quite different picture. Human beings require bodies and the biblical hope points to the resurrection of the body, but not of our present 'flesh', rather than simply the survival of the immortal soul. Moreover, bodies require contexts in which to be embodied and so the hope is held out of a renewed heaven and earth in which righteousness dwells (2 Peter 3:11-13). I suggest here that the language of purging with fire, found in these texts, points to precisely that – the purging of the present creation from everything that contradicts the will and character of God so that it might be renewed and glorified as the dwelling place of God, as envisioned in Romans 8, Colossians 1 and Revelation 21. The apostle fall was very fond of the term 'all things', and I can find no greater vision in his writings than Ephesians 1:8-10: 'With all wisdom and insight he has made known to us the mystery of his will, according to his good pleasure that he set forth in Christ, as a plan for the fullness of time, to gather up all things in him, things in heaven and things on the earth'. Furthermore, when in Revelation 20 God is said to proclaim, 'Behold I make all things new!', it is hard or impossible to make 'all things' mean anything less than 'all things': human, animal, vegetable, mineral. This surely means God will make not 'all new things' but all things new'. Even beyond this, 'all things' must be held to mean not only all those things that are likely to exist at the time of the end, whenever that might be, but all things that have ever existed in space and in time, a retroactive healing of the whole sometimes tragic story of creation itself. Granted that this is an utterly outrageous vision, and its credibility can readily be contested, I am persuaded that it is nonetheless that to which the biblical revelation points and the whole Christian edifice of thought needs to be understood in the light of it. It takes us far beyond what now seems the rather parochial concern of individual souls going to heaven. At the same time, it by no means cancels that future hope but sets it within an even more glorious context. Traditional evangelicalism is simply not evangelical enough.

Post Two: The Bible as both Indispensable and Disreputable

There is a further nodal point for this theological pilgrimage, namely the nature and role of the revelation to which the scriptures of Israel and the Christian church bear witness. I understand this revelation as a 'cumulative process of events and their interpretation' (Henrik Berkhof). The scriptures are the written deposit of this process, by which that which has happened and been spoken in the past continues to be made available today. A moment's thought is enough to realise how central this must be. We have written scriptures that make accessible the testimony and wisdom of the past and these scriptures endure beyond their original contexts. They are durable, portable, translatable, and accessible. Without scripture, there would be no church, and although doctrines and interpretations of the scriptures might vary, there is no contesting the fact that they underlie the basis of any and every movement that lays claim to the name 'Christian'. Doctrines of scripture typically speak of 'inspiration' in asserting this importance and of 'illumination' in their capacity to come to life again and again. The idea that these classical texts are 'God-breathed' (2 Timothy 3:16) is both a reference to the divine energy that inheres within the text such that they awaken awareness of God and repeatedly 'speak' to the human condition and to some understanding of how in God's providence they have come to exist as witness in their present form. At the core of the biblical tradition is the idea that God has acted in particular and crucial ways in human history and that such actions have been authoritatively interpreted for us so that we grasp their meaning. They are able to regulate what truly passes as the truth of God. The prophetic model fits with this in that there are those called and illuminated by God to disclose how God is acting in events: 'men and women moved by the Holy Spirit spoke from God' (2 Peter 1:19-21). Events, therefore have their record and interpretation in words that are inspired by God and so demand a hearing. It is not enough simply to say that the scriptures are 'valuable' for faith: if they are valuable, they must also have authority. They offer us not just a resource but an authoritative 'norming norm'.

The concept of inspiration requires further examination here and I distinguish two avenues of approach characterised as 'deductive' and 'inductive'. The deductive approach is the more common among evangelicals and works as follows: Inspiration means literally 'God-breathed'. To be breathed out by God implies that the scriptures have divine characteristics, and so must be without error as God is without error. From this are derived concepts of infallibility and inerrancy. The Bible cannot be wrong as God cannot be wrong and so full reliance must be placed upon it. It cannot deceive or mislead. Now, this doctrine might be deemed problematic once it encounters the actual text of scripture. With all scripture's evident humanness, it becomes necessary to clarify the word 'inerrant'. For some, this means 'full inerrancy': the scriptures are inerrant regarding all and any topic on which they touch, whether this be cosmology, history, science, morality or theology. This interpretation would generally be thought of as 'fundamentalist'. A second approach is that of 'partial inerrancy' in which inerrancy is understood in relation to the Bible's witness to God and matters of theology rather than incidental issues of history and cosmology. A third is that of 'inerrancy of purpose' in which the central purpose of scripture is understood to be that of personal salvation through faith in Christ, with a degree of leeway in other areas. Of course, a parallel logic works differently: God inspires human beings to speak and bear witness in God's own name. Human beings are intrinsically limited and time-bound and operate within specific cultures; therefore, what is spoken from God through human beings will bear these marks and will be true witnesses but not inerrant on incidental matters.

Clearly one difficulty here is in defining the word 'inerrancy'. What is deemed to be an error, and by what criteria can this be judged? That the word might function as a general statement of confidence in the Bible without the need to undergo precise definition is one thing, but subjecting it to human scrutiny drawn from contemporary practices of historiography or scientific inquiry is another. Worse still is when, in the name of devotion to scripture, there are those who presume to set standards for it before they consider it worthy of them. On two occasions I have encountered individuals who have spoken in bold terms about how perfect the Bible must be to be trustworthy. On one of these occasions, the conversation went as follows, 'If you can show me any part where this book has any mistakes in it then I will throw it in the bin'. This, I found an arrogant statement along the lines, 'This book has to match up to my high standards in order for it to be good enough for me'. It all sounds like such high-octane Christian belief but, in fact, is a form of high-handed arrogance. What is good enough for God should be good enough for us. Because a detailed study of the Bible inevitably raises questions about apparent contradictions and discrepancies between, for instance, the various Gospel records, how does a concept of 'inerrancy' cope with these? One approach is to redefine the word such that it is tolerant of generalisations and approximations or differing cultural perspectives – its words are thought to be 'true' within the times and contexts within which they were written. Fair enough, yet the word 'inerrancy' then suffers the death of a thousand qualifications and becomes useless other than as a symbol. A further approach is to insist that the Bible is inerrant only 'as originally given', that is, as it came from the pen of its original authors, the 'original autographs' now being irretrievably lost. What such a proposal has in its favour is the recognition that in the process of copying, the text has been added to or distorted and that such additions do not carry the authority of 'inspiration'. They are to be discarded in favour of a more accurate reconstruction of the text, a discipline that can be undertaken according to strict, scholarly criteria and passes under the names of 'textual' or 'lower' criticism (as distinct from 'higher' criticism that concerns itself with issues such as authorship and content).

Given that there have been recognisable corruptions of the text, as can be seen from comparing the underlying Greek text behind the KJV with, say, the NRSV, this is clearly a necessary discipline and can be carried through with a high level of scholarly accuracy. Beyond that, however, the concept 'as originally given' risks being a convenient fiction intended to evade difficult questions. It might always be claimed that the original text did not contain some of the difficulties we encounter. But how are we ever to know this apart from conjecture?

The fact is that nobody possesses the texts as 'originally given'. This means that any copies of the Bible that we are likely to have cannot be proclaimed 'inerrant'. They are liable to suffer from faulty translation, faulty manuscripts on which such translation is based and, potentially, faults in what was originally written anyway, though, as already argued, a discussion must ensue as to by what criteria any statement could be characterised as such a fault. Yet despite these barriers to a perfect text, Christians have still had sufficient confidence that the Word of God might adequately be heard through what everyone must agree is a less than perfect reconstructed text. Apparently, God's authoritative Word can still be conveyed through an 'errant' text!

I have struggled along the way to understand exactly what it is people are rejecting when they criticise the teaching of 'verbal inspiration'. If there is inspiration, it seems to me that it must indeed inhere within the actual words used. So, Paul can claim, 'And we speak of these things in words not taught by human wisdom but taught by the Spirit, interpreting spiritual things to those who are spiritual (1 Corinthians 2:13). Surely this is a form of verbal inspiration? Perhaps what is being criticised is something more overblown than this. In one of the seventeenth-century Baptist Confessions, we find the language (spellings original): 'We may be moved and induced by the testimony of the Church of God, to a high and reverent esteem of the Holy Scriptures; and the heavenliness of the matter; the efficacy of the Doctrine, and the Majesty of the stile, the consent of all the parts, the scope of the whole (which is to give all glory to God) the full discovery it makes of the only way of man's salvation, and many other incomparable Excellencies, and entire perfections, are arguments whereby it doth abundantly evidence itself to be the Word of God'. Granted that this is the language of spiritual devotion and, as such, is commendable, and granted that some of these statements may be proportionate to some parts of a remarkable and diverse book, I, nonetheless, after nearly sixty years of Bible reading and study find them difficult to embrace. Biblical authority is not established by overestimating its nature. It is better to think of it, and of much else on the human level, as a clay vessel in which treasure is to be found. The Bible also contains that which is problematic, obscure, morally offensive, time-bound, frustrating and at times barely sufficient for what it is intended to achieve. In other words, it is profoundly and unambiguously human, so the language of perfection is more in the eye of the beholder than in the text. All this said, as with the incarnation, the glory of scripture does not consist of its supposed perfection but precisely in God's willingness to speak though a very creaturely text derived from highly particular historical circumstances that we often find it difficult to recover or understand. For this reason, I also resist 'presentism', imposing present day predilections on past ages and circumstances of which we understand little.

I have come to prefer an 'inductive' approach to inspiration which I believe liberates the Bible from a particular set of prior assumptions and so enables it to be more truly itself. Of course, all of us approach the Bible with assumptions. The issue is whether we have examined them sufficiently. To reiterate what has already been said, If one approach is to pursue the logic (1) the Bible is God-breathed (2) God is incapable of error (3) therefore the Bible is without error and only so can it be trusted, an inductive approach pursues the line (1) The Bible is God-breathed (2) divine inspiration is mediated through human beings (3) human beings are limited, contextual and historical by nature (4) therefore the Bible displays these qualities. In other words, we take the Bible as we find it to be rather than imposing upon it assumptions derived in advance as to what it has to be to demand our assent. Such an approach is more respectful of the scriptures and of the revelatory dynamic of events and their interpretation that lies behind what is written. It is no surprise to me that, say, the books of the Hebrew scriptures display characteristics that were the common coinage of the times in which they were composed. One of these is the use of hyperbole in recounting the ages of those of old, or the numbers slain in Israel's battles, or legendary events such as the sun standing still or the sun going back on itself. Indeed, once read against the background of other forms of ancient literature, particularly from the Ancient Near East, the Hebrew scriptures begin to look quite sober and restrained! Whereas I am fully persuaded that the Bible is a historical book. I hold this to mean both that there is a historical core, a bedrock of history, around which its narratives are written; and that in telling Israel's story, it deploys literary techniques in bringing out the meaning of that history. So, the Bible is literature as much as history and as literature, it sets down the underlying narratives that were part of Israel's story. In the telling of that story, the use of hyperbole and folklore was calculated to hold the attention, at times also to entertain, and above all to drive home how Israel understood itself within the purposes of God as the One who had called, preserved, and established it. Understood in this way, the Bible does not conform to our contemporary standards of historiography or, natural science or even ethical conventions. Rather, it bears witness to God's dealings with Israel from within cultures that operated differently. 'The past is a foreign country; they do things differently there' is perfectly apt, and those who approach scripture with the standards of 'presentism' will inevitably fail to value it. Whereas it is entirely appropriate to ask the question, 'what actually happened?', it might be better to approach this question through a prior one: why has this been written in the way it has, and what are we to understand from what has been written? Only then need strictly historical criteria come into play and, as with many events in ancient history, conclusions might prove elusive. This seems to be in line with Paul's injunctions: 'These things happened to them to serve as an example, and they were written down to instruct us, on whom the ends of the ages have come' (1 Corinthians 10:11). Scripture exists to instruct and enlighten, to convey understanding and wisdom. Spiritual learning rather than strict historicity is the point; but 'these things' did indeed happen in the sense that there is a historical bedrock, the meaning of which is then subject to prophetic interpretation.

I am persuaded that a deductive approach enables us to better understand the scriptures that are our inheritance and deflects us from imposing essentially 'modernist' assumptions on the text. It liberates us from an untenable literalism that reckons that unless the whole can be shown to be factual, then it is without value. As the saying goes, 'Either we take the Bible literally, or we take it seriously'. To take it seriously is to reckon with its diversity and to acknowledge that 'in many and various ways God has spoken through the prophets' (Hebrews 1:1-2). I have gained great and enjoyable benefits from John Barton's book on the history of the Bible,[11] and am comfortable with his characterisation of a believing approach to the Bible as being true (at some level), relevant, important, and profound, self-consistent (though dialectically so), and congruent with the 'rule of faith' of the church. His position on these things might be less conservative than my own, but I find his judgements intensely fair.

There is a fallacy that passes for piety in evangelical circles, that the more literally we can construe the Bible to be, the more devout, believing, or faithful we are. When I was in college, we had a lecturer (an American, as it happened) who gladly proclaimed his adherence to literal interpretation. One of his sayings, delivered with the appropriate accent, about the Book of Jonah, was, 'Do I believe the whale swallowed Jonah? I'd believe the Bible if it said Jonah swallowed the whale!' That says it all. But to abandon literalism means we learn to be better readers of the Bible. We no longer need to assume the defensive attitude towards critical scholarship that has been taken by some conservatives, evangelical or otherwise. To accept the documentary hypotheses in relation to the Pentateuch, or the Synoptics, or a late date for the Book of Daniel, or a deutero-Pauline authorship for the Pastoral Epistles, or the parabolic nature of the Book of Jonah in no way undermines the fact that God has spoken and does speak through these instruments and that God's

---

[11] John Barton, *A History of the Bible: The Book and its Faiths* (London: Allen Lane, 2019), pp. 6-11.

word is true. The limiting factor to such a nuanced approach is the belief, characteristic of Jewish and Christian faith, that God has acted in history. If Jesus never lived and the cross never happened, the faith of the Christian becomes incoherent. If it is this kind of book, with its bedrock core of history and its creative interpretative commentary, that God has chosen to use in making God's own self known, who are we to object? Critical scholarship's individual proposals can certainly be contested and, at times, modified or rejected, but this should be done according to the critical standards it accepts for itself, and admittedly, not everything that is proposed is credible. We should be sceptical about scepticism. Scholarship is capable of leading to (relatively) conservative as well as radical conclusions. But if we are to have integrity, to decide what those conclusions are in advance of examining the evidence is surely wrong.

I would like to develop the parallel with the incarnation at this point. To believe that in Christ, God has become incarnate in a particular human being is a core Christian conviction and one that has been contested from the beginning, both in principle and in detail. So, what do we infer from this? In my experience, it is common for devout Christians to take a maximalist position: Christ was a perfect human being in every respect. I recall once asking the rhetorical question whether Jesus would ever accidentally have trodden on anyone's toe and received the answer No, he could never have done that because he was 'perfect'. On another occasion, I recall a famous preacher claiming that despite being a carpenter, Jesus' hands were beautiful and without blemish because, as the incarnate Lord, he was 'perfect'. Such perspectives prompt further rhetorical questions: did Jesus need to learn, or did he already have full understanding from the beginning? In learning to write Hebrew did he ever make a mistake? Had he studied mathematics would he immediately have got everything right? Did he believe that the earth revolved round the sun? Theologically, does it jeopardise his status as the True Witness and the Way, the Truth and the Life to assert that he by no means had perfect knowledge of all things, that in many areas that did not impinge upon his central mission, he was in fact as ignorant as any contemporaries, and that in this there is no sin, simply evidence of those human limitations without which we cannot, in fact, be human? My answer is not only 'absolutely not' but that it is *absolutely necessary* that he embraced such limitations and did so gladly. This belongs to the divine self-emptying that *is* the incarnation. To judge otherwise is to collapse into Docetism, the belief that Jesus only *appeared* to be a human being. Docetism removes Jesus from us in that he did not truly become as we are, and so could not really fight our battles and redeem our humanity. The parallel with the scriptures should be clear: they are both divinely inspired and genuinely human, and we should not want them otherwise. They both bear true witness to God and do so from within genuinely human contexts and categories. As the fact that God in Christ embraced our imperfect humanity is the true glory of our faith, 'He did not abhor the Virgin's womb', so the humanity of scriptures is testimony to the true glory of God.

Two perspectives or illustrations have helped me along the way. The one I derive from Emil Brunner, who compared scripture to an old 38 record. As it is played on a turntable, there are scratches, distortions and 'white noise', but despite this, the voice that is recorded can be clearly heard. Both inerrantists and 'errantists' acknowledge that there are 'scratches' to scripture since we do not have direct and unadulterated access to what was originally given, and what we do have has been subject to manuscript transition and translation. Yet we can hear the authentic voice that is recorded even if, occasionally, we cannot make out the odd word. We do well not to build too rashly on what is indistinct. The second illustration asks us to imagine the scriptural text as three concentric circles. There is that which is absolutely at the core and without which there would be nothing worth hearing. Around that would be further valuable amplification of the central word that is to be heard. Around that still there is much else that has been preserved but of which the religious or theological value is less obvious or agreed. That this is how scripture bears upon us, in fact, is evident in that the Bibles we use are worn in some places and not in others, that in actual practice some sections are more illuminating than others. Not all parts of the Bible are equally important to us, and, indeed, some parts would not make much difference to the 'grand narrative' if they were not there at all. All the same, just as the background of a portrait contributes to the overall impact, so even the background aspects of scripture can contribute. Perhaps also one day they may speak to us with new force. In constructing our doctrines, we do well, however, to root them in the central witness to which the record bears witness while acknowledging those parts that are more puzzling or of lesser value.

It must be said that in the minds of some, the Bible is also a disreputable text, and to a degree, I find this to be true. As I write, news has come in of a school district in Utah in the United States (a strongly Mormon-populated state) that has decided to ban the Bible for primary and middle schools on account of some of its difficult content. It is ironic that when a child is born, he or she may be presented with a copy of the Bible or that (once upon a time) it would be common for a bride to walk down the aisle holding a white leather edition. There are indeed difficult, even disreputable, things in the Bible: incest, rape, prostitution, warfare and violence, slavery, mistreatment of women, invasion, conquest, and you name it. To be fair, there is a difference between description and prescription. To describe these things is not to commend them as actions to be imitated – they may be warnings of what *not* to do, and narrative as a medium does not always make this clear. What cannot be claimed is that the scriptures are sentimental writings that gloss over the realities of the human condition. In fact, they could be faulted as being out of touch if they did *not* contain such content. Indeed, for some passages, a parental guidance warning or even an X-rating might be appropriate. On the one hand, we are presented with a vision of a better, more just and more peaceful world that is an entirely honourable or noble aspiration for all human beings. On the other we are not spared an introduction to the world as it currently and regrettably is; and it might be pointed out that our television screens do much the same thing on a weekly basis.

My approach to the Bible considers the disciplines of critical scholarship whilst approaching those disciplines with appropriate scepticism. Some of what is claimed to pass as a scholarly consensus is plausible but not necessarily persuasive. Nevertheless, I approach it with respect and look for how it might illuminate the meaning of the text. I note that outside scholarly circles there is an approach to the Bible which is almost fantastical: the Bible is a semi-magical text in which all the parts are held to cohere and fit together wonderfully. I stand apart from this and am more tolerant of those parts that do not easily fit together. It troubles me not that there can be elements of messiness. This is what I might expect of such ancient and venerable texts produced, even under inspiration, by human beings.

To anticipate material yet to come, I take the opportunity to add that, much of the time, when the Bible gives moral instruction it is offering the best possible advice that was available in the circumstance in which it was written. Its world is not our world, and it is foolish, and indeed unfair, to imagine otherwise. A process of interpretation is necessary that may be likened to ascending and descending a ladder: from the specific instances of laws and ordinances we are offered in the Hebrew scriptures in particular, a ladder needs to be ascended into the realm of principles that can be seen to underlie them and have enduring relevance. Correspondingly, a ladder then needs to be descended into our present world and those enduring principles applied with discernment to very different circumstances, possibly with different results. This discussion takes us into the world of hermeneutics, the 'science' of interpretation to which I now turn.

Nigel G. Wright

Post Three: Interpretation – a Crucial Challenge

Holding to a doctrine of scripture and its inspiration is only part of our engagement with its witness. Possibly of greater importance is how we interpret what we have been given. The fact that thoughtful and intelligent people can draw many different conclusions from the same material is a sure indication that this is no simple matter. When we approach the 'horizon' of the text, we are inevitably already shaped by the multiple 'horizons' that we bring to it and that form our pre-understandings of what is possible, ethical, and valuable. The failure to recognise that we are already determined by culture, philosophy, and personal experience to read or not read the Bible in certain ways is naïve. For that reason, it is rightly to be recognised that there is a 'hermeneutical circle' into which we enter when we begin to engage with the text. I suggest, however, that the two approaches to 'inspiration' outlined above, deductive or inductive, bear on this issue and that the deductive runs the greater danger of determining in advance what we believe we are obliged to find. It is further the case that we read the Bible within a 'cultural circle', that is, a community of interpreters that shares a set of pre-understandings that allow or disallow some things to be expressed. Where this community shares conservative instincts, for instance, it may prove difficult to acknowledge the genres of myth, legend, or folklore since these might be thought to chip away at the reliability of scripture where this is understood as 'facticity'. Any who suggest this might have their 'orthodoxy' questioned or be labelled as 'unsound'. At the risk of simplification or even caricature, my suggestion is that the deductive approach views the Bible as a uniform whole, the parts of which might be mined for an overall and coherent theology, with text added to and compared with text on the assumption that they can be harmonised into a systematic theology. One danger of this is that once that systematic theology has been attained, the Bible itself falls into the background as an instrument whose job is done. What is lost here is an awareness that the scriptures are heavily contextualised, and any attempt to treat them as the purveyors of 'eternal truths' risks universalising what is essentially local and immediate in application.

By contrast, an inductive approach sets out to follow the biblical narratives with the fullest possible awareness of the contexts from which they derive, the purposes to which they are put and the ways in which they have been re-interpreted and re-applied internally in new contexts by subsequent (inspired) editors. I value the idea of 'constants in context' that is applicable both to the exercise of Christian mission and to biblical interpretation.[12] There is that which is constant, consistent, and coherent in knowing and thinking of God. But this is variously to be applied to cultural contexts of considerable diversity, and it is awareness of context that has

---

[12] Stephen B. Bevans and Roger P. Schoeder, *Constants in Context: A Theology of Mission for Today* (Maryknoll, New York: Orbis Books, 2004).

assumed greater significance in more recent years. Greater wisdom is required in grasping what is consistent and what is contingent, and in turn, this brings to the fore a greater sense of 'the mind of Christ' within the church in discerning the difference. Thus, in the process of events and their interpretation, there accumulates through time a body of reflection which allows a vision of God and of God's purposes to emerge, in other words divine wisdom. One might consider here, for instance, the way in which Deuteronomy grows out of the Mosaic tradition to bring it to new levels of understanding and application. It is impossible to deny here, at least to my mind, that revelation and responses to it in the growth of wisdom have a progressive character. The principle, therefore, of 'sublation' is operative: concepts and ideas emerge and contribute to a greater understanding that paradoxically leads to an abandonment of earlier understandings and practices even while being inconceivable without them. I find the German word *Aufhebung* helpful here, of which 'sublation' is a passable translation. *Aufhebung* means 'abolition' but also has the sense of 'lifting up' into something new, the very substance of that which was abolished.

From a Christian perspective the sacrificial system of Israel's worship falls into this character. The offering of animal sacrifices as a means of expiation of sins and as an expression of repentance or thanksgiving prepared the covenant community that, in time, broadened out in Christianity into an understanding of the life and death of Jesus as an atoning sacrifice. Yet, having been accomplished, that same sacrifice led to an abandonment of animal sacrifice by Christians, decisively so once the Jewish temple apparatus was destroyed in AD70. So, the system of sacrifice in Israelite worship prepares the ground for our understanding of Christ's once-for-all all self-giving, and then this, in turn, requires the leaving behind of animal sacrifices as 'shadows' only of what was to come. They have done their job, and Paul could say of God or Christ, 'He has abolished the law with its commandments and ordinances' (Ephesians 2:15). Yet there is continuity and discontinuity here: the old form passes away, but the substance it contained is taken up into a new reality. The Book of Hebrews is particularly insistent that the former covenant is replaced by something better, even while insisting that the new is a fulfilment of the old. For Jewish believers, this is a precarious claim, but I cannot see how it can or should be avoided. The same process of sublation can be traced in other ways, such as in the transformation of the temple, or the priesthood, or circumcision, or the 'law' as a marker of identity. Sublation is a key concept for interpretation, though the word may be virtually unknown! It means that all the scriptures are profitable for teaching and revelation, but they are not 'flat' in the sense that all are of equal weight. There is forward movement.

For the Christian, the decisive witness or revelation of God comes in Jesus Christ. Yet Christ cannot be understood apart from the preparation that comes in the history and the scriptures of Israel. Christ intensifies, fulfils, and expands the biblical hopes, all of which are, so to speak, funnelled down into his life and ministry and brought to decisive expression. This is why the Gospel authors are so prolific in applying Old Testament texts to Christ's careers and identity. There would be no normative witness to him were it not for the written witness in both Testaments to him. Without scripture, there would be neither Judaism nor Christianity. The scriptures record and regulate the content of faith, but more than this, by 'indwelling' those scriptures, the narratives that bear their witness, a spiritual vitality, an experience of encounter, an illumination of the mind and spirit takes place through the Spirit who continues to breathe energy into them and through them. Scripture could, therefore, be understood in 'sacramental' terms, an earthly instrument taken up in the Spirit to engage and transform sinners, never to be left behind or treated as a mere repository of information, but 'living and active' (Hebrews 4:12). There is a subtle distinction here. I do not believe in Christ because of a prior belief in scripture. I believe in scripture because of a prior belief in Christ. Christ is the Word of God to us.

Conversion rarely comes as a deduction from having read the whole of the Bible. Rather, it is a result of having been incorporated into a believing community, somewhat like catching an infection. It is then buttressed by attention to scripture. Belief is impossible without the testimony of scripture; the words bearing witness to the Word, and since Christ is the 'sublation' of the promises, hopes and expectations that have gone before, He is the interpretative key to the whole. Whereas the word 'inerrant' is to me unhelpful and problematic, I find the word 'infallible' more acceptable when it is taken to mean that scripture is not liable to deceive or mislead in relation to the knowledge of God in Christ. The more modest words 'reliable' and 'sufficient' are, to me, more than enough for faith, especially when we combine them together and proclaim that the scriptures are 'reliably sufficient' and 'sufficiently reliable' for their purpose. It is striking to me that a key text for divine inspiration in, 2 Timothy 3:16 has it that inspired scripture is 'profitable' when inerrantists would claim much more.

My contention is that the Bible interprets in an authoritative way the acts of God for our salvation, and much else besides. But the interpretations of the biblical 'authors' need themselves to be interpreted and this is the task of the church. The temptation for both believers and unbelievers is to imagine that the meanings of scripture can be simply read off from the page without the profound wrestling that those texts demand. As in so many other areas, we are impatient with complexity, yet complexity is endemic to life itself, not least the life of the spirit. The sheer endurance of the Bible as the world's best-seller is testimony to its ability to yield ever-new depths of meaning. My conviction is that the concept of inerrancy gets in the way of an honest encounter with the text. It is clear to me, for instance, that the Hebrew scriptures love hyperbole and should be understood as rhetoric rather than objective, uninterpreted history (if ever there were such a thing). Though there is a bedrock history behind the text, these books reflect the Near Eastern milieu out of which they emerge, with the exception that they are, in fact, more restrained than their parallels in other cultures. Where they differ from those texts is of particular interest. The large numbers frequently cited in Israel's defensive battles or the huge ages of ancient genealogies, which we are inclined to take at their face value, have rhetorical and symbolic value rather than the attempted precision of modern historiography. Acknowledging this relieves considerable pressure on the devout Bible reader who feels obliged to accept as fact things which, in other contexts or religious histories, they would immediately recognise as literary devices. What we have as the final canonical text has a didactic purpose: to disclose that God was, and so is, at work in the calling, preservation, and formation of Israel. This is not to deny the bedrock history, but it indicates that such is not always easy to retrieve. The 'authors' did not set out to write history as we now understand it but to teach the ways of God in dealings with Israel. Hence, scholars have long made the distinction between *Historie* and *Geschichte*, the former being the attempt to retrieve 'objective' history and the latter being narrated history that draws out the significance of God's past actions for present identity, vocation and hope. This is by no means a form of special pleading but an intensification of the fact that all history, however objective we try to make it, is subject to similar forces. Russians, South Africans, Scots, or Americans will always tell their stories in distinctive ways that serve present ideological purposes, whether these are known or unknown. It may be possible to arrive at degrees of objectivity, but these can never be complete or pure.

A recent film (I am writing in 2022) may illustrate the point. The film *Dunkirk* sets out to tell the story of the evacuation of British and French forces from the continent at the beginning of World War 2 in 1940. As a device, the film is interwoven into three scenarios, one lasting for a week, another for a day and the third for an hour, as it follows respectively the evacuation from the beaches, the arrival and withdrawal of a 'little ship' from Weymouth harbour, and the offensive action of three aircraft of the RAF. Each operates on its own timescale. It is clear throughout the film that this is a tribute to British bravery in the face of extreme threat, a point driven home by a special arrangement of Elgar's quintessentially English *Nimrod*. Having watched the film several times, I still struggle to integrate the various parts and to determine exactly what happened when, especially in the air sequences; so the film itself is a bit of a teaser. It is nonetheless highly effective in representing the meaning of something that did happen, even if not always in the way depicted, given that there are clear fictional reconstructions to the film. Yet the film is *truthful,* certainly from the perspective of the British patriot! In similar ways, the events of Israel's history are packaged in the Hebrew scriptures to narrate their meaning in the purposes of God. In the process, literary devices appropriate to the times are employed and include social memory, sober history, folklore, saga, theological fiction (think of Jonah or Job), allegories and parables, and stories that might best be depicted to the modern mind as soap opera (think of the Joseph cycle, or the escapades of Jacob, Samson, or Elisha). Neither should we exclude humour since, again, contrary to our instincts, there can be no doubt that scriptural drama retains the potential to entertain – a point understood even before the invention of Hollywood. Perhaps then we are to imagine the Bible not as we currently possess it – a discrete literary work to be read in private, but as a wide variety of works to be narrated publicly, dramatically and with the intention of teaching and bearing witness to God's purposes for God's people. As C.S. Lewis said, there is no reason why there should not be sacred myth and sacred fiction as well as sacred history. Scripture is both performative and formative. In such a framework, the use of hyperbole and rhetoric makes sense since the objective is to gain a hearing and make an impression rather than to valorise precision. If it be objected that the telling of the story falls short of being fully truthful, the answer might be that it is precisely to communicate the truth that such devices are used. Only with time have such artefacts been committed to writing to be preserved for future generations and to achieve the status of sacred writings.

Post Four: Election and Predestination

Intrinsic to my early formation in the faith were the concepts of election and predestination, and they have remained so, though with radical shifts in more positive directions than are sometimes associated with such doctrines. I have sometimes been asked whether I believe in predestination and have been greeted with a degree of surprise on answering in the positive. The short answer is that all Christians believe in predestination; any Christian who does not is simply not paying attention. God has a purpose for the world and is working that purpose out through human history. To deny this would be to reduce theology to chaos. Intrinsic to the idea that God has an ultimate purpose for all creation is the idea of election, that God has called a people (or peoples), Israel and the church, to be the primary vehicles of that purpose, although ultimately with the whole world in view. Just here, there are matters of huge importance to be negotiated and divergent paths to be trodden, so much so that the decision as to which path to choose makes all the difference to one's theology. These are sometimes distinguished as the Calvinist and Arminian understandings, but this can lead to an over-simplification. For a start, similar tracks can be distinguished within Catholicism, given the importance that Augustine, the fountainhead of certain doctrines, has for both Catholic and Protestant traditions and the place of Jansenism within Catholicism. Similarly, Arminianism, rightly understood, is a variant within Calvinism, or at least within the Reformed tradition, with which Calvin is closely associated rather than strictly an alternative to it. A token of this is that churches with their origins in Dutch Arminianism are also members of the World Alliance of Reformed Churches. There are, therefore, variant strains of Calvinism which proves to be a more diverse phenomenon than is allowed in the polemics that surround these issues.

In light of this, I would describe myself as being *Calvinian* rather than *Calvinist*. This has to be the case because I position myself somewhere between the Reformed and the Anabaptists, not entirely corresponding to either tradition. As a resolutely free-church believer, I depart from Calvin over his justification of infant baptism and of his version of church-state relations, and, of course, his punitive approach to heretics such as Servetus. On these counts, he wished to perpetuate aspects of Christendom that I find problematic. This is not the full extent of my disagreement. I reject his rendering of predestination. However, I swim in the river of his characteristic doctrines and find his writings more generous and humane than is often allowed: hence 'Calvinian' but not 'Calvinist'.

To enter the discussion of predestination, we start where Calvin himself seems to have started, with the phenomenon that when the gospel is proclaimed, it is not universally embraced by those who hear it. There are two kinds of people - those who believe and those who do not. This is a matter of fact and cannot be contested. Moreover, if the final point for fixing human destiny is deemed to be death, those who die without repentance and faith in Christ are considered reprobate and so doomed to perdition (eternal loss). There may be some nuancing here, but the scheme generally stands. How, then, is it to be explained? Calvin's own perception was that, given all things happen according to the sovereign will of God, it is because God has so willed it. God has, before the foundation of the world, divided humankind into two camps: the elect and the reprobate. God saves the elect to manifest his mercy to undeserving sinners, but he displays his justice by rightly condemning others to damnation. In this way, the mercy and the justice of God are made known, and God is glorified both in revealing his mercy and his severity. Much of this is based upon the apostle Paul's discussion in Romans 9-11, read in a particular way. The fact that this is a divine decision, or 'decree' before any decision God makes to create (though the order of the 'divine decrees' is discussed) means that the sovereign will of God is exalted. Creation and the subsequent decision of God either to decree the fall or simply to permit it are the ways in which God achieves the prior and supreme decree of God to elect some and reprobate others. This is the hardest and most severe form of Calvinism, and it is typically known as 'supralapsarianism'. More moderate forms of Calvinism mitigate the severity of this framework in one way or another, but supralapsarians believe their 'system' brings honour to God by magnifying God's sovereignty. Everything that happens does so because God has decreed it and willed it to be so. This 'system' was formulated in 1617 at the so-called Synod of Dordrecht in reaction to the developing 'Arminian' alternative (of which more shortly) in a way that has been more recently summarised by the acrostic TULIP. This stands for the 'total depravity' of human beings whereby they are incapable of redeeming themselves and so are entirely dependent on God; 'unconditional grace' whereby God determines to redeem the elect irrespective of any works or merit of their own; 'limited atonement' according to which Christ has paid for all and any of their sins (but not for those of the whole world); 'irresistible grace' whereby it is impossible finally to resist the will of God to save those whom God has chosen; and 'perseverance of the saints' whereby God, having elected and called individuals ensures that they persevere in grace to the very end.

I make it clear here that I am fully opposed to some dimensions of this formulation and to the mentality that lies behind it. Indeed, I believe it to be a distortion of the biblical witness, which is not concerned in Romans with some metaphysical and eternal division of humankind into two camps but with the freedom of God to pursue his purposes of election *throughout history* in the way that God chooses so to do. So, God chooses Abel rather than Cain, Isaac rather than Ishmael, Jacob rather than Esau (contrary to the usual conventions of inheritance), and David rather than his brothers to work out God's purpose and promise. God is free. The significance of the verse Malachi 1:2-3, 'Yet I have loved Jacob, but I have hated Esau' (cited by Paul in Romans 9:13), does not refer to a primordial choice for salvation or reprobation but to the outworking of the divine purpose in history: it is without prejudice to the issue of eternal salvation. And even the idea of 'hate' must be understood. It is not that God has viscerally hated Esau, but that God has loved him less by comparison to the way God's favour has been worked out through Jacob. (A similar notion of 'loving less by comparison' can be applied to Jesus' words in Luke 14:26; and it should be noted that Esau prospered in life as did Jacob). The theme of God's free sovereign choice can be pursued through Israel's history and, for the Christian culminates in the choice of Jesus of Nazareth and then of the Gentile church alongside faithful Israel to bring that purpose to the world. The will of God is not to be eternalised as something that was decided before the foundation of the world and, therefore, unalterably fixed even for God's own self in its outworking in history. Rather, the will of God is the freedom of God to be true to God's own self in the ways in which that purpose is worked out. But crucially, the will of God is subordinated to the love of God and not the other way round. Placing the will of God above the love of God is, to me, the fatal and lamentable flaw in supralapsarian Calvinism. It may have a severe logic to it once certain premises are assumed (notice the use of the world 'system' above). This clearly appeals to some people. But it mistakes its own severity for a 'high' view of God. It is a system that lacks warmth and generosity and, consequently, risks creating people in its own image. Or so it seems to me.

Does this, therefore, make me an Arminian? Yes and no. The followers of Jacob Arminius reacted against 'high Calvinism' by positing an alternative system. God loves all that God has made and gave his Son as an atoning sacrifice for the sins of the world. Such a perspective is clearly biblical and reflects the fact that Christ is the 'Lamb of God who takes away the sin of the world!' (John 1:29). If the supralapsarian system can be tested against scripture at any point it is manifestly here since scripture is clear about the universal value of the atonement. And failing at this point, its logic must be seen to fail at other points. God is a God who wills to save and is not willing that any should perish (2 Peter 3:9) and equally 'does not willingly afflict or grieve anyone' (Lamentations 3:33). This is contrary to high Calvinism which precisely asserts that there are those God does will to perish.

How, then, do we account for the fact that in this life, not all believe? The answer for the Arminian is that election or reprobation are the destinies that people choose for themselves by heeding or not heeding the gospel. There are, therefore, indeed two classes of persons, but who belongs to which class is not a decision made by God but by individual human beings. Being given 'free will', they can accept or refuse the offer of salvation. Salvation for all is not in itself in doubt: what determines the 'fate' of the individual is the human will, not the divine will. This is what is anathema to the strict Calvinist and indeed remains a trenchant criticism since it apparently reduces God to an observer of human beings who are themselves placed in a position of sovereignty and thus exalts humans above God and deprives God of glory. The alleged consequence over time of such a theological move is to diminish God and enthrone the human will, and this insight needs to be taken seriously. It is compounded by the fact that it posits a more optimistic doctrine of human ability, the ability to choose the right, rather than the radical inability that is contained within the doctrine of 'total depravity'. We might see, therefore, that the 'great debate' between pure Calvinists and Arminians within the Reformed tradition raises issues of supreme importance and is far from being inconsequential or a doctrinal indulgence. As I am allowing myself the luxury of exploring my own evaluations, I move here towards the expression of my own opinions.

High Calvinism, with its commitment to double predestination, is to me unattractive and biblically, doctrinally, and simply humanly flawed. The heart of the flaw is the prioritisation of the will of God above the love of God. Neither in its approach to human destinies nor in its related doctrine of 'meticulous providence', according to which nothing happens that is not ordained by God (Calvin believed a tile cannot fall from a roof except this be willed by God), does it persuade me or delight me. I find it hard, unyielding, and lacking in compassion. My fear is that it creates and forms people who are themselves hard, unyielding, and lacking in compassion. Theologically, I believe it reads scripture non-historically; it takes the doctrine of election out of the narrative of Israel's history as the freedom of God to work out God's own purpose and eternalises it as a decision (or series of decrees) that God has made from before the foundation of the world. The abstract notion of 'decrees', which I find singularly unsupported in scripture, distorts our vision of God as one who is remote and arbitrary. It is better replaced by the language of loving divine purpose. It also individualises the divine decision such that God decides before time what is to be decided about each individual rather than understanding it as the choice of a people to bear witness to God's own self. It takes biblical testimony and, by means of logical deductions, philosophises it into something it is not intended to be. More moderate forms of Calvinism affirm a universal atonement (sublapsarianism) yet still a limited election; or posit election to salvation and deny that God decrees reprobation but simply leaves sinners to their chosen fate, although an improvement, do not do justice to the love of God. The high Calvinist is faced with the tension of arguing that in one sense, God loves all and yet, in another, loves only some. God loves all in that he 'makes the sun shine on the unrighteous as well as the righteous' and shows benevolence to all God's creatures. Yet such love does not extend to willing the salvation of all so that all might be with God in eternity, at least potentially. This is expressed in the formula, 'God loves all in some ways and some in all ways; but God does not love all in all ways'. This is a snappy formula, but is surely not good enough. It sounds like God preserves sinners for a time, but only with the intention of finally committing them to the eternal torment of hellfire (a subject to which I will return). Expressing this pejoratively, most human beings are being fattened up for their eventual slaughter. I find this problematic in the extreme. Although this tradition makes much of 'the doctrines of grace' and asserts the superiority of its 'high view' of the will of God in that it is inscrutable and unyielding, it seems to me more like divine arbitrariness and, to put it bluntly, luck rather than grace. As the divine choice in eternity past is unconditioned by anything done by individuals who have, in any case, yet to be born, it amounts to good or bad luck on which side of the divide any person happens to be.

None of this is to say that the Arminian position is beyond fault. In fact, my judgement is that Arminius, the theologian, is more careful in his theological arguments than some who are labelled 'Arminian', just as some who are 'Calvinists' actually go beyond Calvin on the subject of 'limited atonement'. Where the Arminian approach gets it right (along with those modified forms of Calvinism that are more faithful to scripture) is in affirming the priority of divine love, the love and compassion of God for all, the universal nature of God's atoning work through Christ and God's will to save. This is the kind of divine generosity that should exercise its gravitational pull on our characters to make us generous and hopeful people. Where it is questionable is in its more hopeful view of human ability - that we are capable of choosing rightly. The doctrine of total depravity, set against this, is a recognition of human radical inability, and at this point, it scores. Yet I choose to interpret the 'total' in this doctrine as meaning not that there is no residual goodness within us since this would render us demons rather than humans and would be a denial of our createdness. Rather, it is the realistic awareness that our sin and fallenness make their impact on the totality of our being – the way we think, feel, behave, act and even the way we love. Luther was right to say that we are *incurvatus in se*, turned in upon ourselves, corrupted, deprived and even depraved. All these things are empirically and observably true, as any reading of history will repeatedly display. When I read or hear people saying that they find reasons for no longer believing in God but do believe in humankind, my response is that reasons for not believing in humankind far exceed those for not believing in God. The claim that human beings are 'basically good' is true in that we are made by God in God's image, and God's creation is a good one. But we are also radically fallen and behave frequently like wild dogs. A Christian anthropology does justice to these twin realities in ways that few other perspectives do. Humanists need to question their faith as much as Christians do. Experience confirms, to my mind, both that the continuing presence of goodness within human beings can be breathtakingly surprising and that the inhumanity of people to each other, to other sentient beings and to the planet can appal. The upshot of this analysis is that Arminianism might, in the event, prove to be even less optimistic about human salvation than Calvinism on the grounds that it is always better to place one's faith in God rather than people. Thinkers such as Wesley were able to counter any drift of Arminianism into Pelagianism by stressing both human inability (parallel to 'total depravity') and God's prevenient grace. Only with the approach and the persistent wooing of God's Spirit does anyone rise above their own fallenness and become capable of faith in a way that ensures that faith is itself a gift of God rather than a human achievement or 'work'. This seems to me to be a fruitful line of thought that might be incorporated into any restatement of the doctrine of divine election that we should attempt.

Before approaching a constructive statement of election and predestination, it is worth wrestling further with the Calvinist tradition of double predestination. I have already indicated not just my dissatisfaction with it from several angles, biblical, theological, and humanitarian, but my sense of horror once one affirms the universal and undeserved love of God for everything that God has created. With this, there goes the conviction that God is a God who wills to save. In other words, all that God has created and which yet has become alienated from the 'ground of its being' is the object of God's will to reconcile and restore to God's own self. This is plainly the witness of Colossians 1. On the face of it, double predestination stands fundamentally contrary to this since it asserts that God eternally and intentionally wills to reprobate and so eternally condemn at least some of those whom he creates. For those who fail to comprehend how this squares with the fundamental idea of a loving and saving God the question arises as to how any thinker in Christian history could countenance such a proposition. I have already noted the drift of Calvin's theology, which sees this as a regrettable, indeed horrible, conclusion that has to be drawn in the light of the empirical fact that there are some, perhaps many, who fail to come to repentance and faith before they die, a point that is considered to be final. Alternatively, it might be that for some, the doctrine had a symmetry to it that over-rode the notion of God's love; that is to say, if God decrees that, on the one hand, some should be saved, and on the other that some should be reprobated, this had a logical or aesthetic simplicity to it that was deemed to fulfil certain ideas of intellectual elegance and style. If so, this represents the triumph of style over substance: we are talking about persons, not cyphers, all of whom are created by God and who are capable of both joy and suffering. There is a deep inhumanity implied in the attraction to a logical system of this form.

Is there anything in all of this that can be redeemed? Having pointed out that Calvinism and the Reformed traditions can be a broader tent than is often assumed, there are things that can be said in its defence. So, for instance, Calvinism might give rise to an 'hypothetical universalism', and as a matter of fact, has done so in that some universalist movements that look to the salvation of all have emerged from it. The reasoning is as follows: If salvation is dependent upon the divine choice, and that choice is irresistible, then who is to say that in the mystery of God's electing grace, the elect are not magnificently more numerous than we might currently see? Reformed confessions typically assert that elect children who die in infancy are saved. This can be extended to claim that all children who die before years of discretion are saved precisely because they are already among the elect, even without the personal profession of faith (of which they are not yet capable). Granted that those who are nurtured in other religions are outside the hearing of the gospel, might it not be that among them also God has God's own elect, even though we might not know who they are? These are God's 'uncovenanted mercies', and no one may dispute that it is within the freedom of God, particularly on Calvinist grounds, for God to save whom God wills. And once it is acknowledged that death, the termination of human lives, is not an insuperable barrier to salvation (as may be so in the case of infants or the mentally incompetent), can it not also be that even those who have lived a full term of life might find beyond their own lives that they are among the elect? Hypothetically therefore, even while preserving a doctrine of double predestination, it might be claimed that so long as there is one person who is in the category of 'reprobate', the 'system' is upheld while at the same time asserting, along with the staunchly Calvinist Charles Hodge, 'We have reason to believe . . .that the number of the finally lost in comparison with the whole number of the saved will be very inconsiderable'.[13] This is not to say that Hodge follows my process of reasoning but that he does come to a more humane conclusion than some others who share the general character of his

---

[13] Charles Hodge, *Systematic Theology* Volume III (London: James Clarke and Co. Ltd, 1960 edition), pp.879-80.

theology. The Calvinist faces the question, if salvation is dependent on God's predestinating choice and is carried through in the undeserved regeneration of the sinner, why could this not, in principle, be extended to the whole of humanity by a loving God?

Two more things are worth saying here. The first is that such a Calvinism might prove to have a more generous vision of salvation than Arminianism if it roots itself in God's will to save and the irresistibility of grace. Arminianism asserts the ability of sinful human beings to choose God under the influence of prevenient grace, but what we know of human nature and depravity gives us no necessary ground to be optimistic about the outcome. God loves us all and has made provision in Christ for the salvation of all, but there is the unknown quantity of how many of God's creatures will respond. For there to be a relationship, there has to be a reciprocal response. As humans are incapable of any response drawn from their own resources, it can only be as God draws near in grace and, in so doing, evokes faith. I do not take the view, therefore, that God offers salvation and then leaves it up to us to 'take it or leave it', as in some popular preaching. What I do believe is that whereas we cannot choose God apart from grace and divine awakening, we can resist grace. All of us resist grace in one way or another. But maybe there are those who resist it to the end and judge themselves to be 'unworthy of eternal life' (Acts 13:46). The Calvinist who celebrates with Revelation 7 the final reality of 'a great multitude that no one could count' can actually be more hopeful than some Arminians, given the capacity of human beings to resist grace. The second thing is that if following Karl Barth, we embrace double predestination but relate it not to God's inscrutable division of humankind into elect and reprobate but openly and manifestly to what God has done for us in Christ, then Christ is both the Elect and the Reprobate; that is to say he is chosen of God, and all human beings are elect in him, and yet chosen also to stand under condemnation on the cross so that no other human being may be so condemned. '(For) as all die in Adam, so all will be made alive in Christ' (1 Corinthians 15:22). Thus, the thorny issue of election and predestination undergoes a transformation by which it becomes good news, which is exactly what it should be.

My own convictions are strongly influenced by Barth's reconstruction of the discussion and resemble closely the kind of hypothetical Calvinism described above. At the same time, they fully endorse Arminian ideas of God's love for all and the power of Christ's universal atonement. In addition, they balance the Arminian idea that the grace of God may not be finally irresistible (this remains for me an open question) with the notion of God's persistence in pursuing human beings, a persistence that reaches beyond and into the grave and does not see human death as the point beyond which it is not possible to be saved. Let me elaborate on these.

Barth's reconstruction of the doctrine of predestination has been likened to a masterly feat of landscape gardening. The individual features of the traditional formulations of doctrine are all present but they are rearranged to ensure that the doctrine can no longer be viewed as implying that 'the Book of Life has a death column'. Rather, the doctrine is transformed into the good news it should always have been, a rearranged garden on which 'the sun has been made to shine' (I refer back to T.H.L Parker). Crucial here is to realise that the eternal will and purpose of God is not inscrutably hidden such that we may never be sure who, for instance, is among the elect or the reprobate. When it comes to the love of God, there is no hidden God behind the God who is revealed in Christ as the One who is 'for us'. Rather to use my own language, God's eternal will to save is open and manifest. It is made known in Jesus Christ that God is for us and wills to be our God and for us to be God's people, a theme constantly reiterated in the Hebrew scriptures and directed not only to the people of Israel but through them to the whole of humankind. In realising this goal, Christ is the Elect person, and in him as the representative or head of the race, the last and redefining Adam, all human beings are themselves elect.

Conversely, Christ is also the Reprobate and bears on behalf of all humanity God's just judgement against human sin and corruption. In him God condemns sin in the flesh but does so in order that there may be no reprobates since Another has been judged in their place. It can be seen here that the constructs of double predestination are prominent but undergo a transformation as they become Christologically focused. A fault of the traditional approach to the doctrine, and one which Barth counters is that it does not travel via the 'narrow Christological defile' which should be true of all Christian doctrines. If the one-time purpose of the doctrine was to display both the mercy of God and the justice of God in the Elect and Reprobate, respectively, and so to glorify God, that purpose is maintained in the newly constructed doctrine. In Christ as Elect and Reprobate, God is glorified both in God's mercy and in God's justice. Yet because one has died for all none other needs so to die, God's work in Christ being sufficient. God is just and merciful in justifying the ungodly without compromising God's own integrity. The relevant doctrines are to be Christologically determined in a way that ensures that all may potentially be redeemed, and none need potentially be condemned. It is clear to me that if Christ incarnate is the Word of God through whom all things have been made (John 1:3) and is the One through whom all things are upheld (Hebrews 1:3), whatever He undertakes and achieves on our behalf must have universal impact. I have rarely heard this note struck in theological discussion, though perhaps I have just missed it. The Creator is the Re-creator. So, contra previous doctrines which called predestination into play to explain how it is that some believe and others not and located the answer in the inscrutable will of God, Barth locates the doctrine in the very being of God as an expression of the universal love of God. It does indeed transform a potentially troubling doctrine into one of good news, the best of news, in that it asserts the possibility of salvation for all. God has, first of all, elected God's own self to be our God, a God who is for us, not against us.

Within this framework, election is not to be understood as a pre-mundane selection of who was to be saved or reprobated but rather as God's work in the history of choosing a people, Israel and then, by extension, the church, who are reconciled to God through Christ and receive the benefits of his redeeming work both as an end in itself and as an instrumental means by which such knowledge of God may be communicated to the whole world. Election is indeed a privileged status, but it is to a vocation not of superiority but of witness and service. When it has been taken, either in Israel or in the churches, as a ground for boasting or superior status, then this is a fundamental corruption of a wholesome doctrine, emphatically to be rejected. In speaking here of election, we are in the realm of the Spirit who enacts the will of God in history by drawing sinners into the reality of God's redeeming love. The Spirit gathers the church so that what is ontologically achieved through the life, death and resurrection of Christ becomes an 'ontic' event in those who are awakened and made regenerate by grace through faith. Rather, then, than conceive election as an outworking of an already-decided fate, it should be seen as the Living God working out a dynamic, free, and sovereign purpose of reclaiming in love what belongs to God, namely the whole of humankind and the whole of creation. We are currently amid this history as the Spirit dynamically expands the circle of the redeemed and those who believe are fellow workers with Father, Son and Spirit of bringing it to realisation. I have often given thought to words allegedly spoken repeatedly by Charles Haddon Spurgeon in the form of a prayer: 'Lord, save all the elect, and then elect some more' (as reported by Spurgeon's biographer W. Y. Fullerton). Whereas Spurgeon might be thought here to be departing from his firmly held Calvinism, he is, in fact, showing excellent instincts. It is not that God has made decisions before all time to which even God's own self is now subject, whether God so wills or not. God is not so subject because God is always the Sovereign Lord, even over God's own will. God is Lord of God's own decisions and is to be thought of as free, free to expand the circle of the 'saved' and to go on doing so throughout the course of human history (and even beyond). God's history is dynamic and so should be any understanding of predestination and election. What we are led to, therefore, is a vision of God that differs from some of our inherited assumptions. It is not that God is a monolithic will, immutable and unbending. Rather, God is living and active, passionately, and personally engaged with the creatures He has made and with the history they are living and bringing it to the promised end intended from 'before the foundation of the earth'. I think this is what Moltmann conceived as 'the Trinitarian history of God'. We may set no limits to God's persistence in seeking and saving the lost. Nor should we seek to do so since we are not God.

Post Five: Universalism and the Human Condition

In his formulations, Barth has frequently been characterised as a universalist, and this is not without good reason. His approach to the doctrine points in this direction even if, according to his own claim and to preserve the freedom of God, this should still be seen as an open question. Belief in a final restoration of all things and so a reconciliation of lost human beings is much more deeply represented in the history of Christian thought than is often supposed. It is also possible to interpret with integrity much in biblical revelation as pointing to this, even if it is also necessary to grapple with texts that undoubtedly suggest the reverse. One helpful distinction here is that between promise and threat. Both promises and threats are well represented within the scriptures, but whereas promises must stand and never be revoked, threats may be withdrawn. The glory of God is not necessarily served by the eternal loss of those who have been made in God's own image nor by the destruction of the creation without which such persons cannot be. Both these represent *prima facie* a kind of failure. Scripture points to the reconciliation of *all things* and the making of *all things* new (Revelation 21:5) and so can lead us resolutely to an intensely hopeful perspective.

It must be insisted that any such hope is rooted in God's grace and not in human ability. I am sometimes asked whether I am an optimist, and usually deny the adjective. But there is a distinction to be made between optimism and hope: I have no optimism about human achievement but abundant hope in God's 'indefectibility', that is, God's intention to fulfil what God has purposed. The belief that human beings need a Saviour and that salvation comes from beyond ourselves as gift must count as definitive for the Christian faith. Those who do not believe that they need a Saviour are not authentically Christian. We cannot save ourselves or reconcile ourselves to God. On this point, mainstream Christianity speaks with one voice. And yet that voice speaks in both major and minor keys: Human beings are made in the image of God to be like God and to be for God, and yet they are radically fallen. I have already explored these things in discussing 'evangelical humanism'. A Christian anthropology combines belief both in human dignity and human depravity neither of which can be surrendered or allowed to cancel the other out. Humans are the glory and the off-scouring of the world, of all creatures, God's most problematic.

The ambivalence of such a doctrine means that we must tread with care and be careful with our formulations. From without and within, the doctrine of original sin attracts frequent criticism and may be considered to imply a degree of negativity that eclipses the goodness of God's human creatures and of God's own self. Alternatively, the doctrine might be held to be the only adequately realistic appraisal of human beings. It is also a great leveller since it applies to all people, rich and poor, 'common' or 'noble' alike, and so is one of the bases for belief in human equality. No caste system can stand in the light of it. My own approach is to distinguish between the idea of inherited guilt being imputed to all people because of the sin of Adam (and Eve), which I reject, and the idea that human beings are structurally and corporately off-centre, eccentric, and compromised in a way that no individual can escape, which to my mind is ineluctably true. All have sinned and fallen short without exception, and in a way, as indicated, that reduces us all to the same level irrespective of social class or position. The first of these approaches, 'original guilt', might be thought to be the standard position and can be traced to Augustine's interpretation of the apostle Paul, a false interpretation in my view. Accordingly, when Adam, the first and proto-typical human being in the biblical narrative, sinned against God and incurred guilt, he implicated all future human beings. They inherited his guilt irrespective of whether they sinned in the same way and simply because they were 'in Adam'. Augustine considered that this was a true interpretation of Paul but based that interpretation on a grammatical misunderstanding of Romans 5:12-17 (he did not know Greek). This is a problematic doctrine in that it consigns all people to condemnation and, to some minds, everlasting conscious destruction, irrespective of anything they themselves have done. Infants that die, therefore, before any possibility of themselves sinning are on this count condemned because they belong to the 'mass' of fallen humanity. The severity of this doctrine, which must be obvious even to those who promulgate it, is sometimes mitigated by qualifying claims such as the belief that those infants who receive baptism are thereby redeemed because it removes the taint of original sin or in Reformed traditions by claiming that elect children are saved, though we know not who or how many these are; or even by speculating that all children who die before the opportunity for faith must be considered among the elect; or, in Catholicism, by constructing a doctrine of 'limbo' to the effect that such children are neither condemned nor saved but in an intermediate state. To my mind, these are failed attempts to humanise an inhuman doctrine and are best excised from the Christian worldview. I am tempted to blame this 'inherited guilt' version of the doctrine for those elements of inhumanity that have been increasingly uncovered in supposedly Christian institutions such as schools, orphanages, or homes for unmarried mothers. I also believe that this version of the doctrine ought not to obscure the elements of truth that are contained in an alternative version. The German language permits us to distinguish between *Erbsünde* and *Ursünde,* inherited guilt as against constitutional, radical fallenness.

This second version acknowledges that human beings, personally and corporately, are structurally fallen, but each of us incurs guilt only for our own personal inclinations and attitudes. We do not inherit guilt, although we cannot evade all the consequences of the guilt of previous generations. If we did so inherit, we would find ourselves guilty not only for Adam's sin but for the sins of all our ancestors and predecessors in whose 'loins' we have previously been. Rather, the Adam narrative is one which discloses what is true of each and all of us, an analysis of human sin. It is properly understood as a myth, not in the sense of being untrue but precisely the opposite of being universally true. 'Adam' represents all of us corporately. The word means 'humankind' and might be thought of as 'Everyman', each of us personally, and every person who has ever lived, reaching back to the beginnings of human history and to the first human beings to emerge, how many and whoever that was. They did from the beginning what we all do and, yes, inclined their posterity in the wrong direction so that the idea of 'original sin', that is, as belonging to our origins, is appropriate. Those among us who were first to sin set up, as it were, a chain reaction that has impacted us and the creation ever since. We take our place within the chain and exacerbate it by our own choice and inclinations. We are thus ensnared in patterns of godless behaviour, are born structurally turned in upon ourselves and are further shaped by the networks of relations in which we are held, reinforcing these as we come to make our own choices and decisions in godless directions. I think Mike Starkey sums it up well, 'It is not so much that we die the death of Adam: rather we inherit from him a spiritual "virus" which leaves us weakened and vulnerable. This tendency towards sin becomes actual sin when people can make real spiritual and moral choices.

We choose wrongly. We are then held accountable for our sins. Those who, for any reason, never reach a point of moral accountability are not judged for their ignorance.'[14] I find Alistair McFadyen's analysis a compelling and realistic one. Sin, he says, is more than isolated wrong acts that we happen to commit but a power that holds us and shapes us: 'Sin now appears as energised resistance to the dynamics of God and, thereby, as constriction in the fullness of being...Sin, therefore, is not an object of possible choice, external to my will, but a dynamic disorientation already internalised in my will and redoubled with the addition of personal energy I provide through my own willing'.[15] I also apply a passage here that speaks to our condition:

"As creatures made in the image of God, humans were suspended contingently over nonbeing by the slender but entirely sufficient umbilical cord of love and trust that linked us to God. Through that connection flowed the divine energy to sustain us indefinitely. Humans possessed no intrinsic immortality, but they were not subject to the necessity of death either, so long as the link held. The breaking of this link through sin cuts us loose and cuts us off. Unnourished by the divine energy, our existence fades into subjection to corruption and death. In such a state, our mortality

---

[14] Mike Starkey, *What's Wrong: Understanding sin today* (Oxford: BRF, 2001), p.119.
[15] Alistair McFadyen, *Bound to Sin: Abuse, Holocaust and the Christian Doctrine of Sin* (Cambridge: Cambridge University Press, 2008), p. 247.

becomes a source of anxiety. Futile attempts to defend ourselves from it lead us into active sin and estranges us from trust in God. Now sinfulness is more a result of mortality than mortality of sinfulness. To say that humans are "conceived in sin" does not mean that some guilt or evil inclination is passed on to them in the act of their conception, but that *what* they inherit is a mortal human nature, which became mortal as a result of sin."[16]

This is a profound and realistic analysis of the human condition, which strikes me as superior to any of its alternatives. When told by those without faith or who have forsaken it that they can no longer believe in God but have turned instead to a more vibrant faith in *humanity,* I find the claim incomprehensible. Whatever reasons may be adduced for not believing in God, the grounds for not having faith in people are considerably superior, given the inhumanity of humans to each other, to other sentient creatures and to the rest of the natural world. I have made these points before and feel them deeply. To say, as people do, that human beings are 'basically good' is a claim that needs to be interrogated. Yes, they are good in that they are created by God in God's own image; yet they are also radically fallen, capable of the most unbelievable cruelties surpassing anything known in the rest of creation. They are deeply problematic, at times 'just being no damn good'.[17] To be sure, my own thinking does not

---

[16] S. Mark Heim, *The Depth of the Riches: A Trinitarian Theology of Religious Ends* (Grand Rapids: Eerdmans, 2001), p.68.
[17] Bakewell, *Humanly Possible*, p.21.

follow the pattern frequently found in the Christian imagination that once, in a supposed unfallen age, all things were perfect, human beings with them, until Adam and Eve sinned, and so diverted the whole course of heaven and earth. The notion of an original perfection squares neither with the facts of nature nor with the more accurate concept that the creation is orientated towards a goal, an Omega point, in which 'perfection' is yet to be achieved. Still less is it the case that humans were once inherently immortal. Genesis 3 sets immortality before us as a possibility to be realised. Rather than in a state of perfection, the first humans were at the beginning of an adventure full of possibilities. They were given a good beginning, and the 'Fall' consists more in the nature of a failure to rise to their potential in God's grace. I like the distinction between 'ontology' and 'existence' here. Human ontology allows for that which we are truly capable of becoming; our actual existence is what we manage to be, and the gap between these two is the measure of our fallenness. The traditional picture, sometimes called 'Augustinian', certainly points up the contrast between what is and what could have been, but the alternative, sometimes labelled 'Irenaean', takes better account both of biblical testimony and human reality. It also underlines that the problem of sin is one that does not so much refer us to 'back then' as identify what *we* do here and now. We fail to rise to the challenge of faith and love of God. Human beings have the capacity to intend evil, to operate out of hatred and it is surely this intention, the capacity for deliberate malice, that makes evil truly evil. The Christian doctrine of sin is realistic. It needs not to be trivialised but stated compellingly and intelligently. But can it become excessive, unbalanced and entangled in the web of evil we humans weave? I find it hard to believe that an unbalanced view of human depravity is not in some ways conducive to the kinds of abuse and cruelty that have sometimes been practised on the vulnerable and which are a stain on the reputation of some churches at sometimes acts that cannot be denied and which vitiate the reputation of the whole church. Even with this said, these very acts are themselves a testament to the radical evil that grips the human heart, even the hearts of the 'redeemed'. Gross evil can be masked even in the pretence of doing good.

Here, we must make the turn that I have implied in my recognition of ambivalence in our estimation of the human condition, which has already been anticipated in what I have said about the doctrine of total depravity. If this is held to mean that in the totality of the human character, we are dislocated and ontologically distorted, then this is a statement of the evident truth. As an illustration, human reasoning capacities are impaired not simply in the sense that they are limited and only have a partial grasp of reality, which is a commonplace thing to say, but more seriously in that we use our reason to rationalise that which is not true, not good, and not kind but destructive of the common good. We find reasons to bolster our own personal or political interests. As I write these words, Vladimir Putin's Russia has invaded Ukraine and is in the process of attempting the destruction of a neighbouring, sovereign, and peaceful nation. Innocent civilians, men, women, and children are being deliberately targeted and slaughtered. These appalling actions are deeply illustrative of radical human evil and are accompanied by a narrative of justification that is a rationalisation of unjust actions built upon deception. There is nothing new in this tragedy; it has been repeated multiple times in human history. Truth, as they say, is the first casualty of war. Human powers of reasoning and argument are being used to deceive and conceal war crimes. Creative human energies that could be turned into good purposes are being used to destroy and kill. Yet 'total depravity' should not be taken to mean that all human goodness has been obliterated.

This is one of those points where we approach a near cognitive dissonance in holding together human dignity and human depravity. This tension is illustrated in the outpouring of human compassion that surrounding nations are showing in the welcome and support being given to refugees fleeing from destruction. It is entirely wrong to imagine that nothing of goodness or the divine image remains within humankind, as my 'evangelical humanism' seeks to argue. People remain capable of the most moving and sacrificial acts of kindness and good will. This is evident daily as we both encounter and expect love within families, between neighbours and friends and towards strangers and enemies. This is to say little of those extraordinary human capacities for music, art, literature, scientific discovery, medical progress, and the like. It would be a tragically distorted person who does not recognise, enjoy, and value the small tokens of graced humanity that are all around us. There is that which is granted to us all in the very fact of creation. Traditionally, we call this 'common grace' as an acknowledgement that God preserves the world in being and draws us back from a collapse into the total negation of our created humanness so that whatever our condition in life, most of us still want to go on living and to enjoy the benefits of this life. Does God take pleasure, as we are able to do, in God's own human creatures? For sure, in the creation narratives it is evident that God sees what has been made and proclaims it good. And with the creation of human beings in the community, such pleasure is escalated to the status of 'very good'. But given our fallen state, does the Creator still find grounds to take pleasure when continuing goodness and beneficial humanness are displayed? I find it difficult to believe otherwise and would deem it a bleak proposition were it not the case – God's face permanently turned away from us. The appeal to 'common grace' helps us here and is properly employed to endorse the good that remains in humanity even amid our human tragedy. God shows grace to all, and though we may have fallen, we have not entirely fallen out of God's hands. God's grace is like the sun that shines on the natural world, causing living organisms metaphorically to lift their heads to God and fulfil their divinely bestowed nature. Yes, indeed, believers are entitled to consider that God takes pleasure in those who believe that faith is pleasing to God. What about those who do not believe? Are they simply odious to God? Such a view would be hard to square with the idea that God loves what God has made (Psalm 145:9), that God has compassion on us and takes no pleasure in our self-imposed progress towards death. I would suggest that the fact that God wills to lead us to faith and to eternal life in God's very presence, that God is not willing that any should perish but that all should come to repentance (2 Peter 3:9), is proof that there is that in all of us that God considers worth redeeming. And surely Christ himself is the guarantee of this, the lasting demonstration that it can be beautiful to be human, that such beauty will someday triumph and all of us might one day bear the image of the one who is himself the image of God. For this, we were made.

So, on the question of universal salvation, where would I stand? There are various forms of universalism with which we could be dealing. There is a universality of divine love that embraces all that God has made. I affirm this. There is a universalism that contrasts with particularism in that God is not solely concerned with one nation, Israel, but with all nations and that sees God's work in Israel as a particular means to a universal end. The biblical evidence for this is extensive, and once more, I affirm it. There is a universalism in describing the work of Christ as unlimited in scope, embracing all humanity and, indeed, 'all things'. There is a universalism in the hope for a new heaven and a new earth in which righteousness dwells, of a time when the earth will be filled with the glory of God as the waters cover the sea, and every knee will bow to Christ as Lord. All this is clear to me, the bedrock of my faith. Does this necessarily mean that every human being who has ever lived will receive eternal salvation? This is not clear to me, and I stop short of such dogmatic universalism. Whatever might be said of some others who affirm universalism for largely sentimental reasons, this does not apply in my case. I would be untroubled if some of history's tyrants, petty and otherwise, were to perish eternally. I could affirm this as the just action of a righteous God, and I do not believe in a cheap grace that fails to reckon with the depth of human wickedness that cannot be glided over. On an equally personal level, having read recently a powerful argument that is not only dogmatically universalist but believes that such a belief is *necessary* for Christian belief, I found myself reading the final chapter of Revelation with its warning: 'If anyone takes away from the words of the book of this prophecy, God will take away that person's share in the tree of life and in the holy city, which are described in this book' (22:19). I could have read any number of other warning texts, but it struck me that if I were to smooth away this warning and override it with the belief that this would not in fact be the case, then I was not taking the Bible seriously. It was my duty as a hearer to heed the warning, not dismiss it, and to live accordingly. There are questions to which the Bible does not give direct answers. Sometimes, it gives reasons for more than one possible answer, and we must live in the tension between the colliding truths – this is where we feel we are approaching cognitive dissonance. And that's fine.

The most satisfactory statement I have discovered is: 'I am not a universalist: But God might be.' This enables me to heed the warnings of scripture and take them seriously whilst acknowledging that I do not have the last word and that human destinies are in God's hands, not mine. In the meantime, I persist in the belief that God our creator wills to save; that the God revealed in Christ has acted and is acting for our salvation, albeit in ways beyond my perception; that this God is a God who comes to this world and in Christ has come to the farthest possible extent, even death on a cross; that through the Spirit God has acted in creation, in Christ, in Israel and in the church to reach those who are lost and estranged and persists in doing so; that this search for the lost is not confined to this life but reaches beyond it into the realms of the dead, death not being a barrier to God; yet that in life and beyond it, it remains possible to resist the grace of God, and in so doing progressively deprive ourselves of the vestiges on our *humanum*. But God does not come to any of us once or twice but many times, and so the idea of a 'second chance' is incoherent, the word 'chance' being inappropriate for One 'who works all things according to the purpose of his will' – God persists because God wills to save. But who can say that even so, even given every grace, there may not be those who resist it and condemn themselves to perdition? Such is 'the mystery of iniquity'. And perhaps for any in this condition to perish is a mercy.

What I am sure of is that however history works out, God will be glorified and will be known to be both righteous and good. When it comes to 'universalism', I am content to rest with that statement: 'I am not a universalist. But God might be'. This resonates with me in that it rejects presumption and complacency on the one hand while leaving room for the mercy and freedom of God on the other.

Post Six: Grace, Merit, and Atonement

This touches on the doctrine of grace that God shows towards us, a kindness and a favour that we do not and cannot merit by our own efforts to acquire it. Everything we do is, at some level, tainted by self-interest and pride. Even when we do good there is part of us that congratulates ourselves for it. This is one reason why Jesus warned his disciples to do good in secret rather than to garner the praise of others. One hand is not to let the other know what it is doing. We do good because the good is good for its own sake and not to acquire a reward or even a positive self-image. I am confident that such an understanding of God's unmerited favour is fundamental to our faith and fosters a healthy attitude to ourselves and to God, one that frees the self to flourish. It is also fundamental to a Protestant and evangelical approach to the faith, as articulated by Martin Luther (though with the years, it has also become clearer that with qualifications, it is embraced by Catholics as well). We don't have anything that we have not first been given. Yet this needs to be disentangled from a deeper reality, without which we are likely to collapse into a Manichaestic subversion of God's good creation. To distinguish these two aspects of 'merit' or 'what we deserve' has come to be important to me. To make the point, I refer to the miracle of birth. When a child is born, it is our duty to accept, love and nurture it unconditionally. We do not require it to deserve such love by its actions, first of all, to 'merit' what it needs to survive and grow. It works the other way round. We give it all that it needs because its very existence as a child is valuable to us; it deserves what it receives because it has an intrinsic, not an acquired, merit. The fact that its very being is good in our eyes, and in God's, is what compels us to do all we can to ensure that its life will be a happy and secure one. To bring a child into the world with any other motive than so to love it is a gross evil. Those cases where any child receives only neglect and cruelty are among the most outstanding examples of human depravity, and no one can deny that they exist. So, the idea of *merit* and *that which is deserved* operates at two levels: that which is intrinsic to our being as creatures made in God's image and to whom justice is due, and that which we acquire by our actions, 'condign' merit to use the terminology. Our inability to achieve the second should not compromise the importance of the first. By extension we might add that all creatures of God, not human beings alone, have their own intrinsic worth and should so be respected. By further extension I wish to argue that God's purposes of redemption make no sense unless there is that in human beings which is worth redeeming. This is itself a recognition of the 'merit' intrinsic to being God's creatures. Salvation is by grace, but so is creation: we have done nothing to deserve being created and granted life any more than a child has done for the privilege of being born. I will go on to make the bold statement that while there is any residual goodness left in any single person, there also exists a will of God to redeem it and reclaim it for the glory of God and the blessing of the creature. To deny this is to deny God's sovereignty. If there is any ultimate damnation it only happens when all claim to incarnate such goodness has been finally lost. But this is to anticipate. For the moment, my purpose is to affirm both the depravity and the dignity of humankind and to argue that the former should not be allowed to eclipse the latter.

So, I turn to the relationship between the work of Christ and the redemption of God's creation. This is a massive field of study and one which is far broader in scope than is often allowed. God's purpose is to restore and redeem a world gone astray, to bring God's own intention and purpose to final fulfilment and to do so in the person of God's own Son and in the power of the Spirit. The trinitarian doctrine of God that lies at the core of the Christian narrative (and that, despite contentions to the contrary, I find deeply embedded in the biblical revelation) enables us to give greater coherence to the multiple dimensions of this doctrine. To grasp what is at stake, I have always found the analysis of the early chapters of Genesis, especially chapter 3, particularly illuminating. It helps, as already suggested, to abandon a literalistic approach to this chapter because its power does not lie in such considerations but in its penetrating ability to disclose the truth about ourselves, about each of us individually, of our race corporately and inclusively, and of all of us since the time when our race emerged from whatever went before to become the *humanum*, that identifiable phenomenon that we call humanity. Whether we describe it as a saga or, myth or parable, what it renders is the truth of our condition. We are alienated from God as 'the Ground of our Being' (Paul Tillich) and so from our true identity as children of God. In place of communion with our creator, we condemn ourselves to psychological, sociological, and ecological forms of disruption, putting ourselves into crisis and vandalising the peace of creation. At the root of all these tragedies is the theological turn away from God and to our own selves as those who challenge the very deity of God and seek to exalt ourselves in God's place. It was never intended to be this way. But neither can it be claimed that none of this was foreseen. From before the foundation of the world, therefore, in the eternal intentions of God, we must imagine that God's purpose was that the world, having become estranged, should be redeemed and, in time, restored to its ultimate goal as the 'new heaven and new earth in which righteousness dwells'. Christ is to be understood as the remedy to all these dimensions of sin. Where my mind has changed in understanding these things is in grasping the depth and the scope of what Christ has done in his life, death and resurrection, and will bring to completion in the fullness of time. Colossians 1 is an elegant expression of these themes: all has been made through Christ, and all will be redeemed through him.

Once we are persuaded that God wills to save, we have gained an indispensable perspective on the world and everything in it. Double predestination in its received form does not affirm this. Rather God wills both to save and to damn, and this is immutable.

If God wills to save, it is to save some and not all. The more moderate form of Calvinism asserts that God actively wills to save some and chooses simply to pass by the rest. This amounts to the same thing, but lacks the courage to assert it. It means God is indifferent to the fate of at least some of those God has made. I deny both these versions and believe them to be inconsistent with that which we know of God in Christ. In Christ, it is made known that God loves the world and wills to save it and that Christ came into the world for this very purpose. It is correct to assert that this is the frame within which to interpret the sometimes diverse and varied biblical writings. It is a far-reaching statement and is the ground of our hope. When we embrace a double outcome of predestination as determined by God and add to this the belief that we cannot be sure into which category we fall, even if outwardly we are conforming Christians, there is the recipe for deep anxiety, and nowhere we can go beyond it. The doctrine so expressed suggests to us that behind what is revealed in Christ, there is a God who remains unrevealed, mysterious, and potentially arbitrary. Asserting that in Christ, God's will to save the whole of humanity is made known decisively and that there is no other God than the God Christ makes known is the basis of hope.

An intrinsic belief of Christian faith is that each of us stands in need of a Saviour. We cannot save ourselves. The external and internal forces that shape us are beyond our power to control and so we are in dire need of God's grace and mercy. Focus, therefore shifts onto what it is and how it is that God brings about our salvation. Here, we add that such salvation is the work, as are all God's works, of one God who is Father, Son and Spirit, one continuous work of God that originates in the Father, is enacted in the Son and accomplished through the Spirit. There is no question of the persons of the divine communion acting against each other as though, for instance, the Son must persuade the Father to forgive, or appease the wrath of the Father, or turn the Father away from the course of judgement to that of mercy. What happens has its origin in the Father's love since 'God is love' and takes no pleasure in the death of sinners but rather wills that none should perish but that all should find repentance and live. These are vital yet subtle themes that are potentially misrepresented and turned into caricatures. At the same time, there is no value in diminishing the reality of God's wrath, properly understood as God's resistance to human sin, nor the depth of that sin, nor the objective power of the cross as an act of atonement, expiation and, indeed, propitiation and satisfaction, properly understood. The crux of the matter is that the cross of Christ is not some kind of mechanism or external accounting transaction that enables God to forgive but a deeply personal place of encounter to which we may come to find grace in time of need. It is for our sakes that Christ has died in fulfilment of the eternal purpose of God, not for God's sake as though it were resolving some kind of dilemma within God's being. These last words are directed against the kind of preaching that reasons, and this may be a caricature, 'God out of love wanted to forgive us but also had to punish us for our sins, and so designed the cross as a place where this dilemma could be resolved'. It is indeed true that at the cross, justice and mercy have 'kissed each other', but not in a way that provides a resolution to God's dilemma but rather to our own plight. Careful approaches to these themes are necessary.

Firstly, the wrath of God. It is a major failing when this theme is seen as a source of embarrassment, and I am persuaded that to attempt to go round it leaves us with an impoverished doctrine of God. The embarrassment stems from the suspicion that to associate God with something like a bad temper is to detract from God's glory and God's love. It is unworthy of the God we worship, the claim goes, and so it would be if this were what it means. The contrary view is that righteous anger and just wrath are a manifestation of the fact that God loves and cares for the world that is God's creation and opposes all that would destroy it. Unlike the gods of Greek and Roman mythology, God is not subject to arbitrary mood swings. It is to be acknowledged that the anthropomorphic language with which Christians, and indeed the Bible itself, image God can lead the unwary in this direction. I am persuaded that the language is necessary to capture the personal nature of the divinity and to avoid abstraction. But the reality to which it refers has nothing arbitrary about it. It is rather God's implacable resistance to that which is evil and destructive of God's good creation, the 'contrary wind of the divine will that he soon discovers who runs against it' (Emil

Brunner). God's wrath is God's refusal to bend when confronted with human sin, a refusal that turns human sin back against itself in negative consequences. There is, therefore, truth in the insight that 'wrath' is like a process of cause and effect that works itself out in the created sphere. Those who set themselves to oppose God will find themselves opposed. This is like a moral law that is shot through the universe, the very grain of things. Evil actions bring down upon their perpetrators their own consequences, if not immediately, then in the fullness of time since there is a justice to the way things are. If we are rightly to imagine that the love of God is mediated to us in the very fabric of creation such that God provides in the things that have been made that which is necessary for life, then the obverse is the case. God's resistance to human evil, God's wrath, is displayed through creation itself in the processes of cause and effect within which we are held. It appears to be a biblical insight that when evil is done, an effect is unleashed that must fall somewhere, either on the head of the evildoer or, tragically, somewhere else. 'Wrath', therefore, could be described as having an almost impersonal character, but this conclusion would not be entirely accurate as beyond and behind the process is the implacable and personal resistance of God to evil. Wrath is God's wrath, not something disassociated from God. God gives us what we choose, and as Paul emphasises several times in Romans, to be judged is to be given up to the consequences of the actions that we perpetrate: 'Therefore God gave them up in the lusts of their hearts to impurity, to the degrading of their bodies among themselves, because they exchanged the truth about God for a lie' (Romans 1:24-5). The good life is to live in harmony with God and with a beneficial creation, the harmony of life with life. The perverse life is to reject such harmony in favour of dissonance.

It is in keeping with this that salvation is understood in an overarching sense as liberation: there is that which holds us captive, and God's action in Christ is to set us free. Luther characterised this as being set free from a series of giants that hold us in thrall: sin, wrath, death, the world and the devil. In what follows, some account of this liberating work needs to be given. Yet it is worth noting how the theme of liberation has gained a new resonance since World War 2. Perhaps this is not unrelated to post-colonial societies in which, entirely understandably, formerly subject nations have demanded the right to be liberated from the empires that came to be dismantled in the twentieth century. We now look back on the imperial past with a degree of amazement that the domination of some nations by others was ever considered acceptable. And the theme of liberation, equally understandably, has been extended to more than nations, to women, the disabled and LGBT groups, and more. 'Liberation' has become a theme to be picked up by any group that has become aware of its victimisation. If the Bible has sometimes been used to legitimise the status quo, it has become clearer that it also lets loose a revolutionary dynamic of liberation, whether in the Old Testament narratives of the exodus of a group of Hebrew slaves from Egypt and later from Babylon, or in the exodus from sin and spiritual captivity accomplished through Christ, his death and resurrection, in the New Testament. We may want to query how useful it is for the Christian when the theme of liberation acquires an independence of its own and is no longer informed by Christ the Liberator, but there is no doubt that the saving work of Christ fits within the overall narrative of liberation. Christ has been given as a 'ransom for many', which sets those in captivity free: 'For freedom Christ has set us free. Stand firm, therefore, and do not submit again to a yoke of slavery' (Galatians 5:1) has always been, for me, a crucial verse, and its ramifications go well beyond the core issues of personal salvation, even if without this, they lose their proper rooting. To be set free through the work of Christ is to acquire a new relationship with God, but also new standing as children of God who are being restored to their status as true and free human beings in all their dimensions. I have said enough here to indicate that any theology that does not reckon with wrath, that is, the divine resistance to wickedness and evil in all its manifestations, should be regarded as fully inadequate. But we are set free.

Secondly, concerning the atonement. The so-called Christus Victor approach, which resonates with the theme of liberation, has become, for many, the preferred perspective for understanding the atonement. It has frequently been the case that doctrines of atonement pick up on the intellectual context in which they have to be made intelligible. In the creedal formulations of Christian theology, there has been greater reticence in defining atonement doctrine than in some areas, notably Christology and Trinity. Consequently, the theological space has, entirely legitimately, invited a variety of attempts to fill in the blanks. The ecumenical creeds are quite clear in affirming that Christ has died 'for us and our salvation', and this must be considered dogma; that is, it is a belief without which the church ceases to be the church. But, a more precise understanding of how Christ's death achieves human salvation requires considerable further exploration. It is rightly to be understood as a 'mystery' not in the sense that it is forever beyond any level of comprehension but in that it is so dense with meaning that no simple 'explanation' can do justice to it. The hymn 'When I survey the wondrous cross' may not originally have intended the word 'survey' in quite this way, but if to 'survey' means to look at something from multiple perspectives, it can certainly apply to the cross of Christ. It is multi-dimensional, to be explored by a multiplicity of metaphors, like the facets of a diamond, to bring out its depths. Some of these may, of course, have priority over others and are best explored as exposition of those statements and metaphors that both the Old Testament and New Testament allow. The theme of Christus Victor serves well as an overall framework for this exploration but is not itself the whole. Indeed, even when well stated, it requires further steps. Sometimes, it is contrasted favourably over against themes that see the atonement as 'satisfaction', but to my mind, this is mistaken. It is impossible to express the atonement doctrine without the element of satisfaction properly understood. One might say that without satisfaction, the doctrine remains unsatisfactory. What cannot be gainsaid is the centrality of the cross in Christian thought and devotion, a centrality to which both baptism as a dying and rising with Christ and communion as a continuing participation in the benefits of his passion point. A cross-less Christianity is no Christianity at all. The proclamation that in the cross the love of God is revealed is absolutely true but remains incomplete without some account of what it is God has actually done in love. For me this must reckon with what it means for Christ to be the 'bearer of our sins' (1 Peter 2:24).

Much debate and commentary in the recent Western context has revolved around the appropriateness of the theory of penal substitution. For some this is the heart of the matter, to be insisted upon at all costs. For others, it is erroneous, possibly even heretical, to define God, or at least God the Father, in punitive terms. At this point, as at so many others, I come out with a 'Yes and No' response. I find myself here in a similar position to my understanding of election and predestination, wishing to do justice to the various elements of the 'theory' whilst also wishing to rearrange them, landscape-wise, into a pattern that recasts them as unequivocal good news. There are significant problems with the theory as commonly understood, though these may be avoided by the best theologians. If the theory casts the incarnate Son over against the Father as one who appeases the Father's wrath and persuades the Father to be merciful to sinners, then surely it is guilty of both incoherence and caricature. If the cross is precisely an expression of the Father's love, then it is incoherent to assert that the cross is the place where the Father is turned from wrath to mercy. It is out of the very mercy of the Father that the Father provides a place of atonement and reconciliation in the cross of Christ. The cross is not for God's benefit, an instrument by which the Father might resolve the tension within God's own self between wrath and mercy and so forgive. Rather, is it for the sake of sinners that we might find a place of expiation, atonement and reconciliation and be assured of the gracious mercy of God. I risk anthropomorphising this discussion by drawing an analogy with what it means to forgive on the human level: In any act of forgiveness, there is the fact that the person who has been offended must internalise the hurt that has been caused and inwardly overcome it by an act of will. Essentially, forgiveness is an act of letting go, but it is a costly and a painful one, not to be considered in any sense trivial. This is what God does in forgiving human sin, sin that is immense. And out of this internal and eternal forgiveness, the Father has drawn near to sinful human beings in the person of the Son to enact that forgiveness so that the cross is an outcropping in time of an eternal reality that both precedes the cross and proceeds from it. Christ bears our sin and bears it away. The cross is not an act that appeases the Father and reconciles him to us, but a revelation and enactment of the fact that God wills to forgive and does forgive where there is contrition and repentance (this is not 'cheap grace'). It is a place of atonement, forgiveness, and reconciliation and, in this sense, corresponds to the 'mercy-seat' of Old Testament practice, the place where the holy God meets us in grace (Exodus 25:17-22).

Once we have resolved this in our own minds, that it is for *our* sake and *our* salvation that Christ is given to us, I see no need to deny the validity of the words 'penal' or 'substitution', the first because crucifixion is inescapably and undeniably a form of punishment, even if only at the level of Roman in/justice (though surely more); the second because I understand a substitute to be someone who does something for us that we are incapable of doing for ourselves. What else can a Saviour be if not one who comes to our aid when that aid is most needed? And Christ is most certainly my Saviour and the Saviour of the whole world. It is common to deny the word substitution and to prefer the word 'representation', though what is gained by this is unclear to me. Christ surely fulfils both categories: he represents us before the Father by the Father's own will and purpose, and in that way he also endures in our place what it means to be judged, condemned and God-forsaken so that this may not be our fate: 'For God has done what the law, weakened by the flesh, could not do: by sending his own Son in the likeness of sinful flesh, and to deal with sin, he condemned sin in the flesh' (Romans 8:3). Yet all this said, I deny that this amounts to the theory of penal substitution as commonly understood, namely that God the Father chooses to punish the Son in place of us, even if once decided upon it is possible to read biblical texts in its light. Rather, in the person of the Son, the Father chooses to endure the consequence of our sins and, so to speak, internalises and absorbs them to bear them away. This is an event in time which reveals what has been eternally true in God's bearing with sinful creatures. With such a large claim, I need to justify my interpretation by setting it out in an orderly form, if only for my own benefit.

The saving work of Christ has long been interpreted by acknowledging that Christ is Prophet, Priest, and King. Each of these words has a considerable 'back-story' in the history of Israel as represented in the Hebrew scriptures. In that sense, they have the distinct advantage of taking up important strands of the biblical story and focusing them on Christ. They have in common that these 'offices' all follow on from some form of divine anointing, equipping the recipient for the task. In the person of the Messiah, these offices are understood to combine into one preeminent, redemptive office. Christ fulfils all the expectations implied in the titles while at the same time 'sublating' them, taking them to a new level that intensifies some aspects whilst superseding others. So, as the fulfilment of priesthood, the offering of animal sacrifices is understood in Christian interpretation to be no longer necessary since the essence of what such sacrifices anticipate is fulfilled in Christ's once-for-all self-offering (Hebrews 9:23-28). In employing this framework to interpret the work of Christ, I may once have homed in on the element of priesthood. More recently, I have found it helpful to give priority to his prophethood.

A prophet is one who speaks from God, conveying a word that addresses a situation and makes known the mind and purpose of God. The prophet receives a specific call and is inwardly constrained to speak, often employing the formula, 'Thus says the Lord', and frequently becomes the object of hostility and contempt for doing so. The word of the Lord is not always welcomed since it is liable to interrupt whatever has become the status quo. To fit Jesus into the category of 'prophet' makes a great deal of sense. He was recognised as such by at least some of his own contemporaries and seemingly was able to recognise himself as such, with the significant distinction that in place of the formula 'Thus says the Lord', which he never used, he would say, 'But I say to you'. This was clearly a claim to exceptional personal authority in interpreting the scriptures and so the will and purpose of God. He spoke with more than prophetic authority, even with the authority of the God of Israel. More than this, he incarnated the word of God so that not only his speech and verbal communication counts as such, but his actions, his mighty works, and his very self: everything he was is the enduring word of God to humankind coming to us from within a particular religious tradition and historical culture. It is for all the world. The movement here is from God to us via the mediation of Christ. In him, God draws near in incarnation for our benefit and salvation. Being a Christian must involve being attentive to Christ both in his incarnation and exaltation as the risen Lord. What is not so evident from this portrayal of the prophetic office is that the prophets also have a role as those who make intercession towards God on behalf of mortals and, by virtue of their office, have an expectation that they will be heard.

The power of such intercession becomes clear in the accounts of Abraham, the father of faith, in his pleading for Sodom based on the conviction, 'Shall not the Judge of all do what is just?' (Genesis 18:25). It is reinforced when God is said to come to Abimelech in a dream and says of Abraham, 'for he is a prophet and he will pray for you and you shall live', with its sequel, 'Then Abraham prayed to God; and God healed his wife and female slaves so that they bore children' (20:7, 17-18). It is further demonstrated repeatedly in the way Moses mediates between the LORD and Israel and, on one occasion, is said to plead with God for their salvation: 'Turn from your fierce wrath; change your mind and do not bring disaster on your people . . . And the LORD changed his mind about the disaster that he planned to bring on his people' (Exodus 32:12-14). Allowing for the anthropomorphic shape of this incident and its accommodation to our understanding, this is plainly an act of propitiation, of appealing to God for mercy and to turn from wrath. But the propitiation consists of Moses' prayer of intercession: 'Yahweh heard my prayer and agreed not to destroy you' (Deuteronomy 10:10 Jerusalem Bible). It shows the willingness of God to listen to Moses in his mediatory and prophetic role.

Similarly, the prophet and priest Samuel declares, 'If one person sins against another, someone can intercede for the sinner with the LORD; but if someone sins against the LORD, who can make intercession?', and then offers, 'Gather all Israel at Mizpah, and I will pray to the LORD for you' (1 Samuel 2:27; 6:6). The Christian has an answer to the first question. Such accounts prepare us for the words in Ezekiel when having enumerated the sins of Israel, the prophet interprets the Lord God as saying, 'And I sought for anyone among them who would repair the wall and stand in the breach before me on behalf of the land so that I would not destroy it, but I found no one; therefore, I have poured out my indignation upon them with the fire of my wrath; I have returned their conduct upon their heads, says the Lord God' (Ezekiel 22:30-31). However much we might wish to nuance them, and I shall, such verses make nonsense of the claim that 'there is no anger in God'. Ezekiel 7 alone contains multiple references to divine anger and wrath. Even if, in this case, no intercessor is found, the fact that one is sought indicates the significant role of the intercessor in the deliverance of Israel and the mercy of God in having sought for one. It is to be noted that there is no mention here of the offering of sacrifice such that God's wrath may be diverted to it. What is required is intercession in the form of pleading for mercy, and it is this that counts as 'propitiation'.

For this reason, I have come to see great significance in the words of Isaiah 53:12, 'Yet he bore the sin of many, and made intercession for the transgressors.' There is no doubt in my mind that this whole chapter offers us crucial materials for understanding the work of Christ, and this verse, in particular, captures the theme of intercession that is well-amplified in the Hebrew scriptures. It also sheds light on the words of Jesus from the cross in Luke 23:34, 'Then Jesus said, Father, forgive them, for they do not know what they are doing.' I used to read these words in relation to those who were his immediate crucifiers but have come to see that they could well apply to all who are implicated in his rejection and destruction, and that is all of us. As the supreme prophet, Christ has made intercession for us all and there can be no question but that his intercession is accepted. The implications are immense, especially when applied universally.

So, where does this take me? It leads me to view the whole life of Christ as an act of intercession for our salvation, which is provided and gifted by God's own self. Christ stands in the breach for a lost humanity and does so in multiple ways. It is not only his death that has saving significance, though the cross must be seen as the ultimate intensification of what has gone before. His whole human existence is the guarantee of salvation. For he has, by the grace and enabling of God, lived the life that redeems humanity, realising the human potential in a way that prevents us from writing off the whole human story as an abject failure. As with God's declaration that God would not destroy Sodom if only ten righteous persons were found within it (Genesis 18:12), for the sake of the one righteous person, Jesus, God spares humankind. Christ is the new creation, the New Being (Paul Tillich) that eclipses the old and holds open promise for us all. The will of God has indeed been done on earth as in heaven. In him, the beauty of humanity has triumphed over its distortions. When in Psalm 8 we are awakened to the possibilities of persons who are made 'a little lower than God', then it is in Jesus the Christ that we see this fulfilled, opening the confidence that we might be conformed to his image'. This same Christ 'always lives to make intercession for them' because his priesthood 'continues for ever' (Hebrews 7:23-25). What was achieved in his life, death and resurrection, has not yet reached its full goal, a new humanity, but the glorified Christ in the presence of the Father is the guarantee that it will certainly be. Christ is our hope, and it is entirely correct to ask the Father to 'look on him and pardon me'. He is the second Adam, the one who comes from God to redefine us, to abolish the old and bring in the new.

This is not the whole story, of course. Although the motif of Christus Victor provides the overarching vision for our deliverance and rescue, as argued, it does not yet sound the necessary note of 'satisfaction'. In Christ, God does what is satisfactory, blending mercy with justice in a way that realises both to the uttermost. I have given a certain priority to Christ's role as prophet, as one who not only speaks *to us* but speaks *for us* in the presence of the Father. This is not to persuade a reluctant Father to forgive but an expression of that Father's manifest will to save, to provide a place to which we may come to ask for and receive mercy. The concept of 'satisfaction' is one that some suspect of being sub-Christian because they take it to mean that God must be appeased by blood sacrifice as though on a par with capricious and vengeful pagan deities. Were this so, they might be right. But they are not. There is a reality in God that cannot change: God cannot cease to be God. Forgiveness, atonement, and reconciliation are fundamental themes in the Christian story, and all are rendered necessary because of God's implacable resistance to sin and evil. Without reckoning with the nature and holiness of God, they become meaningless. There is that which must be overcome on the human side of the divine-human relationship: our coming to a place of contrition, acknowledgement and humble obedience to God so as to accept the reconciliation that is offered. The prophethood of Christ shades here into his priesthood, his self-offering on our behalf. What Jesus brings to this is his life of humble obedience that has led him to the cross.

I want to insist here that what must be overcome exists on the human side of our relationship with God. God already wills to forgive and to reconcile us to God's own self and does not need to be persuaded to do so. It is not some external act of appeasement that is the source of God's will to forgive, but this comes out of the gracious depths of God's own being. It is out of such deep love that God's gift of Christ and cross arise. Yet, of equal importance is the need for sinners to acknowledge the just judgement of God before they can come to the place of reality that leads them to seek mercy from the judge of all the earth. If anything needs to be satisfied, therefore, it is not so much the honour or the wrath of God (though I recognise the moments of truth in both these constructs) but the integrity of God. God seeks to forgive but to do so with the kind of integrity that is consonant with holy and righteous being, in other words, to do so in a satisfactory way. It is not that God 'just forgives' but that God forgives in a way that recognises the reality and depth of human sinfulness. The atoning work of Christ can, therefore, be understood as atonement through *participation*. In a continuous redemptive action that comes from the Father, Christ assumes human nature and identifies himself with sinners in order that he might act on their behalf. This is already seen in the incarnation and is portrayed in his baptism at the hands of John the Baptist, where he 'fulfils all righteousness' by taking the place of the sinner. The baptism prefigures his being engulfed by the waters of death and enduring the just judgement of God, God's inevitable resistance to sin. His identification with sinners enables him to act representatively on our behalf in the priestly fashion set out with considerable clarity by the anonymous yet highly perceptive author of Hebrews. The voluntary submission of Christ to the shedding of his own blood is the consummation of a life of obedience, which is the sign and demonstration that human life can be lived not in disobedience after the pattern of Adam, who represents us all, but at its supreme best in the one who re-represents us. It fulfils the purpose of God and is the guarantee that others will follow. It is the sign of hope for humanity and of the ultimate triumph of God's purpose. In this sense, the intercession of Christ, his 'standing in the breach' for the whole world of humanity, is an act of intercession not only in that he prays 'Father, forgive them for they know not what they do', but in that, his whole life culminating in his death is an intercessory offering before God. There is no need here to excise the idea that on the cross, Christ endures the wrath of God. If God's just wrath is God's implacable resistance to evil, and if that wrath is visited upon humans not as God launches a 'seek and destroy' exercise but as God gives us over to the consequences of our own evil actions, Christ can be understood as the one who steps into the process and endures the alienating consequences of sin on our behalf. He acknowledges the justness of the divine justice. He is the Lamb of God who takes away the sins of the world. This does not reduce divine wrath to an impersonal process of cause and effect that somehow exists independent of God, so distancing God's own self from a concept that some (foolishly) find distasteful. Such wrath is God's wrath, constituted by God's own being as love. There is no way that a rebellious world can escape it. It is the guarantee that sin and evil will not finally triumph. In this narrative of redemption, it is not necessary to evade the concept of substitution. Christ is the one who experiences what it means to be alienated from the Father; and this must be the essence of being in hell. Christ undergoes this in order that we may be spared it, however much it may be deserved. But the power of Christ's cross to atone for sin does not consist in the Father punishing the Son but in Christ interceding for us sinners and seeking God's mercy from within our humanity and condition. And all of this is by the Father's own will and compassion.

I shall have more to say on the scope and extent of Christ's atoning work in due course. I content myself for the moment with the assertion that there is no salvation apart from the intercessory work of Christ. Equally, there is no salvation apart from repentance, that is, our own request for God's mercy made in the name of Christ and based on his work. However, I return for a moment to the much-contested notion of propitiation. There would be an incoherence in any claim to the effect that Christ on the cross appeases divine wrath or that the sacrifice of the cross turns the Father from wrath to mercy or from hostility to love. This would be to make the work of the cross discontinuous, to set the Son against the Father as though their wills were opposed. As already claimed, the work of the cross is the work of the Father, through the Son by the Spirit. John Calvin, who is often associated with the idea of penal substitution, is himself at great pains to stress that love precedes the cross rather than being the consequence of it. Such a view is entirely biblical in that the divine initiative to save springs from God's antecedent love for the world. Nevertheless, this does not avoid the fact that the will of God to save and to reconcile must be enacted, and for this to happen, there has to be the penitent plea for mercy. To say that on the cross, Christ 'makes intercession for sinners' is to claim that by participation in the human condition, though without capitulating to it, he qualifies himself to act on our behalf. In fact, he is doubly qualified to do so, first as the Word of God through whom all things have been made, and secondly, as the head of a new humanity, a second Adam who has come to the rescue and merited his role by his obedience. By accepting on his own self and in our place the consequences of our sin, death, and alienation, he acknowledges the divine condemnation of sin and actively offers up his own life, obedience and prayers as a sacrificial plea. It is a plea for mercy offered by one who is bound to be heard.

I found new light on the word 'propitiation' when reading the parable of the sinner and the tax collector. In Luke 18:13, the 'sinner' cries out, 'God be merciful to me a sinner' and is heard when the self-sufficient tax collector is not. Literally translated his request is, 'God be propitiated to me a sinner'. My point is that God is already propitious to repentant sinners and does not have to be made such. God wills to forgive, but forgiveness must be enacted, and this happens when the request is sincerely made. In Christ, there is one who intercedes for sinners. His cross is the mercy-seat, the place of atonement, expiation, and propitiation to which we may freely come to find help in time of need. Although there is no salvation without our repentance, we can never be sure that our own repentance is deep enough, sure enough, or sincere enough to be sufficient to ensure our forgiveness. We can, however, be sure that when we approach the Father through the Son, his work on our behalf, a work that includes us and perfects our repentance, is more than sufficient to reconcile us to the Father. It is impossible to find a better summation of this than words found in the liturgy for communion in the Book of Common Prayer,

"All glory be to thee, Almighty God, our heavenly Father, for that thou, of thy tender mercy, didst give thine only Son Jesus Christ to suffer death upon the cross for our redemption, who made there, by his one oblation of himself once offered, a full, perfect, and sufficient sacrifice, oblation, and satisfaction, for the sins of the whole world."

Christ's saving offering on the cross is thus to be understood as the culmination of the offering of his whole human existence from conception to giving up his spirit on our behalf. By participating in our human condition and living as the true human being, obedient to the Father and his vocation, he has over-turned that condition, become a sign of hope for a restored humanity and the means given by the Father, through which we may be redeemed. It is occasionally assumed that what matters in Christ's saving work is simply his death. By contrast, I believe, along with many others, that it is the whole course of Jesus' life, his active obedience in living to the Father and his passive obedience in submitting himself to the cross, that is redemptive. Christ has displaced us such that at the cross, we become 'displaced persons' and has taken upon himself God's righteous rejection of sinful humanity. Yet the cross, as the culmination of Christ's life of obedience, is the symbol and sign of the self-giving of God in Christ that seals it all. Christ's whole existence, from birth to death, constitutes his intercessory work. The cross of Christ is the place, the 'mercy seat', to which we must come to seek mercy from God. Even our most sincere pleas for divine mercy are inadequate, failing to reach into the depths of our fallen beings. This is where the intercession of Christ fulfils and completes our own and grants us the grounds of assurance.

Before dealing with the scope of Christ's work I refer to two further points which I believe to be biblically derived and which underscore what has been said above. The first is the idea that sinful attitudes and acts unleash consequences that cannot be ignored. It is, therefore, as though Christ, in his atonement, has intervened in the process to take those consequences upon himself to endure them in his own person and to absorb them and remove them. This, of course, means that God the Father, acting in and through Christ, has also endured them and overcome them in love and grace, opening the way for reconciliation. Although we see this becoming an event in history so that there is an objective realisation of atonement, the event reflects an eternal reality, one that, so to speak, God 'carries' in his very being as a will to reconcile. God is an eternally forgiving God. A second insight is drawn from 2 Corinthians 5:16-21 which asserts that 'in Christ God was reconciling the world to himself'. This points to the atonement as a continuous work that, in a trinitarian fashion, originates in the Father, is enacted in the Son and is realised by the Spirit. The Son is not pitted against the Father but is the overflow of the Father's love. But I have long puzzled over the following words, 'For our sake, he made him to be sin who knew no sin, so that in him we might become the righteousness of God' (v.23). What does it mean for Christ to be 'made to be sin'? Clearly, this is sacrificial language and there is an exchange here, a great exchange. I imagine it takes up what happens on the Day of Atonement as set out in Leviticus 15-16, the most holy day of Israel's year, and still, a signal part of Jewish devotion when atonement was made for the sin of the people by the sacrifice of a bull and a goat by the High Priest. A second, live goat, is also employed: 'Aaron shall lay both his hands on the head of the live goat and confess over it all the iniquities of the people of Israel, and all their transgressions, all their sins, putting them on the head of the goat, and sending it away into the wilderness by means of someone designated for the task. The goat shall bear on itself all their iniquities to a barren region; and the goat shall be set free in the wilderness' (16:21-22). This is the idea of the 'scapegoat', and I find it reflected in Isaiah 53:6, 'all we like sheep have gone astray; we have all turned to our own way, and the LORD has laid on him the iniquity of us all'. It is echoed elsewhere and not least in 1 Peter 2:24, 'He himself bore our sins in his body on the cross, so that, free from sins, we might live for righteousness; by his wounds you have been healed'. The ritual of the scapegoat is the indication that 'as far as the east is from the west, so far he removes our transgressions from us' (Psalm 103:12). For Christ to be 'made sin' is for our sins to be carried away into the wilderness and no longer considered. This is the enormous claim that is at the centre of Christian faith and probably only partially grasped even by most of us who believe. For others, of course, who have no notion of 'sin', iniquity, or transgression, it sadly remains without meaning.

So, I turn to the question of the extent and efficacy of Christ's redemption: Did Christ die for all or only for some? Do all benefit from the work of Christ or only those who consciously take refuge in him through faith? Even within Calvinist orthodoxy there have been divergent views as to whether the atonement is limited to the 'elect' or is sufficient for all. On the face of it, the belief that Christ has made intercession for sinners suggests that all 'sinners' might potentially benefit from the atonement, although this does not necessarily mean that it will be efficacious for all if sinners refuse its benefits. There is an intriguing verse in 1 Timothy 4:10: 'We have our hope set on the living God, who is the Saviour of all people, especially of those who believe'. There is a complexity in the interplay between the 'some' and the 'many' in the biblical witness. Israel occupies a special place within the purposes of God, but correctly understood its role is representative rather than exclusive. It is not that God works for Israel alone but through Israel for the sake of all nations; so Israel is a paradigm for us all and a forerunner. When we take Israel, therefore, as a paradigm case for the revealing and redeeming work of God, we see the significance of this as universal in intent. All nations benefit. When it says of Jesus that 'he will save his people from their sins', it is not Israel alone in view but all people of all nations: 'On that day Israel will be the third with

Egypt and Assyria, a blessing in the midst of the earth, whom the LORD of hosts has blessed, saying, "Blessed be Egypt my people, and Assyria the work of my hands, and Israel my heritage"' (Isaiah 19:24). Remarkable words, and not isolated ones, considering Egypt and Assyria were ancient enemies. There is, therefore, an entirely proper universalism to the gospel, and were this not so we would be left with a form of nationalism in contradiction to the witness of both testaments. This is acknowledged in principle, of course, by all Christians. Yet some traditions impose a different kind of limitation in the claim that Christ has not died for all people without *exception* but only for all people without *distinction,* that is, distinctions of nation, sex, class, colour, or whichever other forms of discrimination we care to erect. Christ, on this account, does not die for all people but for pre-determined persons from all *categories* whose sins are taken and eliminated by Christ on the cross. In these terms, the cross is usually understood as Christ bearing the very specific punishments due to others that are laid upon Christ instead. It might be seen that there could be great comfort in this if one believes oneself to be among the elect for whom Christ died. In turn, what determines destinies is the prior decision of God in eternity, who decrees who is among the elect and who are the reprobates. I have already touched upon some of what seem to me the shortcomings of this system and will have more to say.

My own tradition among Baptist Christians exhibits the polarity of 'general' and 'particular' on this topic. Baptists emerged at a time in the early seventeenth century when these topics were being debated among Reformed Christians in the Netherlands. There have subsequently been variations on the theme in demonstration of the fact that Calvinism and Reformed Christianity are by no means monolithic in conviction. It is typically claimed, for instance, that the work of Christ is sufficient for all but only efficacious for some, those who have faith. This would be widely believed. Personally, I am of the firm conviction that Christ has died for all without exception or distinction and that Christ's life and death are an intercession for all sinners. God wills to save. Christ is the Lamb of God who takes away the sin of the world. God is the God of our salvation, and this is the plain teaching of scripture, so much so that it calls the whole of the limited-atonement version of Reformed Christianity into question. If the scheme can be tested against scripture at any point, it is here, and it is found to be wanting.

However, there is another theological conviction that weighs heavily with me, has already been mentioned, and is usually inadequately developed. This concerns the implication of understanding Christ as the Word of God through whom all things have been made (John 1). All things have come into being through him as God's agent in creation and are forever upheld by him (Hebrews 1). Believing, as Christians do, that this same Word has now become incarnate to renew or recreate the world that has gone astray and become estranged from its creator, what Christ the Word does in redemption must make its impact universally. This means on all human beings, not just some, and indeed on the whole creation at all its subordinate levels, both mineral and animal. This latter statement is grounded in the belief that in becoming incarnate, God in Christ has recapitulated all these levels and as the Word of God redeems them. It coheres with the long-held Christian belief that 'What is assumed (in the incarnation) is healed'. God's saving work is in the incarnation and in the cross as its culmination. Salvation is not only for all people without exception or distinction but for everything whose created reality Christ has assumed. In turn, this sheds light on the passage in Colossians 1 that envisions everything that has been created being finally reconciled 'through the blood of his cross' (v.20). It provides the basis on which Revelation 21:5 can proclaim, 'See I am making all things new!'. The term, 'All things', frequently used by Paul, is hard to exhaust. So is Christ's redeeming work. This is no surprise since God is inexhaustible.

Christ is both prophet and priest, offices that he exercises in a representative role by virtue of his having participated in human nature and freely taken our self-imposed fate upon himself. His ability to act representatively and to recapitulate the human story is intensified by the fact that he is and has always been the pre-existent Word through whom all things have been created and through his ministry will be, and are being, re-created. The third office traditionally ascribed to him is that of kingship and it follows from what he has fulfilled as prophet and priest. Because of his obedience, he has been exalted by the Father to the place of lordship over creation. To be sure, this is already prefigured in his earthly ministry as he demonstrated, or so the Gospels portray it, his liberating power over illness, evil influences and even the created order. Within the New Testament narrative, as emphasised in the liturgical year of the churches, this is instantiated in the Ascension which pictorially illustrates the honour and glory that are Christ's, his headship over both church and universe. He is the exalted Lord. It is entirely appropriate that knees should bow before him, and his kingly status and worship should be offered without reservation. In the face of constant fashionable critiques of hierarchies and notions of super- or subordination, I have not the slightest hesitation in yielding to Christ as the only one who is truly worthy. While some view such subordination as a loss of human dignity, I regard it as the making of us. Neither do I regard such attitudes or language as legitimating oppressive human structures but, on the contrary, as subverting them and over-turning them precisely because the one who now occupies the 'space' of divine lordship is the Crucified One who came to serve not to be served. And in this he defines the true nature of our creator and the proper function of power.

Post Seven: The Resurrection and its Narratives

The kingship of Christ is enacted and displayed in his resurrection, the bedrock event of Christian devotion, an event and reality to which the whole New Testament bears witness. This is truly a 'boundary event, at the point where...the laws of physics cease to apply. It is the beginning of a new creation'.[18] In the event of the resurrection, Christ becomes Lord over death. It is made manifest that he will not and cannot die again. I say 'event' because the resurrection is something that has happened *within* human history, but I do not regard it as an event *of* human history in the sense that it arises causally from what has gone before. If it makes sense at any point to speak of 'divine intervention', then it is here. Something radically new and unheard of happens. It is a profound mistake to envision the resurrection as a resuscitation, the reanimating of the dead body of Jesus. Rather, the body of Jesus is lifted out of its mortality into immortality; it is 'glorified'. It interests me that the Gospel narratives portray the tomb of Jesus as being empty but as still containing the grave clothes of Jesus lying where his body had been. The impression conveyed by this, surely intentionally, is that his body quite literally rose and entered a new condition, that of a 'life-giving spirit' (1 Corinthians 15:45). I value

---

[18] Lesslie Newbigin, *The Gospel in a Pluralist Society* (London: SPCK, 1989), p.11.

the thought that what we encounter here is the entry of the future into the present. The newness of the 'new heaven and new earth' here becomes a reality. This is impossible, of course, for those who discount the possibility of 'newness' but not for those who find it within the gift of God. The body of Jesus is the first created reality to undergo the transformation that will one day be the case for all creation. We ourselves will ultimately be raised as he has been raised (Romans 8:11), but he remains the first fruits of the new creation and the agent of its final coming just as he was the agent, as the Word, of the first and present creation (1 Corinthians 15:20-29). The kingship of Christ is, therefore, sublime. Such thoughts enable us to come closer to the nature of the resurrection appearances. They are both visionary and embodied, but their embodiment is ineffable, according to a form appropriate to the world to come rather than this present age. Christ is portrayed as one who comes and goes, who passes through locked doors, who engages in physical acts such as eating and drinking and can be touched, yet who cannot be 'grasped' in his risen and exalted state. Some sincere interpreters see these elements as apologetic additions to the resurrection tradition. Maybe they bear the imprint of such concerns in the way they are formulated. I do not personally see why they cannot belong to the bedrock of the resurrection witness. It is not that they have been constructed by the early Christians to give credibility to their experience. Rather, the events of the resurrection have created that experience in the first place.

Those are surely right who argue that the primary reality we encounter in the resurrection is the life-giving presence of the eternally living Christ. This was true for the first disciples and continues to be true in the life of the church, wherever it may be located. Christ is present and knowable for all who believe. There is an interplay between the Risen Lord and the Holy Spirit through whom his presence is extended into our present, so much so that the two are blended into one in our experience and need not be overly distinguished. Those of us who live at a remove from the history of Jesus and the origins of our faith know of them by means of witness and testimony and not by direct empirical apprehension. Yet what we know is real and objectively true. This is far more than saying that the resurrection consists in the enduring memory of Jesus, a kind of afterlife because of which it is impossible to forget him, or a reference to the continuing impact of his teaching and personality. These things are undoubtedly and blessedly true. But taken on their own they would be reductionist. Christ's presence is a real presence, that of one who lives now in God and is genuinely present and active in the world for those who have eyes to see. Yet there is more than this. The resurrection is not a product of antecedent history within the causal nexus. It is rather an act of God within history that can be historically discerned even if not historically verified or observed. Historically speaking, the resurrection can be shown to be probable for those whose presuppositions and worldview do not exclude it from the start. It is grounded.

It might be that concentrating the focus on the living Christ who is spiritually present for those who believe relativizes the importance of the need for historical evidence of the event of resurrection. There is a strength in this in that all outside the first generation of witnesses depend for their faith on the sense of spiritual encounter with the Risen Lord. They are not able to touch, see or in any way to associate with an embodied Lord. Much can be made of the fact that the encounter of the apostle Paul with Christ on the road to Damascus was itself visionary rather than embodied. The deduction is then sometimes made that all the reported resurrection appearances of the first disciples had the same nature. This then allows a divergence between those who would dismiss them as 'bereavement visions', which experiences are well and widely documented in the psychological literature, and others who would reckon them as 'veridical', that is, visions of an objectively but not physically present Lord. The former of these views (bereavement visions) might restrict the visions to a few persons, such as Peter and Mary Magdalene, who prompted a form of contagion among others. This sceptical view could certainly point to relatable experiences in the diverse, varied and often incredible history of human religious phenomena. Yet even so, that such bereavement visions should happen to these particular persons surrounding the death of this particular and extraordinary individual at this particular juncture of history with all the remarkable consequences that flowed from it takes a degree of believing that itself borders on the miraculous. If the alternative understanding of visions as 'veridical' carries weight, it is also within the range of human religious experiences that take audible, visual and even sensory forms. The visionary pathway, therefore, is not necessarily reductive but may point us to the fact that the resurrection experiences are *sui generis*; in other words, because they are transcendent events, they do not fall easily within categories we can explain. There could be a category of 'trans-physicality' quite consonant with the belief that in the resurrection, the future is invading the present. What might we expect if not profound mystery when this happens? And maybe the first disciples who were witnesses to it also struggled to find the words to describe it.

I am fully persuaded that Christ was raised from the dead by being exalted from mortality to immortality. This involved the transformation of his body into the life of God, its 'glorification' (a useful word that leaves its precise definition open) in such a way that he could be present in a 'spiritual body'. I can imagine that either in earthly, factual reality or in a veridical, objective vision, he could make his presence felt. I have been taken by the statement of Diarmaid McCulloch that at the heart of the New Testament, there is a 'blank', and that 'blank' is what the New Testament is all about.[19] There is indeed a blank in that there was no-one who did or could

---

[19] 'The New Testament is thus a literature with a blank at its centre; yet this blank is also its intense focus', *Christianity: The first three thousand years* (Harmondsworth: Penguin, 2010), p.57.

have observed the resurrection as such. What was observed was its residue in the empty tomb and its consequences in the apostolic eyewitnesses. If there is solid and observable history in all of this, history that I find irrefutable, it is that those first disciples were convinced that Christ had been raised, that they were neither deceitful nor deluded in their claims; indeed, they paid the price for what they believed in a way that establishes their credibility. If, as is frequently claimed, our convictions should be based upon evidence, the only evidence we have points in the direction of an event unusual in the extreme that the New Testament itself reckons as 'resurrection'. When alternative hypotheses are advanced, such as the disciples having stolen the body or Jesus' reviving in the tomb, they are speculation without evidence. The question then becomes, what happened to account for the disciples' conviction? And what would be sufficient to give rise to the movement that flowed from their testimony?

I freely acknowledge that there are challenges here, and whereas I am keen to negotiate them, I do not wish to minimise them. An older apologetic such as Frank Morrison's well-known *Who Moved the Stone?* Operated with the assumptions that the Gospel narratives were straightforward accounts that could be mustered into a forensic argument. In retrospect, this seems a naïve position to take. The New Testament records are at times inconsistent, well described as 'narrative mayhem'. Whereas it could well be the case that with some creativity they might be placed within a coherent structure, and this has been attempted, this can begin to feel like special pleading. Given the unique nature of the resurrection, one that potentially could redefine our concepts of space and time, this might just be the way it has to be. However, I am prepared to concede that some traditional approaches to these narratives are questionable. To assume they have the nature of direct eye-witness records, all of which are to be taken literally and naively, is surely mistaken. In reality, all of the narratives have a history and have developed over time within certain cultural and theological contexts before assuming written form. They may have assumed this form before being included in the Gospels that came to be canonically recognised. For sure, they go back to some original historical sources. I find entirely credible the scholarship of Richard Bauckham that points to the regulative role of early eyewitnesses.[20] But it is also clear to me that the narratives show signs of the intertwining of history, legend, apologetics, and theology. It would be foolish, for instance, to deny that reports of the bodies of the saints of old being shaken out of their graves after the resurrection of Jesus and appearing to many is a legend (Matthew 27:52-53) - it is not given testimony in any other New Testament document which, given such an extraordinary event, is passing strange. It has value in witnessing the power of that resurrection for those already dead, but

---

[20] Richard Bauckham, *Jesus and the Eyewitnesses: The Gospels as Eyewitness Testimony* (Grand Rapids: Eerdmans, 2006).

to defend it as historical borders on the incredible. It could have originated in a vision, but how would we ever know?

We find here both the controlling and pre-determining role of the doctrine of biblical inerrancy and the 'domino' fear that if one part of the evidence is regarded as legendary then the rest might fall. Yet 'inerrantists' would have little difficulty in recognising legends as such in other ancient documents, religious or otherwise. And 'thin-end-of-the-wedge' arguments can prevent us from seeing things as they really are. I have no difficulty in acknowledging some things as legendary and, in fact, would be surprised if there weren't any, given that the scriptural records we have developed over time. I find a level of meaning in the legend, but not a literal one. I would also find little difficulty in granting the 'tearing of the curtain' in the temple (Matthew 27:51) as a theologically significant legend or including the earthquake and the darkness (27:45) within the same category. Sure enough, earthquakes were common enough in the area, but the events of Golgotha were 'earth-shaking' in every other sense. I see this as a theological interpretation wrapped around a historical event; a feature not unknown in biblical history. Likewise, the presence of angels in the narratives serves both to communicate the numinous nature of the resurrection event and to introduce the voice of God by way of interpretation as to its meaning. Some may see these judgements as devaluing the narratives, but I would take the opposite view. They are ways of communicating their all-but-incommunicable significance. In studying the life of Jesus, as will become clear in what I have to say later, I have much enjoyed and benefitted from the study by Maurice Casey entitled *Jesus of Nazareth*. In part, this is because, although he gave up Christianity and thoughts of ordination as a student, he endeavoured to write neither out of religious motives nor anti-religious ones but to the best of his ability as an objective scholar. Many of his conclusions are remarkably 'conservative', including, for instance, the dating of Mark's Gospel to the AD40s – very much an 'outlier' position. When it comes to the resurrection, he adopts the 'bereavement vision' approach but goes on to say:

"It follows that we should not blindly accept the traditional Christian view that the Resurrection of Jesus was God's vindication of him. Some people will prefer the view of most Jews who were in Israel at the time that the Resurrection did not really take place. On the other hand, there should be no doubt, even on the most rigorous of historical criteria, that some of the first followers of Jesus had genuine visions of him after his death and that they interpreted these as appearances of the risen Lord. In other words, the historical evidence is in no way inconsistent with the belief of the first disciples, and that of many modern Christians, that God raised Jesus from the dead and granted visions of the risen Jesus to some of the first disciples and to St Paul on the Damascus Road."[21]

---

[21] Maurice Casey, *Jesus of Nazareth: An independent historian's account of his life and teaching* (London: T&T Clark, 2010), p.498.

Given that the only access to what happened is through those who bore witness to it, it may be that all these historical questionings are beside the point. On solely historical grounds, we have no way of determining the issue, and it is to be doubted that twenty-first-century historians have greater authority than first-century witnesses. Yet it is reasonable to say that a unique event in human history, such as the resurrection, might quite reasonably attract a diversity of ways of clarifying the reality of what took place and refuting misrepresentations of it. I certainly feel the force of those criticisms that point out that the New Testament world was a story-making world and did not adhere to the kind of historiographic conventions that prevail in modern scholarship. Some of the New Testament constructions attract the suspicion that they derive from theological or apologetic motives. For instance, the account of the sealing of the tomb and the setting of the guards (Matthew 27:62-66; 28:11-15) can be understood as refuting the Jewish claim that the body of Jesus was stolen or removed by the disciples. The probability that such hapless guards should be rewarded for a gross dereliction of duty rather than summarily punished strikes me as unlikely. At the same time, we are dealing here, as often in historical investigation, with probabilities, not certainties. In a similar way, the beautifully crafted account of the disciples on the road to Emmaus could credibly be understood as a theological and devotional product of 'eucharistic' experiences. There are those who question the very existence of Joseph of Arimathea and the consequent accounts of the empty tomb and see these as later inventions intended to support the resurrection claim. Debate in all these areas flows to and fro and its conclusions are usually fashioned by the presuppositions that lie behind it. The point is that from a purely historiographical point of view, it is impossible to be definitive. Nevertheless, we might confess to various degrees of probability in assessing the evidence.[22] Strangely, the fact that not all the details of the narratives can be taken as literal, historical truth does not by any stretch of the imagination mean that the resurrection did not take place. The more 'questionable' elements can be understood as attempts to interpret an event that goes beyond our regular categories. They are commentaries, shaped and winnowed over decades, on the nature of the resurrection and its significance, constructed indeed with theological and apologetic motives but nonetheless bearing witness to the truth. Behind the constructs, there is genuine bedrock history.

I conclude at this point and at many others in the reading of biblical history that the primary question to ask is, 'What am I to learn from this witness?' Rather than jump to the question of historical and literal facticity, the primary questions concern what is to be understood from what is there. On this basis I embrace the thought that there is nothing disinterested about biblical narratives –

---

[22] I have much enjoyed the extensive consideration of the resurrection in the work by *Michael R. Licona, The Resurrection of Jesus: A New Historiographical Approach* (Nottingham: IVP Academic/Apollos, 2010).

they intend to inform, enlighten, and instruct concerning the primary meaning of the events underlying the narratives. To this end, they are rhetorical and are intended to bear witness and persuade. I refer again here to what I have previously written about the film *Dunkirk*. My point is that there is no doubt that the Dunkirk evacuation took place as a positive historical event, but the way it was portrayed in the film for later generations and its significance brought out involved a device that was artificial without being untruthful. It even included, as such films often do, elements that are fictional. When this analogy is applied to the resurrection accounts, I find no difficulty in recognising that they are (and must be) 'constructed'. At the same time, they are evocative and powerful, and when approached with a view to what might be learnt from them, they are life-giving. And details apart, they relate an overall and agreed story: Jesus was crucified, he was entombed, and shortly thereafter, his tomb was found to be empty, and a series of appearances convinced his first followers that he was alive in a way that was beyond death. There are two poles, therefore, to the witness: one is the fact of an empty tomb and the question it raised. The second is the appearances of Jesus as one who had been glorified. This conviction impelled the first disciples into the world as witnesses at the cost of their own lives and well-being. People do not do this without very good reason. And they tell us what that reason is.

Post Eight. The Nature of 'Finality'

To reiterate: I have sought to stress the universal nature of the love of God and of Christ's work of redemption, so much so that I see in it far more than the salvation of human souls from eternal loss but rather the ultimate redemption of our bodies and of the creation itself. This is clearly witnessed to in the scriptures. Inevitably, as we have seen, such expansive beliefs lead to questions about the final destiny of human beings. Will all be saved? The typical evangelical answer to this is one of denial: there is heaven, and there is hell, a double outcome to human history. Our destiny is binary. This accounts for the seriousness with which evangelicals approach questions of human decision: there is much at stake, eternity itself. In turn this concern leads to an evangelistic posture towards the world – it is our duty to preach Christ and to call people to repentance in order that they may be saved. I have qualified this approach by claiming that the narrowness of a preoccupation with 'going to heaven when you die' neither answers to the breadth of the biblical concerns nor to the needs of human societies. There is more to be understood. God's purpose is to gather a people in whom God's presence may be known and transmitted in a way that is redemptive. The search for a 'paradigm' people for the good of the whole world is fundamental to both the Old and New Testaments, with the Christian churches being understood not as an abolition of Israel the people but as a concentration and expansion of what was initiated with Abraham and definitively set forth in Christ. Whereas this might qualify the 'going to heaven when you die' message, it does not, however, abolish it. Our future destiny and that of others is far from a matter of indifference. That we should inherit eternal life, the life of God, remains part of the Christian hope, only to be broadened out in that it includes 'a new heaven and a new earth in which righteousness dwells'. There can be no doubt that this represents a universal perspective.

Evangelical Christians tend to be profoundly averse to the nation of universalism because they typically understand this to be the belief that whatever individuals may have done, God our Judge will overlook it all and decline to exclude any from eternal life. Evangelicals are inclined to believe that whatever lies beyond this life it must grow out of the decisions of the present one. This accounts for the seriousness with which they approach the subject – how we set our lives now determines the future beyond this life. I agree with this, though with significant qualifications. My contention is that this is only one way of understanding what is meant by 'universalism' and a 'non-doctrinal' one at that. Universalist doctrines have been held in the church more widely than is often supposed and have been rooted in more significant theological and doctrinal concerns than the simplistic belief that God will turn out to be 'nice' to everybody. 'Soft' universalism fails to reckon with the radical nature of human corruption, the unbelievable cruelties that human beings inflict on each other and their other companions in the journey of life, and for which justice and truth demand that they be held accountable. It renders almost incidental the redeeming work of Christ on the grounds that it was not necessary after all. I have asserted my twin beliefs that there is no salvation apart from Christ and that there is no participation in Christ apart from repentance. My task now is to further expound these themes.

The rejection of 'soft' universalism, a rejection with which I entirely sympathise, overlooks the fact that there are other cogent universalisms, some of which have been prefigured in what has appeared above. At one level, there is the fact of the particularist focus on Israel outlined in the Hebrew Bible whereby God elects one ethnic people for a special relation with God's own self: 'You only have I known of all the families of the earth' (Amos 3:2). At the same time there is from the beginnings with Abraham a universal concern that these people should be chosen for the blessing of all. The particularism of the revelatory and redemptive role of Israel is instrumental within a universal intention. There are good reasons for this within an understanding of the 'sociology of knowledge'. Knowledge is constructed within communities that develop their own 'plausibility structures'. There can be no abstract or universal knowledge independently of specific groupings. To convey a revelation to the whole, God has chosen a part for the sake of the whole in which a certain way of knowing develops.

Biblical revelation makes it clear that the choice of that part is by grace, not carried through because Israel was in any way superior to the other nations: 'It was not because you were more numerous than any other people that the LORD set his heart on you and chose you – for you were the fewest of all peoples. It was because the LORD loved you' (Deuteronomy 7:7-8). It was the very insignificance of Israel that qualified it to be used by God so that glory might be given to God alone, leaving no room for 'boasting'. Understood so, it is a major perversion of the divine intention when God's gracious choice is interpreted as a form of ethnic or human superiority. This aberration is easily committed and has occurred both in Israel's self-understanding and that of the church. However, my point here is that this form of universalism is entirely true to the biblical testimony. Viewed as the expansion of God's purpose initiated (and arguably continuing) in the people of Israel, Christianity has nonetheless broken beyond any form of ethnic definition and understands itself as necessarily inclusive of all nations on the grounds of faith in Christ rather than ethnic origin. This universalism constitutes an element so fundamental that Christianity would not be Christianity without it. It represented a major tension in the early church. 'There is no longer Jew or Greek' (Galatians 3:28). It also constitutes a major difference with contemporary Judaism, which, although it can be generous to the religious status of the 'nations', still adheres to a strongly ethnic particularity. (In relation to Jewish fears that Paul's theology leads to a loss of Jewish identity, I would respond not that such identities are abolished but transcended. There is a higher reality in which we participate, and this binds us together without our ceasing to be distinctive. So also, with male and female.)

At further levels, therefore, the Christian faith takes into itself and reinforces the elements in the Hebrew Bible/Old Testament that look towards a universal salvation and blessing of the nations. It proclaims that God loves the world and gave his Son for it. It understands Christ's atoning work as one that 'takes away the sin of the world'. Christ is portrayed as the Saviour not only of those who believe but of all people. It looks towards a final ingathering of the nations and a consummation of the whole creation. It asserts that 'God is not willing that any should perish but that all should reach repentance'. The apostle Paul repeatedly speaks of 'all things' being included in Christ's redemption, of a universal and final gathering back to God of what was made by God in the first place. I celebrate the trinitarian perspective that encompasses God's work as Creator, Recreator and Transcreator. The distinction sometimes made and already referred to between 'all without distinction' and 'all without exception' comes into play here. The former perspective negotiates the universal statements of scripture as embracing all kinds or degrees of persons without regard to class, ethnicity, gender or any other such difference. The second asserts the saving intentions of God for every single person. I embrace this latter understanding and regard the former, though it contains important truth, as an attempt to evade the plain meaning of scripture, paradoxically by those who otherwise insist that this is what we should be seeking!

There is not only strong biblical testimony to the universal intentions of God but equally strong theological consideration to undergird it. It makes sense that God, having created all things, should redeem them when they have gone astray. It is unthinkable to imagine that God would abandon that which has been purposed in creative love from eternity. There is a symmetry between God creating all things and God redeeming all things. It is impossible to follow this logic without at least entertaining thoughts of universal salvation as the horizon towards which we are being drawn. Once more, we find a degree of paradox in discovering that universalist impulses have sometimes arisen within the Calvinist tradition that is often associated, as in double predestination, with more restrictive approaches. This I have referred to as 'hypothetical universalism'. The argument proceeds as follows: Election to salvation is by grace alone, irrespective of human merit. It is also 'irresistible' in the sense that, the decision to save having been made, no elect person can finally resist the divine choice and must come to believe and to persevere. Moreover, the work of Christ on the cross is of infinite value sufficient to cover all sin. Hypothetically, therefore, the prevenient divine choice could embrace every human being who has ever existed if God should so choose. If God is indeed love and God's compassion is over all that God has made why and how should any be excluded from salvation? On this ground, even if to demonstrate God's justice, something less than the total number of human beings is to be saved, this number may yet be very considerable, with the greatest number of persons attaining salvation. Extending this line of thought even further, since by the will of God Christ has borne God's judgement and condemnation in our place, the justice of God has been manifested in Christ in such a way as to make it unnecessary for any others to be condemned. In this sense, Christ alone is the 'Reprobate', and there need be no other. Hypothetically, therefore all could be saved, although we do not know for certain this will be the case.

There are other considerations that could be added to this train of thought. A crucial shift in thinking already indicated, and an unusual one for an evangelical to entertain, is to allow God's search for the lost to reach beyond death. Accordingly, the end of a person's life is not the end of the hope of salvation, the 'final' point beyond which change is not possible. I believe that this must be the case and do so on several grounds. This shift of thought, which many with my theological background would find problematic, involves redrawing the lines of 'finality'. It is widely assumed that death seals a person's eternal fate and is to be followed by the double outcome of heaven or hell. Hence, the importance of not dying in unbelief and the value sometimes placed on the 'death-bed conversion'. Once more, although these patterns of thought are widely assumed in both Protestantism and Catholicism, they are not easily substantiated by scripture. I have no desire whatsoever to abate the challenge to repent and believe in Christ and to do so before one dies. To die in Christ is to die securely. But I have come to believe that 'finality' does not necessarily occur at individual death but at the final judgement, however, this reality is understood to take place. This belief is to be distinguished from the Catholic doctrine of purgatory, which has to do with the purification of the already baptised to fit them for the vision of God. There are, to my mind, many reasons for positing the possibility of 'post-mortem salvation', and it is clear to me that many Christians tacitly and pastorally already embrace the possibility.[23] Death remains a mystery for us all, but this does not mean that we cannot reverently, if tentatively, enter this territory in our thinking. Even more so in the light of a God who has compassion on all that has been made and who wills to save.

It makes no sense to me that such a God should abandon the majority of those made in God's own image to what is sometimes called 'a Christless eternity'. The more severely this fate is conceived of (as in 'everlasting torment'), the more problematic and inhumane the belief becomes. I have already suggested how 'hypothetical universalism', emerging from one of the more stringent of the theological traditions, can mitigate the severity of this position. Confessions of faith might, for instance, assure us that 'elect children' who die in infancy are nonetheless saved. As there

---

[23] Stephen Jonathan, *Grace Beyond the Grave: Is Salvation Possible in the Afterlife? A Biblical, Theological and Pastoral Evaluation* (Eugene, Oregon: Wipf & Stock, 2014).

is no way of knowing who or how many this might amount to, some go further and assert that *all* children who die in infancy are 'saved' and inherit eternal life because they are all elect. Immediately, this pushes the number of the redeemed into majority figures if we take account of child mortality rates throughout history and, possibly, extend them beyond natural death to include abortions and miscarriages from the beginning of the human story (though this raises unanswerable questions). It is entirely imponderable to reflect on the status of the unborn in the eyes of God. To say that 'life begins at conception' seems irrefutable since what is conception, if not the conception of life? But at what point one begins to become a person with a destiny in life and beyond is securely only known unto God, though the question is significant in evaluating the ethics of medical abortion. If we take a suggested figure of 60 to 100 billion as a credible estimate of the number of human beings who have ever lived, we can only conclude that the number who have come to conscious faith in the God of Israel or Jesus the Saviour must be considerably fewer and provokes the question of how many must be lost for some to be saved? Is there an acceptable wastage rate in the divine plan of salvation? Or should we conclude that there are those 'uncovenanted mercies', that God has his other peoples,[24] sheep that are not of the immediately obvious fold? I cannot avoid this conclusion based on the claims of justice and the belief that a loving God wills to save. Though we are certainly to be judged based

---

24

on what we have done in this life, and all will be revealed in the finality of the last judgement, we should reckon with the persistence of God who seeks the lost, a search that reaches beyond death into the largely hidden realms that lie beyond.

The claims of justice are considerable. It is rightly pointed out that the Hebrew scriptures present us with only the dimmest perceptions of an afterlife. When the claim is made that religion is about 'pie in the sky when you die', then the religion of Israel is a standing refutation since its hopes were deeply 'this-worldly' rather than other-worldly. The hope of a resurrection emerges only slowly and clearly when the author of the Book of Daniel (one of the latest Old Testament books) contemplates the problem of Israel's martyrs, those who are eliminated in a time of persecution because of their fidelity to the LORD. The writer envisages a future in which they are restored to life and vindicated, and so justice is delivered to them: 'Many of those who sleep in the dust of the earth shall awake, some to everlasting life, and some to shame and everlasting contempt' (Daniel 12:2). Hope of resurrection emerges from the claims of justice rather than the dread of death: true justice cannot be done in this life alone. This trajectory can be extended to address my present concern, which is sometimes described as 'the fate of the unevangelised' and embraces every human soul, even outside the circle of those to whom God's truth has been revealed in history. These latter persons are indeed privileged to see things into which 'angels have longed to look'. They occupy a pivotal place in the history of salvation. But they are not the sum of those who are to be saved. It appears inevitable, therefore, that we should extend the line of salvation beyond them and beyond death itself. Admittedly, the scriptural evidence appears minimal and perhaps too much weight is laid upon 1 Peter 3:19 and its reference to Christ being made alive in the spirit and 'making a proclamation to the spirits in prison'. What this means is uncertain. But the *theological* case that extrapolates beyond scripture yet is consonant with it, must be judged a strong one. There is something unseemly about the arguments of those who would resist this conclusion. They argue as those who are safely inside the circle, certain (or complacent) about their own salvation. A true understanding of divine grace, of the willingness of God to show grace extravagantly where in our limited outlook we consider it should not be done, surely forbids such an attitude and demands that, at the very least, we be reverently agnostic about what happens next. I wish to be more than agnostic, though only in general terms, since it is not given to me to rule on the fate of any individual. I see no reason why death should constitute the final limit of the possibility of salvation if God in Christ is Lord of death. Death cannot defeat God's purpose, and God is not powerless in the face of it. I can well conceive that God persists in seeking the lost until the true point of finality in the last judgement is attained. And this means that none should be abandoned prematurely. Since it is the case that Christ has 'made intercession for sinners' and it is inconceivable that such intercession should not be heard, then none can be excluded from such a hope. Christians are taught to pray 'in the name of Jesus' because when they truly do so, they are assured of an answer (John 14:14). How much more is this the case when Jesus himself has prayed and continues to make intercession for us (Hebrews 7:25)?

Does all this make me a universalist? Only in the sense that we must adopt a universal perspective when we think theologically. I have asserted two things: there is no salvation apart from Christ; and there is no salvation without repentance. If Christ has made intercession for sinners and is bound to be heard, then his intercession, achieved in the entirety of his life, death, and resurrection, is the ground of salvation for all and is the only such ground. In that sense I am not a 'pluralist' who asserts that the paths to salvation are many and that Christ is only one among them. I regard this to be a rejection of the Christian faith as it has been normatively understood from the beginning. Departure from this is defective. Yet neither do I believe that adherents of other faiths, for instance, are thereby excluded from salvation. Christ has made intercession for all without exception. The focus shifts, therefore, to the need for repentance, the reception, either consciously or unconsciously, either in this life or in a world beyond of what Christ has done for us. This is the work of the Spirit who activates the church in its work of proclamation and witness. It should be clear, therefore, that I rule out the notion of 'automatic salvation' unaccompanied by the personal reception of grace. At this point, I pay attention to the message of the whole biblical revelation. It contains a minor key: the gospel of God requires a response, one which has eternal consequences and calls us to adopt an attitude of contrition before God, to acknowledge the radical evil that is within us and to seek for God's mercy. This means we need to come to the cross, which is a place of atonement and reconciliation. There is no salvation without repentance, but even at our most contrite and humble, we must confess that part of us remains proud and unyielding. We remain attached to our sin and imprisoned within our sinful natures. This is, above all, why we need the atoning work of Christ, his full and acceptable sacrifice on our behalf. He takes up our incomplete repentance and completes it so that we may, through him, confidently 'approach the throne of grace'. These words celebrate the doctrine of participation – that what is ours becomes his and is nullified, and what is his becomes ours and is so realised (2 Corinthians 5:21).

The scriptures contain a dialectic between the radical and hopeless nature of human sin, which deprives us of any ground for hope within ourselves, and a larger narrative of a gracious God who can save us. I find this particularly striking in the narrative of Jesus' encounter with the rich young ruler recorded in Mark 10:17-27. Confronted by Jesus with the demand to 'go, sell what you own, and give the money to the poor', the young man turns away in dismay, prompting Jesus to exclaim how hard it is for the wealthy to enter God's kingdom and the disciples to wonder how anyone can be 'saved'. Jesus agrees that this is impossible. But, almost with a sense of surprise at their comment, he goes on that what is impossible for us is possible with God. The tension between these two possibilities illuminates a great deal. Looked at this way, the story of humankind is one of failure and hopelessness. Until we grasp this we are missing the point. Not only personally but historically and prospectively, no good outcomes are to be expected. The human story is one of failure and judgement. But against this is set another narrative, one that finally will eclipse the former. It is the story of what is possible by God's grace. If the lower human horizon tells us that we cannot redeem ourselves and salvation is impossible, there is a larger horizon that overwhelms it and is the sole ground of our hope for better things. 'For the grace of God has appeared, bringing salvation to all . . . when the kindness and loving-kindness of God our Saviour appeared, he saved us, not because of any works of righteousness that we had done, but according to his mercy' (Titus 2:11; 3:4). It is the 'impossible possibility' of saving grace, that finally cancels out our inability. But grace must be received in repentance and faith; so, if there is a factor that limits the reach of the grace of God, it is not on God's side but our own. The persistence of grace reaches beyond this life in drawing people to this point. Because the work of the Son reaches into human lives through the Spirit, it is not enough to imagine that salvation, either in this life or beyond it, is 'automatic', imposed upon us by the will of God without our divinely enabled response. We are justified by grace through faith in this life and the next. I have, therefore, to posit a realm beyond death in which human beings still have space and time to become. Children who die young do not miss out on the opportunity to grow and respond. So do those others who in life have been beyond the reach of the gospel or its adequate expression. Admittedly, this is a speculation but a warranted one. Biblical insights into it may be minimal, but the theological demands of justice and the divine will-to-save give it credence. The speculation is sometimes referred to as 'probation' in the world to come or that there is a 'portal' before final judgement. God's gracious persistence forbids us to set limits to the ultimate scope of salvation. Some dismiss this as the theory of the 'second chance'; I see no reason why there should not only be a 'second chance' but many more besides if it is indeed the will of God to save. The notion of a 'chance' with the suggestion that this is somehow unfair has little to do with any conception of grace. The grace of God overrides ideas of retributive or distributive justice without abolishing them. One of Jesus' parables, that of the workers in the vineyard (Matthew 20:1-16), precisely makes this point in portraying God as free to do what God wants with that which is God's own, even when this conflicts with human notions of what is 'fair'. In the parable, none are treated unfairly, and some exceedingly generously. Grace goes beyond fairness. Scripture portrays God very much as the persistent Lord who remains faithful to God's people and repeatedly returns to them in mercy.

To think universally like this attracts the criticism that it is wishful thinking and reflects our inability to come to terms with the realities of judgement. I feel the force of this but am not overawed by it. Perhaps I have a vengeful streak. In certain moods, I would be content to see some of my fellow humans condemned to eternal fire, given the evil they have done. I have a sufficiently robust sense of anger and even wrath about the shockingly criminal and inhumane actions of many. If any are to be saved it can only be on the basis that they (we) have been faced with the harm our attitudes and actions have done and learned to repent of them, and through Christ to have them atoned for. An adequate if terrifying understanding of hell and judgement would be to be confronted with the hurt I have caused to others and made to feel such hurt myself. 'Nothing is covered up that will not be uncovered, and nothing secret that will not become known' (Luke 12:3). 'I tell you, on the day of judgement, you will have to give an account for every careless word you utter; for by your words you will be justified, and by your words, you will be condemned' (Matthew 12:16-17). 'For all of us must appear before the judgement seat of Christ, so that each may receive recompense for what has been done in the body, whether good or evil' (2 Corinthians 5:10). 'And before him, no creature is hidden, but all are naked and laid bare to the eyes of the one to whom we must render account' (Hebrews 4:13). Perhaps such exposure is the torment in final torment, that of conscience. In some cases, this would literally take a hell of a long time. I don't doubt that

Christians will experience the same in the light of the God who is a consuming fire, but they will do so with the solid assurance that their sin has been atoned for: 'Speak tenderly to Jerusalem, and cry to her that she has served her term, that her penalty is paid' (Isaiah 40:2). This will be their cause for thanksgiving. Even so, at its end, when every sin has been exposed, I can imagine (and this *is* an exercise of the imagination) that there might yet be those who defy God's grace. I can only envisage that at such a point, every drop of goodness would have been forfeited, and they would have ceased to be human in any meaningful form: is it possible to be an ex-human? In which case their best option would be to perish. But perhaps things will never come to this, and while there is any residual good (not merit) left in any one of us, I can only imagine that God working through the Spirit will seek to redeem it. By 'residual goodness' I mean more than moral goodness alone but those creative and productive skills and abilities that are proper to humankind as such and that are in some way a reflection of prior divine creativity.

So, once more, I am not a universalist, but God might be. I can see arguments in favour of both positions, for and against. On one occasion, I had been reading a cogent book asserting that for Christians, universal salvation was not only a possible belief but a necessary one: it is wrong not to believe it.[25] Shortly after, I read the verse in Revelation 20:15, 'Anyone whose name was not written in

---

[25] David Bentley Hart, *That All shall be Saved: Heaven, Hell and Universal Salvation* (New Haven and London: Yale University Press, 2019).

the book of life was thrown into the lake of fire'. I am fully aware that there is a difference between a threat and a promise: a threat can be withdrawn, and a promise cannot be. This verse is certainly threatening, and it might, within the greater horizon of God's grace, be withdrawn. Yet I also concluded that I could not take its warnings seriously while at the same time, in my mind cancelling it out and giving it no weight. I would do better to take this verse and others like it with deep seriousness and to make my election and calling in Christ secure. And what applies to me needs to apply equally to all. We cannot afford to be complacent about our own fate and that of people in general.

Post Nine: Hell and Damnation

To anticipate for a moment discussions to come, if the final horizon of God's purpose is one in which God is 'all in all' (1 Corinthians 15:28), and all things are restored in communion with the triune God, there are two options: either the final victory of God consists in the winning to contrition and repentance of all evildoers such that justice is done; or else prior to the final consummation there will be an eradication of all evil from within the creation. The second pattern of thought does, I think, allow a way of integrating the scriptural testimonies. On the one hand, there is a vision of creation sharing in the glorious liberty of the children of God; on the other, there is that of the dissolution of the present universe in cleansing fire and of the passing away of the present form of this world (2 Peter 3:7). Is this another evidence of 'cognitive dissonance'? I understand the minor key as the expectation that the present universe will be cleansed of its present imperfections, only after which will it attain its final glorified condition.

Which leads me to address more specifically the questions of hell, final loss, and eternal torment. I find this more straightforward. From the beginning of my journey of faith, I have espoused the doctrine of conditional immortality. This involves the rejection of the doctrine of the 'immortality of the soul'. In this connection, the word 'immortality' can be used in both a weaker and a stronger sense. In the weaker sense, it denotes the fact that the soul, or the essential human person and consciousness, can exist independently of the body, and so can survive physical death. This I affirm without fully understanding it. A doctrine of 'non-reductive physicalism' suggests that out of our human nature there emerges a consciousness and spiritual existence that survives the dissolution of the body. The stronger sense implies that the human soul cannot die but is indestructible. In this case, each soul must live on beyond death, perhaps initially in an intermediate state, sometimes known as Hades, before being consigned after the final judgement to either heaven or hell where continued existence consists either of eternal, conscious blessedness or eternal, conscious torment. This notion of hell I reject as neither scripturally warranted nor theologically consonant with the Christian vision of a just and merciful God. Scripturally, it confuses the distinction between 'everlasting' and 'eternal', a confusion that is shown in some translations. 'Eternal' refers to the life of the age to come and is to be understood qualitatively rather than quantitatively. It refers to what it means to be confronted with the eternal God. I have no wish here to repeat what I and others have written in more detail elsewhere to prove the point. The root of the confusion lies in the tendency to literalise and over-interpret the apocalyptic language employed in scripture. The reality to which it refers is the threat of the eternal loss of God, than which no more precarious thought can be imagined. Arguably, the language of eternal torment is intended to point to the seriousness of this fate, and those who advocate it wish mainly to give weight to the seriousness of sin as an offence to a holy God. But it amazes and appals me that good people can defend a doctrine that entails extreme cruelty. To burn to death is a horrific thing. I imagine someone being caught in a fire and screaming in torment in the short time it would take them to die. Any humane person would wish it to be swiftly over or to do what they humanly can to bring it to a close. But to extend this into eternity, to insist that such suffering can never come to an end because they have a 'never-dying soul' strikes me as a contradiction of any notion of divine compassion or of divine justice. To punish a weight of sin incurred in a finite existence by an infinite weight of suffering is surely out of proportion and does not correspond to the much-misunderstood biblical stricture of 'an eye for an eye' (that is to say, no more than what is proportionate), let alone any concept of grace or mercy. Justifying the notion of eternal torment by claiming that offence against an eternal God requires eternal punishment strikes me as a case of logical slippage. I fail to see how such a doctrine can be justified either by the demands of love or justice and leads us with a terrifying image of God. It does not surprise me that critics have progressively rejected it. I fear to think how it might shape and form its advocates; there are anecdotes about devout Christians contemplating the eternal fate of the wicked with something approaching glee because they find the justice of God being glorified by it. I imagine that most who blandly accept it because it seems to them to portray a 'high' doctrine of God have failed to use their imaginations as to what it implies. This does not, of necessity, contradict what I have said about being fully confronted by our own evil, but it does mean there is an end to it.

To count ourselves unworthy of eternal life (Acts 13:46) and to resist the grace of God that wills our salvation is indeed a terrible thing, the egregious nature of which is unlikely to be fully realised until we are finally confronted with the beauty and goodness of God. The doctrine of conditional immortality rejects both the idea that human beings are inherently immortal and that *everlasting* torment awaits the wicked. Instead, immortality is a property belonging to God alone (1 Timothy 6:16), and in so far as humans will share it, it will be as undeserved gift mediated through Christ and the Spirit. Immortality is something to 'put on' and is 'conditional' for this very reason (1 Corinthians 15:53). The doctrine is sometimes referred to as 'annihilationism', but this could be taken to mean that the wicked, and such there are, simply cease to exist, say at death. But this is a misunderstanding. Instead, the doctrine imagines each person being confronted with God, with the offences committed against God, against ourselves and each other and knowing ourselves to be judged. This would be far from a painless process, possibly, in fact, the most painful of all. The pain exists in the accusations of conscience. It is a process that would last as long as it takes to exhaust the awareness of wrongs done – the 'unquenchable fire' of judgement and the worm of Gehenna that 'does not die' (Matthew 3:12, Mark 9:45-48) are so until their fearful task is done. It can only be envisaged for those who knowingly reject God's saving grace and have abandoned the possibility of salvation. This ultimately could be few, many or none. But its outcome would be to cease to exist, a cessation that would be accompanied by the knowledge of everything that had been made forfeit, of looking into the beauty of God and losing it all. This is serious stuff, the most serious of all.

As already noted, it is several times asserted in the New Testament that Christ is the Saviour not only of those who believe but of all people. Christ is the Lamb of God who takes away the sins of the world. It is possible to understand this by concluding that Christ's saving work is actual in the lives of those who participate by faith in Christ and remains potential for those who have yet to believe. If we follow the train of thought outlined by Karl Barth, Christ is both the Elect and the Reprobate, and consequently, there need be no further reprobation in that in Christ, the full weight of condemnation has been borne and abolished for all. As all die in Adam, so all will be made alive in Christ' (1 Corinthians 15:22). This does not mean that there is not still the possibility of eternal loss, but it takes the form of self-exclusion, the refusal to be incorporated organically into Christ. This remains consequent on resisting the grace of God in salvation but becomes inevitable when the One who is the source of eternal life is finally resisted. The words of C. S. Lewis are pertinent: 'Those who are saved are those who say to God, "Your will be done". Those who are lost are those to whom God says, "Your will be done"'.

I have been critical of my own evangelical tradition in pointing out how concerned many have been with the question, 'But are you going to heaven?' as though what happens to our souls after death is what the Christian faith is all about. I have also argued that this remains far from being an insignificant question. Sure enough, though, 'salvation' is far more than this. It includes being part of the divine purpose in the present of gathering a people in whom God may dwell and who may share in the mission of God in bringing the fullness of the kingdom. So, it includes the realisation of justice, peace, and love within the world. However, it would be right to conclude that I remain a 'salvationist' and so firmly embedded within an evangelical faith. Personal salvation, reconciliation with God in the Spirit through repentance and faith, leading to baptism and a life of discipleship remain for me a supreme priority, not to be displaced by other concerns, however important they may be. I can follow that definition of mission that identifies it as a proclamation of the gospel, social action, the struggle for justice and care of the creation. It concerns me, however, that because the first of these imperatives, gospel proclamation, appears in the present climate not to be making significant headway, at least in the lands I know best, there is a tendency to make other forms of missional activity more prominent as a way of the church feeling useful and fruitful about itself. This may be understandable. A danger lurks, however, when ideologies are adopted that are insufficiently theologically or biblically grounded and which risk swamping the church's primary mission of gospel proclamation. Feminism, anti-racism, environmentalism, and other currents are all ideologies that have much to commend from a Christian viewpoint, but none of them should be uncritically adopted on the grounds that they are progressive. They need to be interrogated by more strictly theological criteria in a way that effectively maintains Christian missional imperatives, most of all that none of them on their own are sufficient for the restoration of humanity to its true end. This is found in Christ and in being reconciled through him to the Father, the Ground of our Being, and the Lord of the future. To anticipate future reflections, there is a difference between *integration* and *assimilation*: integration speaks of the church's constructive participation in society and state while maintaining its own distinctives and loyalties, which forbid it to accept any ideology uncritically. Assimilation, by contrast, bespeaks uncritical accommodation to whatever ideology reigns, whether 'progressive' or 'conservative' and consequent loss of Christian identity. As has often been claimed, 'those who marry the spirit of the age in the present generation will find themselves a widow(er) in the next'.

I say all of this by way of reasserting my evangelical instincts and maintaining continuity with the faith I have from the beginning embraced. I stand in no doubt that I am a Pietist in the mould of those such as Johann Albrecht Bengel and Phillip Spener, who, within seventeenth- and eighteenth-century German Lutheranism, reacted against the Protestant scholasticism of previous generations with its close concern with doctrinal rationalism to reassert the importance of the transformed life, living experience of God. This certainly disposes me in an existential direction but also accords with the 'experimentalism' of the English Puritans. The description of the kind of evangelicalism that arose in the eighteenth century as a cocktail of these two legacies, Puritanism and Pietism, is very congenial to me. It embraces both the priority of the experiential knowledge of God, the kind that accords with the Wesleyan emphasis on assurance of salvation, and serious theological reflection not as a form of desiccated intellectualism but as spiritual theology. The essence of evangelical faith for me is not in the defence of certain doctrines such as inerrancy, penal substitution, or eternal torment, that are regarded as the secure perimeter guarding the evangelical estate and not to be transgressed, but the experience of a heart made alert to human sin and issuing in justifying faith in Christ and regeneration to a new life and hope. And here I am keen to repudiate the pejorative use of the word 'pietism' to denote a solely world-denying mentality. Pietism was immensely fruitful in producing both social and missionary initiatives and was also rather influential in contributing to later theological reflections. Equally, the common use of the term 'puritan' to denote judgemental and prudish attitudes falls far short of the theological and political progressiveness of that movement and its contributions to the emergence of liberty and democracy in the Anglo-world. Even more do I wish to distance a healthy evangelicalism from the 'fundamentalist' aberrations of the twentieth century. Amidst these affirmations, however, I do wish to identity what I consider to have been an evangelical weakness and that concerns the doctrine of creation.

Post Ten: God's Good Creation

The fundamental belief that God is the Creator of all things, that the origins of life and purpose are to be found in God and that this God is the sustainer of all that has been made is, of course, fundamental to all forms of Christian belief. So is the idea that there is a purpose to things, that the world and everything in it has a destiny that is intended for eternity and that will one day be realised. It may well be the case that belief in one God who claims our exclusive loyalty, from whom, in whom and to whom all things exist, originated in Israel's tribal devotion to the LORD to whom they attributed deliverance from captivity. But if so, they came in time to see that the LORD was able to save precisely because this same LORD had created all things and was the God of all creation and of every creature. So, we have the emergence of monotheism and the repudiation of any of its alternatives – atheism, polytheism, dualism, pantheism, deism.

Furthermore, Israel's God is transcendent and exists above and beyond the world of finite reality as One who is infinite and eternal, free from the limitations of created reality while utterly free to act for and within it. All of this is the backdrop to Christian belief. Yet arguably, both within that tradition generally and its evangelical variation in particular, the theme of creation and related concerns has not been given the prominence to which it is due. The New Testament, in particular, being wrapped around the saving purposes of God realised in the death and resurrection of Christ, may be thought, rightly or wrongly, to give less place to the doctrine of creation and to narrow down the focus onto personal salvation and the redeemed community in which the Spirit of God is particularly active. If so, a corrective is needed and there are abundant resources to bring this into play as we draw on the whole of the canonical witness. If there is an apparent neglect in the New Testament, it is largely because creation is assumed as part of the legacy of Israel. Yet the resources are there, and appreciation of the cosmic Christ, the universal Spirit, and the hope of a renewed heaven and a new earth are among them. In an age when the very survival of creation is believed to be at stake, we are inevitably prompted to enlarge our theology in continuity with scripture to get to a better place. Perhaps this, too, is an example of how cultural context can provoke the retrieval of neglected themes that truly belong both to scripture and to our tradition.

The massive insight that transforms my thinking is the role of Christ as the agent of creation and the proper exegesis of a trinitarian understanding of that creation: 'He is the image of the invisible God, the firstborn of all creation; for in him all things in heaven and earth were created, things visible and invisible...all things have been created through him and for him' (Colossians 1:16). It is nothing less than astonishing that the New Testament makes this conceptual leap from Christ as redeemer to Christ as creator. This might well mirror a similar shift in the Old Testament whereby Israel's celebration of the LORD as saviour following the deliverance at the Red Sea (or Sea of Reeds) leads to the belief that one who has such dominance over the elements is antecedently the one who is the creator. The same thought emerges in John 1, where Christ is the one through whom all things have been made, nothing excluded, as it also does in Hebrews 1:1-3. We are taken here beyond the incarnate Lord who participates in our limited humanity to the one who is now risen, glorified, and ascended and can be proclaimed as the cosmic Christ, the head and agent of all creation, albeit he never forsakes his humanity but in it pioneers the new creation that awaits us. Christ is, therefore, the mediator of both the old creation and the new. Behind these thought forms is the informing of Christology by both Word and Wisdom thinking in the Old Testament background. God's wisdom is expressed both in creation and its redemption.

Read canonically, from back to front, Genesis 1's narrative of creation by the word of God and references such as Psalm 33:6 ('By the word of the Lord the heavens were made, and all their hosts by the breath of his mouth'), conjure up the image of one who speaks, that which is spoken and the breath with which it is impelled. The Logos Christology of John 1 surely draws both on the Old Testament background of God's powerful word and the contemporary philosophical background of the Logos as the rationality that underlies all things. To focus this exalted pattern of thought in the life and fate of a crucified Jewish prophet and 'the blood of his cross' (Colossians 1:20) strikes me as beyond astonishing. That it could be conceived without the transformation of perspective worked by the resurrection is unlikely in the extreme. The more I have thought about it, the more significant Christ's pre-existence in the life of God and his agency in creation have become. For creation to have come into being through Christ determines what the purpose of creation is. Creation should be understood teleologically as destined for an ultimate purpose, and that purpose is inherent in its creation through Christ and for Christ. The end of creation is in its beginning specifically that all things through Christ should be aligned to the God who is Father, Son, and Spirit, and this means that there should be peace, harmony, and shalom. Until that time the creation is subject to frustration since it is hindered in achieving its goal, and what hinders that realisation is that human beings themselves are not aligned to the divine purpose. Since it is the will of God not to realise the goal without or apart from human beings, the creation must wait until those human beings achieve their liberty in Christ. This I believe to be the meaning of Romans 8:18-25, one of scripture's most sublime passages. Yet this is the hope opened to us by another such passage, Ephesians 1:10, 'as a plan for the fullness of time, to gather up all things in him, things in heaven and things on earth'. These words indicate that God's purpose is that all things will finally be aligned with, through and in Christ. This is not in itself an indication of universal salvation since what does not align with Christ is destined to perish and to have no part in God's future, as is suggested by Revelation 21:8 and the image of the 'second death'. But Christ the Lord is the embodiment of the 'Alpha and Omega, the beginning and the end' (Revelation 21:6, 22:13), and the 'end' is not a thing but a person, one who meets us from the future.

The consequence of a Christological dimension to creation is that creation concern is profoundly part of Christian discipleship. To love Christ is to love what belongs to Christ, and that means 'all things'. This implies disagreement with those strands of the evangelical tradition that rate the creation as the dispensable waste product of salvation. Creation is to be left behind, replaced once souls have been saved. It is to be wrapped up and dissolved, its job having been done. Admittedly, there are texts that can be appealed to here (e.g., Hebrews 1:10-12, 2 Peter 3:10), but within the context of the canonical whole, they can be misunderstood. Creation itself is to be set free from its bondage to decay (Romans 8:18-25). The resurrected body of Jesus is the breakthrough point where mortality is swallowed up in immortality, with the promise of more to come since he is the 'first-fruits'. He is the Pioneer of our salvation in more ways than one. As Christ was raised, so we shall be raised, and as we are raised, so will the context in which we have come to be also raised as something valuable and loved. God has compassion for all that God has made (Psalm 145:8-9). All things are intertwined, and nothing in creation can be what it is, human beings, most of all, without everything else that makes it.

Reading the Old Testament creation texts from back to front and in view of the *telos* of creation in Christ (Ephesians 1:10) helps us to move beyond the idea that God created a perfect world, which only after the human fall was diverted and spoilt. This remains a powerful structure of thought for many and is not without its insights. But perhaps it makes limited sense to think of an originally perfect creation. Rather, the early creation narratives depict a good beginning and movement towards a divinely willed goal in which human beings play a pivotal role, one in which, as it happens, they have failed. In this sense, human beings are suppressing the creation in the hope of attaining its perfection, diverting it from its potential. Romans 8:18-25 might be read in this light. This is a more evolutionary view of creation's history and of humanity's place within it. It views history as a project in which God works towards a goal and in which the journey towards that goal is as important as the goal itself. I resonate with the concept of the 'trinitarian history of God' in which creation, redemption, and consummation come from the Father through the Son in the Spirit and are enacted by being drawn by the Spirit through the Son to the Father, that our loving Creator may finally be all in all. I have also valued the three-fold description of the Father as the Creator, the Son as the Re-Creator and the Spirit as the Trans-Creator posed by Philip J. Rosato SJ.[26] God's work of creation is itself an act of *justification* and

---

[26] *The Spirit as Lord: The pneumatology of Karl Barth* (Edinburgh: T. and T. Clark, 1981).

deliverance as the Father summons the world into being out of nothing and then preserves it against the threat of non-being. In parallel, the work of redemption is *creative* as God responds to the history of human rebellion and sin and enables a new creation. There is a constructive interplay here of the themes of creation and redemption.

The 'creation and fall' pattern of thought was (and for some still is), in part, an attempt to come to terms with the presence of 'natural evil' within the creation. This is a big challenge. It has become plainly impossible to attribute the suffering of the animal creation with all its waste, predation and 'red-in-tooth-and-claw' character to human sin, the diversion through Adam and Eve of all things in heaven and earth. There is a dark side to creation that is rapacious and cruel and which precedes humankind, with which it is hard to come to terms. This is to say nothing of the existence of parasites, destructive viruses and creatures built, so it seems, to prey on others. All of this speaks against a straightforward creation-fall asserting the uncomplicated goodness of things until after the human catastrophe. This is not to refute a doctrine of creation and even less to lay scripture aside. It is rather a call to reconceive how these are to be received. Working this through has been on the agenda for the last several hundred years as the discoveries of geology and evolutionary science have emerged in tension with a previous literal and somewhat static framework of thought. This struggle is on par with that required to emerge from the cosmological assumptions of the Ptolemaic system and to embrace the Copernican revolution that all but flat-earthers now take for granted. It asked interpreters of the Bible to shift to metaphorical rather than only literal modes of thought to draw the proper value from biblical teachings. I wish to guard here against the kind of arrogance that looks back on pre-modern generations as though they were unintelligent. They simply did not have the means to investigate the created world that is now available to us, and increasingly so, and many of those who contributed to these shifts, or do so now, were or are believers. It is understandable that those in pre-modern generations worked with common sense categories – the earth was stable, the sun and moon revolved round the earth, heaven was above, and Hades/Sheol was below. It was a challenge for everybody, not just the religious, to adapt to the fact that the world was not as it seemed. Equally, in those pre-modern times, a literal understanding of Genesis was a useful 'creation myth' in the light of which life could be efficiently lived. But I have no doubt at all that it is possible both to honour the science and to emerge with a truer grasp of the inspired and didactic role the scriptures have among us. Whatever science can disclose to us (and there are multiple dimensions of practice embraced by the simple word 'science'), there is much that lies outside its disciplines. I follow the late Chief Rabbi Jonathan Sacks in believing that though science can tell us much about how things 'work', it has nothing to say about what things 'mean'.[27] This is not to say that there is not an interplay between the worlds of scientific investigation and that of meaning: a more careful attention to the methods of science reveals that intuition, imagination and even revelation (Eureka!) play their part in the process. Amid the billions of 'facts' that arise on a moment by moment basis there must be some sense of significance and meaning to choose which are to be further investigated. Similarly, the search for the meaning of things engages with the way the world objectively is in all its dimensions. Science and theological methods are closer than is often imagined.

It is illuminating and enriching to think of God's creative work as a 'letting-be'. God lets creation be. God grants to it its own agency over against God's own self. The idea is reinforced in the Genesis 1 creation narrative when, having called a structured world into being from chaos, God repeatedly commands the various dimensions of the created world to 'bring forth' after its own kind. It is as though God lays the creation under a necessity, that of surviving, growing, and realising its potential. This is not the portrayal of a divine architect who determines every aspect of a structure but is more 'parental' in mood. When we give up the attempt either to force this passage into the mindset of modern science or to force modern science into the categories of Genesis 1, then we can grasp it for its true worth. This passage is undoubtedly best understood as poetry,

---

[27] *The Great Partnership: God, Science and the Search for Meaning* (London: Hodder and Stoughton, 2011).

liturgy, or hymnology but not as modern science. It is most certainly theology and, as such, is rich in significance. God calls the world into being and then engages it in the ongoing work of creation which is an unfolding of its potential. This is compatible with the general idea of evolution. In this sense, the creation can rightly be described as 'autopoietic', self-creating or self-realising, going on progressively to actuate organically the potential that has been granted to it. This approach, which is sometimes fairly or unfairly thought of as Irenaean rather than Augustinian, makes the most sense to me. The notion that creation, and humankind within it, has agency granted by God yet also over against God conflicts with the assumption of 'meticulous providence' whereby everything that is and all that happens is determined by God. Instead, there is within creation both a randomness and a freedom, yet the random functions as a creative reality, throwing up possibilities that are subsumed within the wider trajectory of creation's becoming. I reflect on this in relation to varying aspects of the order of life.

Card-games might be one sphere in which this applies. The very fact that a hand of cards cannot be infallibly predicted and must be played as it comes is what constitutes both the pleasure of the game and the skill summoned forth in playing it. The same general idea can be applied to all and any ball sports. On a larger scale, the idea that creation has its own kind of freedom sheds light on the fact that in the evolutionary process, there is that which may be produced that is threatening and dangerous. I firmly endorse the idea proposed by

Karl Barth that there is a shadow written into creation, and yet the shadow is not to be identified with what is evil. It may be challenging and destructive, ugly or frightening in the present, but in the ultimate providence of God has its place, one that will finally (eschatologically) be turned to good. Creation is to be understood as much from its future destiny as its origins.

Celebrating the role of Christ in creation and not only in redemption enables us to understand the purpose of God in that creation: It exists through him and for him and finds its coherence in being drawn into harmonious relation with the ground of its being revealed in him. The 'omega point' of Christian faith, that to which we are being drawn, is for all things to be made to add up in Christ (Ephesians 1:11). More than this, the role of Christ in creation commits the serious disciple to love of the creation since all things are Christ's and we are called to love what Christ loves. This is not a 'creation-centred spirituality' but one which is thoroughgoingly Christ-centred. Creation exists for Christ and, through him, for God. Care for creation is an aspect of discipleship, though not the only one. Conversely, to enter the enjoyment of creation whenever this becomes possible is an aspect of enjoying Christ. This line of thought illuminates all our attempts to 'seek the welfare of the city' or to penetrate the scientific or mathematical mysteries of the created sphere or to interpret it through art, literature, and music. 'All things are ours' because all things are Christ's and Christ is God's. This indicates a truly life-affirming lifestyle, but one which is in no way blind to all the ways creation, and we within it, fall short of the fullness it will one day achieve.

Once we rid ourselves of the category mistake that reads the early chapters of Genesis literally, we are liberated to appreciate it as theological literature. As well as identifying God's act of creation as a 'letting-be' that confers a freedom to develop on the creation with the mandate to 'bring forth' and realise its potential, we may also be able to recognise creation not as a supposed past state of affairs in which everything was perfect but as a good beginning towards a future goal. It is an amazing and perhaps inexplicable thing about the natural world that all living beings are under that seeming compulsion to survive and to become. Why is this? Creation is *in via,* on its way towards the future and called to address and overcome obstacles in its way. I see no reason why, to this end, we might not also understand creation as experimental, pursuing the avenues that might lead to its goal. We may read Genesis 1 teleologically as setting before us a destiny that is to be realised, a destiny that will issue in a world at peace, with which the creator is pleased because it is good, indeed very good. It is striking that in the successive days they are portrayed, the final one is a sabbath in which there is rest, or shalom, a day to which there is no end. The seventh day in the narrative has no end, unlike the preceding days.

I posit the idea, therefore, that the creation is under a divine mandate to *become* and that this resonates with the experience that creation exists under some kind of necessity; it must move forward and advance towards its goal. If this is credible, the emergence of intelligent and purposeful life in the form of human beings who might bear the image of God is crucial, and everything that has gone before has the nature of compiling the elements that are necessary for such life to exist. The world must be as it is so that human beings might emerge as they are destined to be. The fact that this takes billions of years to happen is incidental once we understand that God is not imprisoned in time as we mortals are but 'has time'. Time may exist in some sense in God (God's own time), but it does not exist over God to constrain God. God is the Lord of time in eternity. This is not to say that time has no meaning for God, simply that what it means to us is different. The place of human beings within this drama in space and time should be grasped in terms of destiny. The nature of the image of God in humankind has been much debated, and each approach offers valuable insights, but I prefer that which locates the image not so much in a once-held-but-now-lost structure of being so much as in a destiny set before us. It is the God-intended destiny of humans to bear the image of God within the created sphere, an image which is truly realised in Christ who is the authentic image of God and to whom we are invited to become conformed in the Spirit. This does not abolish the idea of the image of God as somehow linked to the structure of human beings since there must be that in a human being that is capable of imaging God, capable in terms of intelligence, reason, personhood, stewardship, and relationality.

In place here is the discussion as to whether, were creation not fallen and in need of redemption, Christ would nevertheless have become incarnate. It is possible to understand the incarnation as an 'emergency measure' rendered necessary because of the episode of human sin, although this suggests that the fall was something not foreseen. Alternatively, the incarnation could be understood as continuous with the work of creation whereby God has always purposed to unite humankind, and therefore creation in its entirety, to God's own self by participating within it and raising it into communion through the Son and by the Spirit to the Father. To be sure, the actual nature of that incarnation is indeed shaped by the need to overcome sin and accomplish redemption, a need that has been foreknown in the mind of God from the beginning. I revolt, however, against any suggestion that God has been taken by surprise and has needed to revert to a 'plan B'. No, God has always known how things would be and has always known how to respond in sovereign and creative love to all that the many agents God has created would do. God is sufficiently omnicompetent as to turn all things to the ultimate divine purpose.

The theological value of affirming that creation has come to be through Christ and for Christ is immense. It delivers us from an anthropocentric obsession according to which the value of everything is assessed as to how it relates to human beings. Things do not exist because they benefit us but because they have their being through God in Christ. For Christ's sake, glory, and pleasure, they exist. It does not matter, therefore, that human beings are late arrivals on the evolutionary scene. God has valued and appreciated everything that has gone before, even the free creatures that sport in the sea (Psalm 104:26). It is striking that in the teaching of Jesus, he appeals not only to history's salvation as enacted in Israel's story but to the world of nature. He perceives the kindness of God in allowing rain to fall on the righteous and unrighteous and, in the beauty of the flowers of the field, and God's omniscience in the fall of a sparrow. Of course, compared to those who bore their witness in biblical times, we moderns are immensely more aware of the sheer breadth and size of the creation in ways they could never have been. Our own planet is, comparatively speaking, a mere speck in an unimaginably large universe that consists of at least a billion planets within a billion galaxies. This boggles the imagination.

An apt illustration may be that of an Olympic-sized swimming-pool being filled with grains of sand, of which only one is Planet Earth. These are, of course, imprecise illustrations! In addition, some physicists speculate whether our universe is only one of potentially millions, that we should speak of a 'multiverse' rather than a 'universe' and that there are other dimensions alongside our own where the governing laws are different. It remains unclear whether such a speculation could ever be empirically confirmed since, if it could be, then whatever emerged would have to be within our universe rather than beyond it. Some versions of the multiverse theory certainly seem to me to be 'ontologically extravagant'. Yet I don't find any of these speculations necessarily incompatible with belief in a divine source of all things but rather enhancing It. The God in whom Christians believe has always been believed to be the Power behind all powers, the transcendent Mind behind all rationality. If such a God purposes to create other universes besides our own, this belongs to God's own freedom. What it should underline is the humility appropriate to the scientific project, that what we do not know far exceeds what we do know and probably always will, and what we do know is what we *think* we know and remains always provisional. I do not forget that reputedly, something between 85 to 95 per cent of the universe is hidden from us and consists of 'dark matter' with which we do not even have the 'language' to communicate and possibly never will. Nor do we know whether 'dark matter' constitutes one 'thing' or many. After all, how can we assume that our finite and limited brains, even collectively applied, are equipped to penetrate the mysteries of the universe? Any assumption to this effect would itself be a statement of faith. Yet even a properly modest posture leaves us with extremely extensive capabilities.

The above discussion, however, certainly raises the question of the significance we allow to human beings. How can we ascribe value to ourselves who are so infinitesimally small within a universe (or universes) so unimaginably large? The answer, of course, must be that size isn't everything. Significance is not solely a factor of size. I recall with amusement a long-ago correspondence in a national newspaper in which an article appeared rehearsing the above description of our planet's insignificance and of ourselves within it. It ended with the question, 'Astronomically speaking, What is Man?' Shortly after, the paper published a letter from a farmer in Sussex which simply replied, 'Astronomically speaking, Man is the Astronomer'. Gender-specific language aside, the letter made the necessary point. Human beings have the capacity to understand (uniquely so far as we know) precisely how small they are and are possessed of the kind of consciousness that enables them to observe, analyse and hypothesise about the creation and to harness the relevant predictions as to how it works. This is the proper discipline of science, and it is only one of that matrix of rational disciplines that enables us to make sense of life, the universe and everything. As far as we are currently aware, the human brain has a degree of complexity and organisation that far exceeds any organism or entity in the known universe, and this, with all its ramifications in language, art, music, humour, and literature, etc., rather than brute size constitutes human significance.

The kind of anthropological discussion engaged above carries a risk, one that is evidenced in the history of Christian thought and that I discern in myself. Christian thinkers are not alone in this. The risk is that of devaluing the rest of the animal creation and of finding little place for a proper 'animal theology'. There may be exceptions to this, such as in the case of Francis of Assisi, but the exception proves the rule. Animals have not been theologically regarded as they should and have been allowed a largely instrumental value. I do not believe that such neglect can directly be attributed to the scriptural tradition.

As portrayed in the creation stories, the animals are commanded into being by God and laid under that mandate to 'bring forth'. God takes pleasure in them and calls them good. There is a delightful vignette in the temptation narratives of Jesus in the wilderness where he was 'with the wild animals', perhaps a reference back to Adam and Eve in the Garden of Eden and signifying a restoration of harmony within creation. There are also prophetic anticipations of a day in an imagined future when 'the wolf shall lie down with the lamb' or 'the lion shall lie down with the lamb' Isaiah 11:6-9). Of note is the poignant and compassionate final statement in the Book of Jonah, where God's concern is expressed for humans trapped in confusion 'and also many animals' (Jonah 4:11). It can be overlooked that in the creation narratives of Genesis, the envisaged human diet is a vegetarian one (1:29-30) and only later is meat-eating conceded, though with certain restrictions (9:3-4). Arguments for vegetarianism seem to me to be strong, though less so for veganism. All in all, therefore, the kind of reappraisal of attitudes to the animal kingdom is entirely appropriate, and the decline of other species wherever human beings achieve dominance is to be deeply regretted and, wherever possible, countered. This is surely pleasing to God and an expression of stewardship of God's world. Human beings are themselves animals. To assert this is in no way to devalue them since animals are part of God's good creation. Our bodies function in similar ways even if mental capacities and qualities of consciousness differ. To describe some human beings as 'behaving like animals' is an insult to animals that rarely behave with the depravity that humans do and, when they do so, act through instinct rather than choice. This re-valuing of animals does not obliterate the fact, one that some would dispute, that there is a hierarchy of value within the animal kingdom. We might helpfully ascribe 'rights' to animals as a way of asserting human responsibility for their welfare, but given that it is not possible to assign to them corresponding responsibilities, the 'rights' discourse takes place on a different level from that of human beings.

Above all, if all things have come into being through Christ and for him, it should be clear that discipleship of Christ intrinsically involves care for the integrity and well-being of that creation.

Post Eleven: Christ and Incarnation

For all Christians, it is of enormous significance that in Jesus Christ, God has become incarnate. Whereas for Protestants and other Western believers, the locus of salvation is often focussed above all on the cross and Christ's bearing of our sins, for Orthodox believers, it is in the Annunciation, that moment that Christ is conceived in Mary's womb, that salvation draws near. Here, eternity enters time, immortality into mortality, and the hope of a new creation within the old begins to be realised. I have never struggled with the idea of a 'virginal conception' as others have done. Granted, some have done so because they find in this doctrine a preliminary but mistaken attempt to 'explain' the inexplicable, the appearance of one who is truly divine and truly human. I nonetheless celebrate it for what it indicates – a new, creative beginning in the economy of God. Sometimes, the virginal conception is mistakenly confused for the 'immaculate conception', but the two need to be distinguished. The latter is a Roman Catholic doctrine unsupported by the New Testament that refers to the mode of Mary's birth from *her* mother's womb. The presumption is that to protect the sinlessness of Jesus and to interrupt the contagion of original sin, a kind of *cordon sanitaire* needed to be thrown round Mary. This is wrong on a whole variety of levels and is one of those Marian doctrines, such as the assumption of Mary into heaven and her perpetual virginity, that have emerged from tradition and have no sound biblical basis. Rather, the doctrine of the virgin birth is entirely appropriate in that the coming of God should be heralded by a sign.

The life of the Son of God is framed at one end by the miracle of the womb and at the other by the miracle of the tomb. True to an approach to scripture that I have come to find helpful, I have chosen to prioritise meaning over questions of historical possibility. I first ask, What am I intended to learn from this? And only then to ask, What is the history that lies behind this? In other words, I approach scripture as first a theological document, or series of such, and subordinate historical questions to their witness. In truth, although I do not doubt there is an historical core behind the birth narratives of Mathew and Luke (Jesus must, after all, have been born somewhere somehow to someone), I am content to read those narratives primarily for their theological and testimonial value. Drawing upon the language and imagery of the Hebrew scriptures that root them in the ancient tradition and so give them legitimacy, they draw out the meaning of the coming of the Son of God as a continuation and concentration of the biblical drama. Most of all, Jesus comes from God. He is not primarily the product of human flesh, not even of the best, most pious Jewish flesh: he is absolutely the gift of God, a saving intervention of God in the human story. It is the notion of 'intervention' that some seem to find problematic in that it suggests a breaking of the 'causal nexus' that otherwise is deemed inviolable. I don't share the assumptions that lie behind this reticence because

I do not share the plausibility structure on which it is based. Indeed, I regard it as the remnant of an outdated mechanistic science that is being superseded. If it were true, then there would never be the possibility of the 'new' when manifestly the Christian gospel is precisely that, and the resurrection, without which there can be no Christianity, would be unthinkable. God in Christ has done and is doing a new thing.

Even to speak of 'intervention' veers off in the wrong direction. Because I am confident that we live and move and have our being in God, I also believe that God may act within creation to vary what otherwise might be the case without this being a threat to the regularity and order of creation. The idea of a 'causal nexus' is a useful hypothesis and one that finds constant confirmation, but it cannot be empirically confirmed in all and every case and so is not absolute. The virginal conception is congruent with and appropriate for a new and decisive stage in salvation history, an opening up of new horizons. In a parallel way, where some might struggle with the paradox that the infinite can become finite, or the omnipotent might be 'contracted to a span', the incarnation is a manifestation of omnipotence rather than its abdication. It is the kind of thing that God can do since God is not imprisoned within the divine attributes such that they prevent God from doing certain things. God is sovereign over God's own sovereignty. God is free and can embrace the weakness and limitations of the incarnation to achieve those ultimate aims that have been eternally intended. This is very much a manifestation of power, but power of a certain and creative kind, one that contradicts typical human concepts and practices of power that major on coercion and domination.

The virginal conception, therefore, is primarily a sign of a new and creative act of God. When the Holy Spirit is said to 'overshadow' Mary, this is reminiscent of the statement in Genesis 1 that the Spirit was 'hovering' or 'vibrating' over the waters. The God of creation is the God of continuing and of new creation. Some otherwise orthodox theologians find it necessary to question the virginal conception, sometimes pointing out that the birth narratives of Matthew and Luke have originated in traditions separate from the bulk of the Gospel materials, as though this, therefore, makes their value secondary. In reciting the Apostles Creed in worship, they may mentally place the words 'born of the Virgin Mary' in quotation marks and look beyond them to the theological truth that Christ's origins are in the eternal God. I can understand this, but I do not feel the need to do it myself. The God who created and the God who raised Jesus from the dead is fully at liberty to grant the miracle of the womb, and this does not particularly stretch my credulity. It does, of course, raise the question as to the solidarity of the humanity of Jesus with our own. If he was extraordinarily born, does he fully share the humanity that he was destined to redeem? It is an axiom of theological thought that Christ had to assume our humanity to heal it, so is this axiom threatened by the virginal conception?

My answer is that Christ quite manifestly was human as we are human and became like us in every respect, yet 'without sin'. The objection simply does not apply. It is theoretical rather than actual. Not only was Christ human as we are human, but the kind of humanity he embraced was the kind we all inherit: humanity in its flawed and fallen condition. There has been an impulse in Christians to protect the humanity of Jesus from any form of taint, almost to suggest that his humanity differed from our own in being 'Adamic', unfallen, and pristine. Some Anabaptists embraced a doctrine of Christ's 'heavenly flesh'. So, as mentioned, the virginal conception has been understood as a way of throwing that *cordon sanitaire* around Jesus to protect him from our inherited sin. The theological innovation of the immaculate conception of Mary protected her from sin in her mother's womb, presumed by the tradition to be called Anne, to become a safe vessel for the birth of her son. This doctrine has been proclaimed in the Roman Catholic Church to be a 'dogma', something that must be believed despite its extremely late provenance. To my mind all of this is wrong-headed and stems from a failure to value the Holy Spirit, that neglected member of the Trinity. Christ was conceived in the womb of the Virgin by the Spirit, and in him, humankind has been made regenerate. The saga of fallen humanity has been interrupted so that Christ is himself the raising of humankind out of the cycle of sin and distortion and the sign of hope for us all. Although Mary occupies a place of honour in Christian thought, she is most of all a sign of the Spirit, who is the ultimate origin of the Christ, the one who 'gives birth' both to him and through him to the new humanity.

Having arrived at this train of thought, I can carry it further. In the attempt to resolve the seeming conundrum that in a finite human being, the infinite God has become manifest, some theologians have developed the idea of 'kenosis', the self-emptying of God to embrace a specific human identity. This is based clearly enough on the Christological hymn of Philippians 2. Christ has emptied himself and become obedient unto death. Suppose this refers to the self-humiliation of the eternal Son rather than being simply a contrast with the first Adam who exalted himself. In that case, it implies the restriction of some of the attributes of deity, the laying aside of omnipotence or omniscience or omnipresence to be 'contracted to a span'. For some, this represents an impossibility and counts against any direct sense in which Christ could be considered to be 'God'. My own thoughts run in an opposite direction in seeing the self-imposed limitation of Christ not as a contradiction of the divine attributes but as a manifestation of them. It is precisely because the Son of God is free from limitation that he can, in the divine purpose, embrace limitation and make it a vehicle for the manifestation of God's glory and love. Omnipotence carries with it the capacity to do this, to display God's power through weakness as well as strength, to show God's omniscience through the wisdom by which he redeems a fallen world. It is wrong, therefore, to ascribe all knowledge or all power to Jesus of Nazareth, the incarnate Lord.

The most orthodox heresy to which sincere Christians fall prey is Apollinarianism, the view that the soul of Jesus was replaced by the divine Word. If this were the case, he would not have been human as we are human, and the corollary would be that we have not been redeemed. I have encountered this kind of view from time to time in popular fashion. When I once asked a church member if Jesus ever accidentally trod on anyone's foot, the immediate response was that this could not have been the case since he was 'perfect'. I recall hearing a famous evangelist eulogise Jesus' hands by saying that although he was a carpenter, they would not have been scarred or bruised in any way because he was a 'perfect' man. My own thoughts lie in the opposite direction. I regard it as an article of faith that Jesus did tread on someone's foot accidentally (or the equivalent) and that his hands showed all the marks of his trade because this is how it is with human beings. Were it other with Jesus, he would be at a distance from those whose humanity he came to share, or at least from mine. It is necessary for Jesus not to have been Superman. In teaching students, I have sometimes posed the question as to whether when he was learning Hebrew, Jesus automatically got everything right, or had he had to learn mathematics, would he have known the answer to every question? The Book of Hebrews presents us with a Christ who is like us in every respect and yet without sin. In him, God has come close to us, closer than ever before, and in a humanity that is recognisably our own, yet one that is not entangled in sin and so part of the solution, not part of the collective problem. It is perhaps easier for us than it was for our ancestors to recognise that in the incarnation, Christ did not assume a version of humanity that was 'Adamic' or unfallen. Alternative views were sometimes condemned as heretical. By taking his human nature from Mary and so from a long line of problematic ancestors, such as his genealogies (with all their problems) indicate, Jesus, was intersecting the human story as it was to redirect it and bring it back to where it should be. Many Christians have found it more difficult to let Jesus be human than to be divine. The wisdom of the church through the ages has been to insist that he is both God manifest in the flesh and fully and authentically human. I have certainly come to value the sheer humanness of the Lord and the details of his earthly life a glory to behold.

A prejudice among evangelicals has been to valorise the New Testament epistles, especially those of Paul, above the Gospels on the basis that the former gives us doctrine and the latter stories. Implicit in this is the assumption that stories are inferior to doctrinal propositions. Equally unfortunate has been the claim, still made on a regular basis, that Jesus, the Jewish prophet of righteousness and of the coming kingdom, was transformed by Paul into something very different. Paul introduced that terrible thing, 'dogma', and so has the greater claim to be the real founder of Christianity. This claim has itself become a near 'dogma' and is found in the writings of Jewish interpreters of Jesus, of critics of Christianity and of certain Christians who want to divest Christianity of its burdensome beliefs. Jesus is celebrated, Paul is execrated. I resist all of this and find it intellectually well off-target.

We have come to see that 'story', the use of narrative is the primary form of human verbal communication and that it contains immense formative capacity because of its ability to appeal across cultures. The narratives in the Gospels are not 'just' stories but are shot through with theological implications. This has become increasingly clear as scholarship has developed. The apostle Paul was not a distorter of what Jesus taught but a servant of its interpretation, albeit employing different theological tools. What Jesus embodied, Paul (and others) had the capacity to conceptualise. As an illustration, Paul's articulation of 'justification by faith' apart from acquired merit is a theological way of expressing the ways in which Jesus associated with the outcasts and 'sinners' and declared that they would enter the kingdom ahead of the overtly religious. Jesus' acceptance of the alienated and lost embodies God's mercy and will to reconcile undeserving outsiders.

There are many ways in which past generations of Christian thinkers have failed to do justice to the historical Jesus. In truth, the very idea of 'the Jesus of history' becomes more problematic the more it is thought about. Does this term mean Jesus in so far as modern historiography is able to reconstruct him and his environment? Or is it simply a recognition that Jesus did live as do the rest of us and it is possible, at least to a measured degree, to say something about his world, his passage through it, and his impact upon it? For many, believers or otherwise, the historical Jesus is swallowed up either in his glorification as universal Lord or in 'the Christ of faith', that is, the overlay of theological belief that, to the mind of the believer, sets out his divine nature, and to the sceptic conceals rather than reveals Jesus as he was. I have always been confident that there is a coherent transition from the Jesus of history to the Christ of faith. New Testament theology is, therefore, the faithful exegesis of what was implicit in Jesus himself and by no means a distortion of his nature and mission. I regard this as one of the most important issues in theological debate. If orthodox Christians are not being true to Jesus, we should give up the game. This implies, therefore, that what we know of Jesus, almost exclusively confined to the Gospels, is a topic of constant interest. I find it so.

Ironically, the analyses I have found most helpful in this regard are almost all from non-Christian sources. Not that I distrust overtly Christian accounts of Jesus, but it is hard to discount the fact of unconscious bias, a will to make the scholarship turn out in a way that is favourable to faith, and perhaps more so when one is serving a community of faith that is sensitive to what may undermine that faith. Those who are both scholars and ordained ministers have accountability in both directions. In Jesus studies it is a notorious fact that reconstructions of the historical Jesus tend to turn out in particular ways, that is, to make Jesus look like we would like him to look. One of the most famous sayings is that investigating Jesus is like looking down a deep well and finding there only the pale reflection of a 'Liberal Protestant face'. Too true. And this fact leads some to believe that there is no way of penetrating behind the accounts we are given in the Gospels and that the 'quest for the historical Jesus' is misguided and perhaps impious. For the moment, I content myself with the belief that it should be possible modestly to look for historical bedrock behind the Gospel interpretations and that it is edifying to do so.

To indicate some of the sources I have found helpful: Bart Ehrman is an American New Testament scholar who is highly critical of fundamentalist approaches to the Bible. He believes them to ignore genuine critical problems. Yet he is an accomplished and, to my mind, judicious scholar. His writings have not only resisted fundamentalism but the equal and opposite form of that phenomenon that refuses to allow that Jesus ever existed. He titles these the 'mythicists'. To abolish Jesus and claim he never existed would be very convenient for those who stand opposed to Christianity. Ehrman does not allow this and mounts a well-informed refutation of the charge, utilising as he does so the standard tools of biblical scholarship in which he is well versed. His scholarship has integrity. His book *Did Jesus Exist?*[28] exposes mythicist arguments as 'weak and irrelevant'. There is clear bedrock history to be uncovered by an unprejudiced mind. He does not,

---

[28] Bart D. Ehrman, *Did Jesus Exist? The Historical Argument for Jesus of Nazareth* (New York: HarperCollins, 2012).

however, let the Christians off the hook and points to the perennial tendency of Christians, as he sees it, to make of Jesus something that he was not. Indeed, the nub of his argument as one who now stands outside the faith is that once we have penetrated through to the historical Jesus, we find him to be uncongenial, an apocalyptic prophet inhabiting a symbolic world that is no longer credible. Jesus is at a distance from us, not one to be embraced. In this he stands in a line of scholarship reaching back into the eighteenth century. Historical study so inclined does not undermine the historical Jesus but uncovers him as being less than attractive to modern people. My response to this is that whereas there is undoubtedly a deep apocalyptic strand to Jesus that we may or may not find congenial, this is far from being the whole Christ. There is much more to him in the Gospels than this. Where I fault Ehrman, having valued the positives he brings, is with the countercriticism that just as Christians for their own ends can make of Jesus an attractive figure worth believing in, he is doing the very same but the opposite way round. He paints a picture of Jesus as one in whom the modern 'enlightened' person should not want to believe. And just as Christian scholars belong to a cultural and confessional circle that inclines them to support positive images of Jesus, so Ehrman belongs to a cultural circle hostile to fundamentalism, especially in its American versions. Nevertheless, his work offers solid refutations of the mythicist prejudice. Jesus is rooted in solid history. Ehrman is far from the only scholar who establishes this – the great majority of Jesus scholars are clear on the matter, but his position outside the faith perhaps lends him credibility in his judgements.

My judgement is that the Jesus whom I confess is securely rooted in history. There is no need to doubt this, however, many interpretations of him are divided between Christian, Jewish or secular perspectives. There is bedrock with which to work. As biblical studies developed, it may sometimes have been a surprise to Christians to discover that the Bible is not as unique as it may have once been supposed. The more we know of the ancient world, the more we can see the overlap between biblical writings and what was also available in the ancient Near East – this is particularly marked in the category of Writings in the Jewish Tanakh (Old Testament) where, for instance, large sections of Proverbs replicate other sources. Why not if all truth is God's truth? Similar things can now be said of Jesus as demonstrated in the scholarship of Jewish author Geza Vermes, regarded by many as the foremost 'Jesus scholar'. Vermes, originally from Hungary, was a one-time Catholic priest who returned to his native Judaism in its Reform or Liberal variation. His book *Jesus the Jew*[29] and other writings revolving round similar subject matter have done a huge amount to re-establish Jesus' Jewish identity and to situate him within his first-century context. Vermes did this by uncovering the fact that there were other charismatic Jewish teachers and wonderworkers roughly

---

[29] Geza Vermes, Jesus the Jew: *A Historian's Reading of the Gospels* (London: SCM Press, 2001)

contemporary to Jesus, notably Hanina ben-Dosa and Honi the Circle-Drawer, functioning in Galilee and attracting followers. This in addition to John the Baptist (although John was never a worker of wonders). On the one hand, this might be thought to reduce the uniqueness of Jesus, but on the other, it adds authenticity to the Gospel accounts as it displays Jesus against his cultural and religious background. That Vermes does not accept Christian interpretations of Jesus does not trouble me. Rather, in his work, I see how those interpretations could emerge as an unfolding of who Jesus was, what he did and what he taught. Vermes not only highlights the elements of wonder-working, wisdom and disciple-making in some of Jesus' contemporaries but shows how they were given titles of honour such as 'lord' (a flexible word that could range in meaning from 'sir' to 'Yahweh') and 'son of God'. It is readily conceivable, therefore, how these titles could be given to Jesus in his lifetime and how they might accrue greater meaning retrospectively in the light of his resurrection. We are, therefore, on the road from the prophet Jesus of history to his denomination as exalted Lord, Son of God, and Saviour.

Thirdly, but secondly, in that she is a Jewish scholar rather like Vermes, though in her case from the orthodox Jewish community in the United States, is Amy-Jill Levine whose work I find both challenging and enjoyable. She possesses an immense field of knowledge of both Christian scholarship and denominational life and is a well-versed New Testament scholar. She could be described as a critical friend, though the challenge of her writings is not to be underestimated. Her most relevant book for my purpose is *The Misunderstood Jew*[30], and the nature of the misunderstanding in question is two-fold. First, it refers to the Christian failure to understand the central figure of its devotion in thoroughly Jewish terms. The book rectifies this balance and reveals Jesus as thoroughly Jewish in dress, context, practice and thought forms. He is far from being understood as one seeking to replace Judaism. If he is prophetically critical this is in line with the Hebrew prophets generally. Given that the Judaism of his day was diverse rather than monolithic, his criticisms were against certain strains within the religion of his day but in accord with other parallel voices. Levine clearly admires Jesus without conceding a Christian interpretation of him. In this argument, I can happily affirm what she writes in the belief that once more, Jesus emerges as a credible historical figure and certainly not a mythic invention. Jesus is faithfully and unambiguously in the prophetic Jewish tradition. Yet the second level of misunderstanding, delivered with humour and persuasiveness, is to imply that Christianity is simply mistaken about its central figure. As Levine is aware that at this point, Jews and Christians will part company, her concerns are to combat 'supersessionism' and to seek the best possible accommodation with the Christian faith. This is to be achieved through frank but

---

[30] *The Misunderstood Jew: The Church and the Scandal of the Jewish Jesus* (New York: HarperCollins, 2006).

respectful disagreement, leading to intelligent and enriching conversation. As a model for this, she is outstanding.

Before the writing of my fourth conversation partner, Maurice Casey, I took the time to divert into that subject of 'supersessionism', the Christian belief that the Christian faith has gone beyond biblical Judaism in such a way as to supersede its validity in some sense. Supersessionism, it is claimed, leads to anti-Judaism, to disdain for the Jewish people and in turn to pogroms, persecutions and to the Holocaust. There is therefore a present concern for informed Christians to reject supersessionism. Without further interrogation, I would find this problematic, and it is not clear to me what the terms mean precisely. On the surface, it suggests that nothing new came into being with Jesus and there is no sense in which the Christian faith should be considered as a fulfilment of the Old Testament hope of a new covenant. Perhaps there is something I simply do not understand. On the other hand, in the spirit of Amy-Jill Levine, if there is disagreement, it is best to acknowledge it and progress from there. To surrender the fact that in Christ, 'everything old has passed away; see, everything has become new!' (2 Corinthians 5:17) is to surrender both what seems plain enough in the New Testament (especially the Book of Hebrews) and to strike at the core of Christian belief and identity. Equally, to discount the continuing place of Jewish people within the purposes of God is to contradict Romans 9-11 and to question the faithfulness of God. The Jews have not been 'replaced' in the sense that they have been rejected but, as with all the nations, are loved by God and have a crucially distinctive place within the divine purpose. Yet surely, post-AD70 Judaism is itself 'supersessionist' in that it has, of necessity, adapted to life without a temple, its sacrifices, and its priesthood. It is no longer what it was. It is a mistake to view contemporary Judaism as the parent to Christianity. Both Jews and Christians are, at best, cousins deriving from a common root and both stake a claim to authentic ownership of the biblical heritage developed along diverging routes. There is no point in denying this, but every point in learning from each other why such differences exist. Judaism, in its various denominational formulations, still has a witness to bear from which Christians may benefit. Jews and Christians also do well to recognise that Islam makes the claim to surpass both in its confession that Mohammed is the last of the prophets. Whereas these competing claims have disgracefully led to religious conflict and still do, there is surely much to gain from the conversation and co-learning within a shared theological discipline that could be called 'Abrahamics'. This does not abolish the differences.

I turn here, therefore, to Maurice Casey, one-time Professor of the New Testament at Nottingham University and author of the volume *Jesus of Nazareth: An independent historian's account of his life and teaching*.[31] I have already referred to his judgement that

---

[31] London: Continuum, 2010.

the resurrection could be, or not be, a plausible interpretation of the historical evidence, even once that evidence has been rigorously scrutinised. The significant word in his title is 'independent': Casey sets out to be neither pro nor, anti- religion but to be a disinterested historian and scholar. He is an example of a type of biblical scholar approaching the Bible with historical and literary interests rather than religious ones. From that point of view, what he finds is interesting. His conclusions can, at points, be remarkably conservative. For example, he ascribes a much earlier date to the Gospel of Mark than the consensus allows, placing Mark in the 40s rather than the 70s and 80s. He is followed in this by James Crossley, one of his doctoral students. As an expert in Aramaic (unlike many New Testament scholars), Casey detects an Aramaic substratum in parts of the Gospel of Matthew, which he attributes to Matthew the tax collector, positing the view that he was necessarily literate and could, and probably did, make contemporary notes of Jesus' teaching. He also proposes that Luke, after a period as an effective evangelist, turned his attention to researching and gathering information about Jesus from eyewitnesses and possibly was financially sponsored in this by his patron, Theophilus. To my mind, this takes the reader back behind the New Testament documents themselves into intriguing questions of their origin and formation. These 'conservative' conclusions might be less intriguing if put forward by a religiously committed scholar and are consequently more striking. This does not mean that Casey lacks scepticism at other points. He can say that certain events, like the raising of Lazarus, are simply 'not true'. Even so, he shows himself surprisingly open to Jesus as a worker of wonders. Critical scholarship has found itself largely unable to attribute to Jesus the mighty works he is said to have performed, sometimes looking for naturalistic explanations. But Casey can say,

"So we have seen him heal a blind man (Mk 8.22-26) and a paralytic who was then able to walk (Mk 2:1-2). He cleansed a man with skin disease (Mk 1.40-44) and healed a deaf man (Mk 7.32-37). It has been generally possible to see how an outstanding traditional healer might do all these things. Further narratives and relatively early summaries by the evangelists are sufficient to show that such healings were a central part of Jesus' ministry."

To these, he adds some at least of the 'resurrection' or resuscitation narratives on the grounds that 'death does not necessarily occur when a person first appears to be dead'. The conclusion:

"There should be no doubt at all that Jesus carried through a dramatic and successful ministry of exorcism and healing. He and his followers were completely convinced that this successful ministry was due to the power of God working through him, and this was a major feature in his ability to attract such a significant following. These were the mighty works of a great prophet. This is why he was known as a prophet and teacher rather than as an exorcist and healer. Important as his ministry of exorcism and healing was, it was part of a larger ministry in which he called upon the lost sheep of the house of Israel to repent and prepare for the coming of the kingdom of God".[32]

Unlike former generations of scholars who have been working with a narrower understanding of what is 'natural', Casey can allow for a broader scope, no doubt, because anthropological studies and psychosomatic medicine have opened areas of human potential that go beyond what was previously assumed. Still, he would see the mighty works of Jesus as operating within natural bounds without the need to look for explanations that were any more 'supernatural'. The total effect is to add to the credibility and authenticity of Gospel accounts of Jesus and to give grounds for their reliability.

The writers I have referred to have greatly added to my appreciation of the Jesus of history and to the view that later Christology is a coherent unfolding of what was implicit in him. In preaching the coming of God's kingdom in his own life and ministry and given that God's eschatological kingdom is not some intermediate structure between God and humankind but the very reality of God's own self, Jesus was the mediation of the reality of God's being in a human person raised up among us for that task. This justifies the idea of a divine incarnation. Furthermore, I draw from Luke Timothy Johnson the perception that a 'historical' person

---

[32] For this discussion see pp.273-75 of the above.

is not only the singular identity of one limited in space and time but the impact that person has made or does make upon those around them who come under their influence.[33] I recently saw an elderly man wearing a tee shirt that announced, 'Grandad: the Man, the Myth, the Legend'. It makes a serious point. There can be no 'isolated' Jesus naked of contextual influence and impact. The quest for such a person is futile. Jesus needs to be understood in all his roundedness, of which first the Gospels and then the rest of the New Testament are a part. Of course, there are differences of presentation – most of all between that of the Synoptics and of John's Gospel. But I resist the temptation, apparently common among commentators, to transmute differences into contradictions. The fullness of God in Christ requires multiple perspectives to make sense of it, and even then, there is mystery.

---

[33] *The Real Jesus: The Misguided Quest for the Historical Jesus and the Truth of the Historical Gospels* (San Francisco: Harper Row, 1996).

Post Twelve: Jesus, the Spirit, and the Church

Former generations located the mighty works of Jesus in his divinity. Jesus could do remarkable things because he was divine and so other than our more meagre selves. To my mind, and that of an increasing number of others, it is preferable to locate these and many other aspects of Christ's life in his Spirit-empowered humanity rather than his divinity. So, Christ, as do we, comes in dependence on the Spirit of God to work the works of God. As he was conceived by the Spirit in the Virgin's womb, so are we to be born from above by the same Spirit. As he was enabled by the Spirit to live in God as the supreme agent of God's kingdom, so may we be effective actors in God's purpose by the same Spirit. In short, Christ is the prototype of a new humanity and his kind of humanity, having first been worked in him, can be extended through him into the community that is gathered around him and that is being remade in his image. All this is from the Spirit and is the firm foundation on which we can speak of Christian humanism. The incarnation by which God does not hesitate to take human nature into God's own self is not only a manifestation of the divine humility but of the value and dignity of being human. It is impossible, therefore to place a higher value on the *humanum*, essential human nature, than is placed by Christian theology. Paradoxically, this is alongside a realistic appraisal of the radical evil so evident in human history. Yet a paradox is not the same as a contradiction. There is nothing more tragic than a good thing spoilt, and the most tragic of all is when the very best acts as the very worst. It is shocking and deeply regrettable when Christian institutions act inhumanely. The apostles of unbelief no doubt celebrate this and find evidence of the wickedness of religion. Yet it would never be the case that without the burden of religion, human nature would spontaneously show itself to be 'basically good'. To be sure, human beings are not 'basically evil', as is sometimes claimed (perhaps understandably when confronted with the most egregious forms of human depravity). Rather, they are basically good as God's creatures, though radically fallen from their calling to become the image of God. They are God's most problematic creatures. The depth of the cruelty they are capable of takes one's breath away. The Christian movement, rightly understood, is an enterprise devoted to shaping a civilisation of love and forming a humanity that achieves its highest potential rather than its worst. Despite the corruption, we are graced.

Having introduced the Holy Spirit in relation to Christology, it may be best to continue along these lines. My own thinking here, as in all the other areas I touch on, is one of broadening perspective. While gratefully acknowledging the role of God's Spirit in awakening, calling, regenerating, empowering and sanctifying believers, in other words, in being the life of the church, I have come to see the Spirit as the very energy of the whole of creation, in other words as the Spirit of Life. The Spirit of God is God in action throughout the universe, the breath of God that breathes through all creation. Whereas it is entirely right to see the Spirit as the gift of the Risen Lord to the church, it is equally right to see the Spirit as the Giver of Christ himself and to trace the Spirit's activity in preparing the way for his coming, in generating the Christ in the womb of the Virgin, in guiding, empowering and sanctifying his life, in enabling his atoning sacrifice on the cross and in raising him from death to life immortal. We might thank the Risen Lord for bestowing the Spirit on us, but equally should thank the Spirit for gifting us the Lord in all his fullness. Having established this context, we may then understand the Spirit as the one who reproduces the life of the Christ, the second Adam, the 'New Being' or 'ultimate man', within the church and its members. We are being conformed to the image of the one who is the image of God and are being transformed from glory to glory in him. If Christ is not only a *real* man in the same sense we are, he is even more the *true* man, the pioneer of a new humanity, something we are not yet but which in him we have the potential to become.

As already mentioned, I have long thought that the time is ripe for the articulation of a new Christian or even evangelical humanism in the light of the above. It is not least through the Christian faith that being human has been elevated and dignified against the background of more brutal and dehumanising views. Taken on its own, a merely evolutionary view of human development can and has led to the projection of a social Darwinism that valorises conflict, dominance, and subjugation of alleged lesser races. In that sense, secular humanism's insistence that we must rise above our genes has shown itself indebted to a religious tradition that it frequently despises. I do have sufficient experience of religion to know that it can be used to oppress and that there is a kind of religious person best avoided. To call this 'Pharisaism' is probably unfair to Pharisees – themselves a religious group that Christianity may not have fairly treated. An understanding of humankind is needed that remains realistic as to the 'evil that is within' and yet does not allow this to eclipse the potential for being in God's image. 'Radical depravity' rather than 'absolute depravity' might be a better way of putting it. Christ makes intercession for us, not least in that he is the sign of hope as to what we can be. He makes intercession for us in the Father's presence (Hebrews 7:25) in that he wills us to become as he is and is the guarantee that this goal will be accomplished. Such a confidence should determine the way we understand our own race. Christians are on the side of humane values. In so far as declarations of human rights point in this direction and are ways of indicating how we should treat others and might expect to be treated, they help us live well.

The life of the individual Christian should always be understood within the life of the Christian community. Election is not some mysterious decree made by God in eternity touching on whom God chooses to save or not, but a historical work of God in seeking out and calling a people among whom God may make a dwelling. It is not based upon human merit but, to the contrary, is the choice in

Israel's case of an undeserving nation and its constituent members in whom God's purpose and glory might be displayed, ethnic Israel first (Deuteronomy 7:7-11) and then the expanded Israel of the church. The community of God's people, therefore, precedes its individual members. In this sense, the Catholic notion that 'outside the church, there is no salvation' has a certain validity, but it is not that of excluding from the joy of salvation any who do not give loyalty to the Roman church. Rather it identifies the centrality of the church in bearing witness and then incorporating into its social existence those who believe. The church is the community of the Spirit, dependent for its existence on the presence of Christ through the Spirit in its midst. When it comes to those individual members, the work of the Spirit is to be identified in awakening them out of the spiritual death of sin into an awareness of God and of their own need. The awakening brings the conviction of sin and of our human falling short, then to repentance and then to the reality of forgiveness in Christ and his work, and so to regeneration or new birth in the Spirit. Awakening leads to regeneration. This 'order of salvation' is disputed in that some regard the work of regeneration as preceding all its other aspects rather than being their outcome. This is held to safeguard the sovereign grace of God in choosing who will be saved and removing any sense of merit from the choice to believe – all this is of God and is part of God's unconditioned and irresistible grace. I question this interpretation and maintain by contrast that God's grace can be resisted. Whereas human beings are incapable of choosing God out of their own resources, this being part of the condition of radical depravity, they nonetheless have the power to resist. I am persuaded that against this resistance should be placed the persistence of God in pursuing the lost and not taking No for an answer. Herein lies the mystery of election, not in some decision taken in a hidden eternal decree of the will of God, but in the interaction between a person's will and the prevenient grace of God's Spirit. The mystery touches on why some respond readily, some reluctantly, and some apparently not at all, and why and how it is that the Spirit presses on to elect some and not others. In saying all this, I do not foreclose on the question of whether God's search for the lost reaches beyond death, in fact, I am fully disposed to believe that it does for reasons I have previously touched upon. It is not for me to proclaim any human soul finally lost but to hold open the confidence that God's grace is larger and broader than any one of us knows. But this is no reason to be less urgent in calling people to repentance and faith and baptism.

Baptism, I understand to be a potentially powerful encounter with God, as it was in the case of Jesus himself, propelling him into his ministry and mission. I say 'potentially' because I do not believe that it is effective without the presence of faith and the grace of the Spirit. When there is, faith baptism is more than a bare act of witness which is humanly generated, a work of our own will. Rather, it is a response to the call of God in which what baptism symbolises is worked into the life of the one who receives it. In this regard I stand at odds with some in my own tradition who, anxious to avoid any sense of *ex opere operato* or quasi-magical significance, all but deprive baptism of spiritual vitality. I find the idea of baptism as a place of rendezvous helpful. God in divine freedom may meet us at any time or place God chooses but has yet appointed specific places where we may meet him, baptism and communion being the primary ritual acts where this may be the case, but only when approached in faith and not as rote actions. Baptism should, therefore, be understood as part of the process of conversion, one which anchors internal faith in an external action that is datable and identifiable in a way that the birth of faith may not be. It is also certainly an act of witness, but more than this, a way of deepening and intensifying faith. It is not, in my understanding, an exclusive action in which grace is available here and nowhere else. Rather, it represents a focusing and deepening of the grace that is already being received in conversion and new birth. It does not add something new but deepens what is already being made available in the Spirit of God. It is a blessing, and since it is commanded in scripture, it is unwise to neglect or refuse it. In regular parlance this is a more sacramental understanding of baptism than is common among Baptists with their prioritisation of faith over ritual. Properly understood (and I freely acknowledge that in all sections of the church, there is a confusion of practice, including in my own Baptist tradition), baptism belongs to the gateway of the Christian community and is a beginning to the living of a baptised life, of living 'under the water', a sign of having made a start, not of having arrived at the goal.

Israel as the people of God, and then the international reality of the church as God's enlarged people are central to understanding God's purpose and so to interpreting history generally. This represents an over-turning of the common perspective, which locates the meaning of history in the political and the powerful rather than the weak and insignificant. Yet within the church, or better said 'the churches', for all their faults, there are signs of God's future reconciliation of all things in Christ. The churches can, therefore, be the *avant-garde* of the promised end of all things. In the church, the Spirit of God allows a foretaste of what is to come, a redeemed and reconciled community that is the provisional dwelling place of God in advance of the day when the kingdoms of this world will become 'the kingdom of our God and of his Christ'. I value the idea that I derive mainly from Moltmann of the 'trinitarian history of God': namely, that history represents the progressive revelation of God through creation, redemption, and consummation. The church is rightly understood as the community of the Spirit and cannot exist independently of the Spirit. It is the temple of the Holy Spirit as well as the Body of Christ. Two instincts follow from this that have been determinative for my understanding of church and my ministerial practice within it. The first is that the church is a community before ever it is an institution. It is constituted as a church by the presence of Christ within it and the interplay of relationships between its members rather than by its relationship to a hierarchy. I do not follow the logic that affirms the church to be constituted by the eucharist that, in turn, is validated by the priesthood that, in its own turn, derives its authority from the line of bishops in the 'historic episcopate' and beyond that in the Pope. Rather, I follow the logic that finds Christ in the intentional gathering of those who believe in him who may be identified by their faith, their proclamation, their baptism, and their celebration of the Lord's Supper. This places me firmly in the category of a radical Protestant. I do not believe that this status is confined to self-identifying Baptists. Rather, it is a broad believers' church movement that reaches far beyond any one grouping and that is identified by its intensity of faith in Christ as Lord and in discipleship in the community. Truth to tell, this tradition constantly runs the risk of fragmentation and sometimes even of destructive sectarianism. But more positively, it can be understood as an expression of diversity and adaptability, of coming to expression in diverse but coherent ways. All 'ways of being church' have their own temptations. Hierarchy can become authoritarianism, and a free church may become anarchy. Each form may even represent a concealed form of sectarianism. In short, any of the 'ways of being church' could be viewed optimistically according to their best expressions (often overlooked by outsiders) or pessimistically according to their aberrations (glaringly obvious to those same outsiders). Our task is to live up to our best ideals, a task that sometimes, given the still problematic condition of our human nature, can at times feel impossible.

An instinct that shapes me is to see the church as the realm of the Spirit. As a Protestant, evangelical and Baptist (all of which I choose to be – it is not as though they have been imposed upon me), I give a distinct priority to the New Testament in deriving my understanding of church life and practice. In the Protestant way, scripture has priority over tradition and exists as a critical principle by which our traditions are tested and scrutinised against their supposed origins in the New Testament. This is not an outright rejection of tradition since the New Testament itself contains a handing on of what has been received, and because the living flow of the church always precedes personal faith, we are indebted to the 'handing-on' process and those who are its agents (2 Timothy 2:1-2). Yet the Protestant approach recognises that tradition can go two ways: it can unfold the witness of scripture faithfully, or it can deviate from that witness by incorporating within itself elements derived from elsewhere that obscure it. Only by constantly looping back to the New Testament can the good form of tradition be distinguished from its rival. This is what the Reformation attempted to do. But it also enunciated the crucial principle that the church is both reformed and being reformed, that it stands constantly 'under the Word of God' as a continuing process, and that such a work is likely never to be complete. This is unsettling in that it commits us to a life of pilgrimage in which we can never totally settle down and feel we have arrived. Moreover, even churches of the Reformation or its radical progeny fall prey to 'bad' tradition. We all have a natural need for stability and security, and church life should offer a proper degree of regularity, continuity, and familiarity. But it remains to be judged when this becomes complacency and institutionalisation. A robust understanding of the Spirit 'blowing where it chooses' helps to maintain appropriate equilibrium (John 3:8)

The Reformation established the priority of scripture over tradition and applied this principle first to issues of salvation, such as justification by grace through faith. This represented progress. The radical wing of the Reformation represented by the Anabaptists took this same principle further and insisted that the mainstream Reformers had only gone halfway. Further reform was needed in restoring the church to its New Testament pattern. This required, in their view, a break with the church-state settlement of Christendom that had long prevailed and was symbolised not least by the practice of infant baptism as an induction both into the church and to the state conceived as both a political and religiously defined institution. The radical shifts in Anabaptist understanding were at the root of the slow emergence of democratic states as plural communities safeguarding religious freedoms. The crucial point for me, however, has been and continues to be that church, as we have inherited it, cannot be assumed to be church as it is supposed to be. 'Normative church' is rather the church of New Testament theology and especially of the three primary images of the people of God, the body of Christ and the temple of the Holy Spirit. This is not to say that we can straightforwardly adopt the practices of the early church as though there were no cultural differences between then and now, nor does it deny plurality in the early church, but it sets out that we should be both inspired and informed by what we find in the New Testament. The alternative is to make the inherited church normative and the church of the New Testament abnormal, which I refuse to do. It is this theological pattern of thought that keeps me open to the charismatic dimension of church life that is so evident in the New Testament.

I declare my identity as a 'card-carrying charismatic' and as a 'continuationist' rather than a 'cessationist' when it comes to the New Testament gifts of the Spirit. I fully accept that there are peak times in the church's story when such gifts and manifestations are more evident than others, yet I reject the idea that they were only for the church of the New Testament and must be proclaimed false at any other time. My perspective here is not only that the Holy Spirit remains the same and is not confined by our restrictive theologies but that human nature remains the same through the ages, and under the impact of the Spirit, the same energies and capacities are likely to be awakened. From the beginning, the Christian faith has been experientialist: it was born out of the experience of the resurrection and the coming of the Spirit as life-changing realities. It speaks of a realised communion with God, and throughout its history, outbreaks of 'enthusiasm' have been constant across its different streams, not always beneficially. Rather than deny this fact or keep such moments firmly in the past to avoid their present challenge, it is wiser to accommodate them, to treat them as normal and revitalising. It is certainly the case that from the earliest moments on, there has been a need to 'test everything; hold fast to what is good' (1 Thessalonians 5:21), but these sober words are indicative both that there is a good on which to hold fast and an admixture of the true and the false within all spiritual manifestations. The reason for this is that we human beings, even in a regenerated condition and at our best, tend to corrupt the best of things. So, to intense spiritual experiences there need to be added both sound doctrine and plain common sense, above all in discerning what points to and glorifies the Christ who is our touchstone for all things. Human experience of God remains precisely that: *human* experience of God. In so far as we bring to it our fractured humanity, the potential for deception and delusion always remains. There is no straightforwardly supernatural phenomenon to which we can point, as our often dualist mentalities suppose. As an example, though speaking in tongues (glossolalia) is sometimes regarded as a divine overriding of our normal humanity, and so proof of the transcendent realm, it is more insightful to regard it as an innate capacity of the human brain. It only becomes a spiritual gift when it is ignited in the service of God by the Holy Spirit, who inspires us and who breathes upon and into us. Anecdotes may abound of people allegedly heard to be speaking in some known foreign or ancient tongue, and there is some pressure to believe them, but in my experience, they are always impossible to trace back to their source and so have the character of urban myth rather than solid reality. Recognition of the human dimension in all our experiences of God helps us understand their nature but does not discount their value. The charismatic dimension signifies to my mind a fuller recognition of the intuitive dimension to our knowledge of God to be placed alongside the cognitive dimension but not divorced from it. So, Paul can speak in 1 Corinthians of worshipping God with both the spirit (intuitive) and the mind (cognitive), what we might helpfully recognise as a 'Word and Spirit' emphasis. The role of the intuitive dimension can be traced in other phenomena such as prophecy, interpretation, and discernment, in 'words of wisdom' and 'words of knowledge' though none of these should be reckoned as incapable mistakes. Humility is essential, and a degree of tentativeness is advisable in the operation of spiritual gifts.

The issues at stake here have been discussed in the tradition by asking the question, does God abolish human nature or perfect it? The former regards something more likely to be 'of God' if the human factor is removed from the equation, whereas the latter approach sees God as working with the grain of human nature, enhancing and elevating it to a place where it can become a vehicle for divine action. My approach is the latter, and I take seriously the possibility that the Spirit of God 'plays upon' human nature. To that end, all spiritual experience has a human side that can be described psychologically without being reduced to the merely psychological. For instance, when sceptics locate religious experiences in a certain area of the brain and deduce from this that they have 'explained it away', they are under a rather naïve misapprehension. If there were no brain activity involved, then there would be no human experience since all human experiences pass at some level through the brain. To describe what happens in the brain when listening to a piece of music does not invalidate the piece of music as an objective reality, even if, in certain states of mind listening to music can be simulated. Given that there are areas of the brain that may be geared towards religious experience, this rather explains why 'religion' is a constant within human communities. All that we know about humanity anthropologically indicates that the religious instinct is innate and universal both through and across time. Atheism, or at least the absence of a religious sense, in that sense is the aberration, the departure from the norm. This suggests, at the least that it is not possible to live a fully human life without a religious dimension in some form. It also raises the question as to why all of this should be so. If the evolutionary process is about adaptation for reasons of survival to the environment, what is it that the human species has adapted to in its religious sensibilities? It is widely accepted, even among sceptics, that religious belief affords an evolutionary advantage, but an orientation towards a transcendent or non-material goal suggests that there might be something seemingly 'out there' to which it is appropriate to adapt. This does not, of itself, validate one single religious pathway, but it does go part way to seeking for one. It might also imply that when people claim to be atheists, they may not fully understand themselves but retain more of a religious instinct than they suppose. *In extremis*, even atheists have been known to let out a prayer to the One in whom they do not believe or alternatively to blame the One who does not exist for the world's misfortune. Many appalled by suffering express their anger to a God who just isn't there.

Life must be lived, and to live it at all, let alone to live it well, requires some kind of framework that borders on the philosophical or the religious. Even in the most secular of contexts, thoughtful people who wish to do more than bury themselves unthinkingly in the sensual and the mundane require a way of interpreting material and personal realities as they present themselves to us. Belief in God (however we define that word) is ultimately a way of interpreting things. It is a hermeneutical stance that goes beyond seeking to locate 'God' within the world of things. 'God' is a way of putting it all together in a meaningful narrative. When I consider my own faith, there are several advantages, call them evolutionary ones if you choose, that I can identify. They include a sense of purpose, participation in a supportive community, and spiritual and experiential resources that make for a sense of fulfilment and hope about the future.

We live in an age that suffers from the theft of meaning. If we do not have a purpose in life, then it threatens to become meaningless. Of course, we all create purposes that are local and limited yet still to be valued, such as love of family and friends. But there is a difference between finding purpose *in* life and finding the purpose *of* life, which is the outrageous Christian claim. The Christian faith offers me just this and locates it in a divine purpose for all things revealed in and fulfilled by Christ. Moreover, since moral and ethical living must be rooted in an understanding of what life is for, a sense of purpose leads to moral and ethical ways of living that embrace my attitudes toward others, the planet, myself and to God. I have heard it said in both Jewish and Christian circles that doctrines or 'beliefs' (that supposedly seek to express the purpose of life) are unimportant compared with practice, in Jewish terms with Torah-obedience and in Christian contexts with care for the poor. Granted, the point being made has its merits, but I fail to see how either of these can be detached from some level of belief, conscious or unconscious, about the way things are and what really counts. Since none of us can live as isolated units, belonging to a community that itself is guided by both shared beliefs and practices is immensely helpful, and probably essential in keeping them alive and determinative. Living communities reinforce and refresh the sense of purpose to which beliefs and doctrines point. Moreover, through worship and other spiritual practices they serve to keep the flame of faith alive, to impart spiritual energy and inspiration to those who believe. Added to this, hope enables us to rise above the tragedies and disappointments of life through believing that ultimately, though certainly not immediately, God will make 'all things work together for good' (Romans 8). There is a future that transcends and fulfils this present life. This is a massive statement of faith and one whose final form asserts that not even death can finally separate us from the love of God in Christ and that God's purposed future is one that is inconceivably generous.

I was once listening to an interview with Jordan Peterson, a Canadian professor and clinical psychologist. He has a reputation for holding contested and reactionary views and is attacked for them, but I usually find him a paragon of common sense. He was told by the interviewer, almost in an accusatory tone, that he believed in the existence of God, didn't he? He answered that he did not know whether God existed or not, but he lived as though He did. He then added that perhaps this was what believing in God meant anyway. I was intrigued by the answer, mainly, I think, because it highlights that there are benefits to such a belief contrary to what the *bien pensant* elite who find it all oppressive commonly imagine. One of these must be that of living an observed life and of being accountable not just in this life but beyond it. What I do, even in secret, is known, and so faith becomes a kind of 'walking in the light'. Furthermore, it points me to a resource beyond myself, which, even if it remains mysterious, I might 'tap into' in times of need and not just of need. There are many creatives that speak of a kind of inspiration that seems to come from outside themselves. I recall the story of the poet Siegfried Sassoon, who had one of those days on which he could not settle for anything but was restless and bored and generally without focus. He decided he would go to bed, and as he was halfway up the stairs, a poem, whole and entire, was 'given to him': 'Everyone suddenly burst out singing; And I was filled with such delight /As prisoned birds must find in freedom'. Inspiration can come seemingly from beyond ourselves. The 'beyond' might well include the depths of our own subconscious or perhaps even the corporate and 'racial' unconscious. But these may also be the medium through which something even further beyond impinges upon us for our benefit.

Post Thirteen: Church – An 'Impossible Possibility'

Having touched upon it in the last post, I return to thinking about the church. Church life has occupied my attention for much of my life. I have increasingly come to see the church as an impossible possibility. By this I mean the difficulty of the church of God living up to its own high ideals and to all that is implied by those primary images of the people of God, the body of Christ and the temple of the Holy Spirit. As somebody wrote, the church is like 'building with bananas'. We are all of us bent to a degree, perhaps more than any of us will readily admit, and the truth that sin continues to dwell within believers is obvious at every point. The pure church nowhere exists except perhaps in a visionary form in the finally gathered church of Revelation 7, the host that no one can number drawn from every tongue and nation. Along with this, I class the impossibility of fulfilling the demands associated with bearing a vocation within the church of which a prime example is that of the pastoral ministry, sometimes called the ministry of the gospel or the ministry of word and sacrament. For fifty years I have sought to fulfil the latter and come to my present point only too aware of how poorly I have done it. And this is not false modesty.

If I have had a theological specialism, I have chosen to call it 'comparative ecclesiology'. I am for sure not the originator of this term, but it is one with which I resonate. There are various ways in which sincere believers have sought to be the church, and each of them has its own kind of integrity. This is not to say that I believe them all to be equally valid but that each, taken at its best, can make an appeal to the New Testament and has defensible insights that are worth weighing and possibly incorporating into a fuller doctrine of the church. At the same time, each manifestation of the church has a pathological version that is to be guarded against. Episcopal churches that are strong on relationships and continuity with tradition, for instance, risk becoming authoritarian prisoners of clericalism. Free churches that have a constant inclination to divide risk the dangers of insularity and sectarianism. Pathological forms of church are obstructive to true progress, but neither should babies be thrown out with the bathwater in correcting them. My intention is always to be ecumenical, to find the elements of 'true church' within whatever forms of church exist and to unite with them at some level. Yet I deny that any church body can claim to be *the true church*, which is precisely what many have done, with the consequence, intended or otherwise, of unchurching others and denying them their place within the spectrum of God's people. The idea of the true church is useful when it is employed as an eschatological category when it is that to which we are moving in God's future and is envisaged in Revelation 7 as that 'great multitude that no one could count from every nation, from all tribes and peoples and languages, standing before the throne and before the Lamb' (Revelation 7:9). What is beautiful about this vision, and vision it is, is that it comprises a vast number of the redeemed and that they are diverse, catholic, inclusive, and therefore immeasurably rich. Such a community nowhere currently exists except in anticipation, fragmentarily and certainly imperfectly. The primary problem that the church, or better the churches, faces, or face, is the same as within humankind generally that the seeds of destruction lie within. I find this to be a constant biblical theme. Adam and Eve precipitate their own fall. In the flood narratives that portray the destruction of humankind and the reconstruction of humanity around Noah's family, it is not long before the virus of sin reasserts itself. In the great heroes of the faith, such as Abraham and Moses, it is not eradicated. Saul, who was head and shoulders above any others of his day and began so well, proves to be a tragic disappointment. Glamorous and much-admired King David fails morally, and his own faults and failings are reflected in those around him, even his own family. And so on. So, it is within the churches. We never completely rise beyond our own destructive tendencies, even when we think we are at our best and most spiritual. There are saintly exceptions of course, but too few. Romantic views of church should be banished, but not to the point of despair. It strikes me that the shortfall between religious vision and actual achievement is constantly present in the scriptures. The land flowing with milk and honey never quite proves to be so. The hope for a righteous and godly king is never quite realised (and so becomes the ground for the expectation of the Messiah). The promise of a glorious and triumphant return from exile is not unambiguously fulfilled. The coming of the Messiah is a definite event, but the 'now' is accompanied by a 'not yet' that leaves us still looking to the future for a second coming and a complete consummation. For now, we live in the penultimate, hoping for better. In every generation, we must be resilient.

I often hear that critics are suspicious of 'organised religion' and am never sure what they mean. The comment suggests that 'personal religion' is acceptable, presumably because it remains in the private sphere. But at what point does it become 'organised'? Once I start meeting with others, it becomes communal, and community is one of religion's greatest contributions. Beyond that, once it shades into institution building, it admittedly becomes more problematic, with all the potential for self-exaltation and abusive power games from which institutions suffer. A degree of suspicion is appropriate and suggests the need for constant vigilance.

Having offered these cautionary words, let me state my enduring conviction that the church is central to God's purpose, and that infused into it is the reality of a people belonging to God. Sometimes, it must be searched for. I have declared my indebtedness to the radical tradition associated with the so-called 'left wing of the Reformation' and, otherwise known as the 'believers' church' tradition. I resonate with words uttered by the early Luther concerning his preferred church order:

"[They] should sign their names and meet alone in a house somewhere to pray, to read, to baptize, to receive the sacrament, and to do other Christian works. According to this order, those who do not lead Christian lives could be known, reproved, corrected, cast out or excommunicated, according to the rule of Christ, Matthew 18 [15-17]. Here, one could also solicit benevolent gifts to be willingly given and distributed to the poor, according to St. Paul's example, II Corinthians 9. Here would be no need of much and elaborate singing. Here, one could set out a brief and neat order for baptism and the sacrament and centre everything on the Word, prayer and love".[34]

Luther may not, under the press of circumstance, have held fast to this early radicalism, but I have identified myself with the kind of ecclesial aspirations he indicated (mostly) and that were taken up by others such as Anabaptists, Baptists and kindred groups. So, concepts such as conversion, regenerate church membership, believers' baptism, non-clericalism, voluntarism, and simplicity in worship have determined my thinking. Whereas some traditions wish to express the beauty of the gospel in ever more elaborate forms of architecture, vestments, music, and liturgy (and I cannot gainsay the aesthetic attraction of these things), that to which I

---

[34] Cited in Donald F. Durnbaugh, *The Believers' Church: The History and Character of Radical Protestantism* (London: Macmillan, 1968), p.3. In my earlier years this was a particularly seminal text for me. Spellings are as recorded.

adhere finds beauty in simplicity and the light of Christ in the faces of fellow pilgrims. In his biographies, the Anglican priest, broadcaster, and former rock musician Richard Coles describes how, for a time, he joined the Roman Catholic Church on the grounds that it was 'the original and best'. By contrast, the radical affirms it is the church of the New Testament that is the original and the best, if only in the sense that there we see laid out in stark images and narratives that which will guide us most securely to our desired end. The areas where that thinking has changed for me include a willingness to concede the legitimacy of other ways of being church and a recognition that the boundaries of church life are much more porous. I have held to a 'high' doctrine of conversion که along traditional Baptist lines, has insisted that repentance and faith, baptism, formal church membership, participation in communion and life-long service in and beyond the church is what constitutes conversion proper. Anything less than this might smack of 'cheap grace'. Indeed, I still hold to this pattern as normative and utterly desirable if churches are to be the stable, effective, and self-propagating organisms that will endure and transmit the faith to the next generation. If my mind has changed, it is in accommodating to the messiness of things and being willing to acknowledge that God is savingly at work in ways that go beyond the humanly and theologically desirable pattern I have outlined. God has uncovenanted mercies. It is a simple matter of fact that belonging to a church in the prescribed manner is just not temperamentally or socially possible for swathes of people. We underestimate the challenge it is for some or many to be socialised into church life as we know it, even into those 'fresh expressions of church' that might appear to some to be a response to the challenge. God bless them and their efforts, yet I am unwilling to restrict the Spirit of God to the churches while at the same time wholly rejecting the siren calls for a religion-less or churchless Christianity with which some have been enamoured in secularised cultures. To the contrary, vital communities of Christian faith are essential in keeping the fire burning not only for those who are participants but for those who might at some point become so. Many who do not belong to the churches are nonetheless glad that they are there and that they let their light shine. Jesus had compassion on the crowds because they were helpless and harassed like lost sheep. He prayed that God should send workers into the harvest and so plainly envisaged that there was a community into which to be gathered in the service of the kingdom. But my hope extends also to those who are not 'gathered in', and I hope that their time will come.

When I recently engaged in a piece of oral history, I surprised myself. I have regularly thought of myself as a non-pedigree Baptist in that I was not brought up in that faith, or indeed in any faith. On reviewing my early life, however, I did realise that from the beginning, I have been in the 'orbit' of a certain Baptist church and that it was through it that I was, in time, awakened and came to believe. This prompts me to ask whether I hold Baptist convictions because I was conditioned to do so or because I became persuaded. The answer must be that I was disposed by background to believe in a certain way but needed to find that way persuasive on my own account, and I did, whilst being aware of its possible weaknesses. While not brought up in the faith, my own religious heritage is decidedly nonconformist and includes Methodist, Salvation Army, and Quaker strands. These dispose me against ritualism, formality, hierarchy, and what Charles Haddon Spurgeon unkindly described as 'salvation by haberdashery' (viz. vestments). This was not his only disparaging comment. His comments are both reprehensible and amusing. I don't dare endorse them but enjoy relating them.

As I came to understand more, I located myself firmly within the traditions of radical Protestantism, in the left wing of the Reformation, part of which found expression in the sixteenth-century emergence of General Baptists and Particular Baptists among English-speaking believers. I am not a state church or established church person. On the other hand, I am certainly a mainstream, orthodox believer who seeks for maximal rather than minimal engagement with other ways of 'being church'. Scholarship tends to categorise my own way of being church as 'sectarian'. This is acceptable when understood as a sociological description and contrasted with the 'church' or 'mystical' forms of Christianity as described by Ernst Troeltsch. Regrettably, the sociological term is sometimes construed theologically as being insular, narrow, and disinterested in wider societies, and I reject this as a distortion. In fact, all forms of Christianity have the propensity in their own way to be exclusive and narrow and are capable of 'unchurching' others. My intention is to be as ecumenical and generous as possible to others (and not just within the Christian churches). Where I find myself something of an oddity within my own tradition is in relation to bishops, and I have repeatedly argued the case for 'Baptist bishops', not, it must be said, with a great deal of overt success.

I think I am probably the only Baptist minister who can claim to have preached by invitation at the consecration of an Anglican Bishop! This was in York Minster when my friend and colleague Cyril Ashton was appointed as suffragan Bishop of Doncaster. A great privilege, of course, and one that was offered without hesitation by the Church of England to its credit. In days of yore, this would have been unacceptable, probably on both sides of the ecclesial divide. Bishops in both Catholic and Anglican traditions were a focal point of 'sectarian' opposition since they represented at one time the kind of ecclesiastical dominance that demanded religious conformity. Such power links to the major shift that took place in the fourth century when the Christian church became, at first, the favoured religious partner of the Roman state and then its official and persecuting religious agent. Bishops then assumed the status of Roman aristocrats (being raised to the 'purple') who continued the Roman exercise of power and were, in time, regarded as lords and princes, often wielding as much secular power as religious. A good dose of *Romanitas* was thus infused into an increasingly dominant church. Those who refused to conform to its beliefs and practices were excluded, discriminated against, and sometimes imprisoned or executed. Resistance to the office of bishop was consequently instilled in nonconformists (though, truth to tell, some of its alternatives could prove similarly coercive). Despite this, I have seen the need for a form of ministry that reaches beyond local churches to offer missional, theological and pastoral care, especially to those in leadership, a kind of 'charismatic episcopacy'. In fact, this is very difficult to achieve. It does exist in that several denominations and newer church movements have developed ministries that seek to fill the gap, sometimes even using the term 'bishop', though in a not-so-hierarchical way. Often the function goes under some other name, more bureaucratic in nature; it is strange that these should be employed when a word that has at least some claim to a scriptural origin is not. That trans-local oversight or resourcing is widely considered of value is an indication that the need is a real one. In the United States these collective if varied structures beyond the local church are generically known as the 'judicatory' since so many church movements have developed them. Often, they are understood in an administrative way. Effective administration is a good thing to have, but my argument has been that the language we use creates certain expectations, and the term 'bishop' should evoke spiritual and pastoral expectations rather than merely organisational ones. I am resigned to not winning this argument, but I have deposited it in people's minds, and in one way or another, it might bear fruit, not least in encouraging those who belong to 'judicatories' to practise 'bishoping' in its most pastoral and spiritual ways. It is noticeable that across both episcopal and non-episcopal communions, a lack of support for those on the front line is frequently lamented.

Post Fourteen: Church, State, and Politics

A significant part of my theological reflection in the past has been concerned with the relationship between church and state. I have carried this through in a rather traditional form and, in the process, have confirmed to myself, and possibly to others, that I am a genuine Baptist. I have taken a keen interest in Anabaptism and its variants and have been much stimulated by it. Where I have come to differ from it is in sitting loose to its supposed pacifism and that of its modern expression in Mennonite communities. I say 'supposed' pacifism because the evidence suggests that some of the first Anabaptists were not pacifists. Rather, pacifism developed precisely as a rejection of some of these early impulses towards violent revolution. The same might be said of Quakers in their emergence after the English Civil Wars, in which some of the early adherents were involved. For the first decade of life the Quakers were certainly not pacifist and only became so after 1661 once the monarchy had been restored and they needed to clear themselves of violent associations. Anabaptists and Baptists may have agreed on the proper distinction between the 'order of preservation' represented (in its proper function) by the state and the 'order of redemption' represented by the church, but they drew different conclusions. They agreed on the need to preserve the freedom of the church and of the religious conscience but disagreed on the extent to which the obedient disciple could participate in the coercive functions of the state in curbing criminal behaviour. There was no question that such a coercive function was necessary in a fallen world, but whether Christian disciples should participate in it was the issue. For Baptists this was acceptable since the order of redemption was also ordained by God for the preservation of the peace. For Anabaptists, this was unacceptable since the vocation of the Christian was to redeem, not to punish. This position led to a greater critical distance from the orders of the state deemed necessary in guarding against evildoers. In fact, all Anabaptist/Mennonite confessions that I have consulted are clear about the need for the coercive function (the 'sword') of the state to keep criminal behaviour, which is a constant in most societies, at bay. Without it, most ordinary lives would be engulfed by chaos, those of the poor most of all. I am at odds with 'justice warriors' who neglect this element. For them, justice is about achieving freedom from oppression and an ever-increasing movement towards equality and fairness, all of which is laudable. But justice is also about vindicating those who have been sinned against and redressing the scales of justice. A decent and equitable society should care about taking the side of those who have been wronged and ensuring through the penal system that wrong-doing is shown to be just that, wrong-doing that is unacceptable and that incurs consequences. We used to call consequences 'punishment', but there is a noticeable reluctance to use this word even though it is precisely what we mean. We talk about 'holding people accountable' instead, but there is a place for retributive justice. Punishment should be in proportion to the wrong done but should not exceed it. Where not, those who have been wronged are not seeing justice delivered; rather the offences committed against them are being minimised. But retribution is not a prescription for individual behaviour but for the civil authorities, in whatever form they exist, by which to be guided. In ancient Israel, these would have existed in rudimentary form as 'the elders at the gate'. The principle of proportion, not revenge, is exactly how they should be guided, tempered by wisdom and mercy but not by moral weakness. There is a distinction to be made between revenge and vengeance. The former is personal and perpetuates the vicious cycle of recrimination to nobody's benefit. The latter is the objective redressing of the scales of justice by a competent authority in a way that delivers justice to the poor and downtrodden and is intended to put a stop to the search for revenge. Without this, the law of vendetta has free reign. The words of Jesus in the Sermon on the Mount are best understood when we clarify these distinctions. However, I am not sympathetic to those who decline to address the idea and the language of retribution. At the time I am writing, the murder of a young girl in Liverpool has shocked society. Commenting on the situation, the local bishop advised the world that this was 'not the time for retribution'. If she meant that this was not a time to seek revenge she was surely right. But the time is precisely right for retribution by the authorities to avenge the brutal death of an innocent child. Retribution is related to wrongs committed and should be proportionate and sure in maintaining stability and upholding the values a society stands for. It is recompense for what has been done, not what has not been done. Of course, it is to be tempered by mercy and, far from being contrary to the ideal of rehabilitation, stands in proximity to it. Punishment brings home the severity of wrongs done and alerts evildoers to the unacceptability of their crimes. This itself is a step towards the amendment of life.

I have indicated here some of the ways in which I have come to distinguish myself from an Anabaptist-Mennonite position and a degree of reticence towards some contemporary and 'fashionable' trends in 'justice' thinking. For the moment, I shall linger on the topic of the Christian church as in itself a political community. I do find inspiration here. In short, the Christian enterprise is not solely to be understood as a lifeboat or an 'ark' into which we gather those who expect the imminent destruction of all things but is an experiment in fashioning a new humanity. I return to the idea that God's church is an 'impossible possibility'. But I don't cease to hope that within a world wracked by hatred and toxicity, it might be possible to be part of a 'civilisation of love', even a faltering one. I conceive of the church as a community of communities who are learning to love in thought and deed in a way that contrasts with 'the world' understood as human society organised without God. The church is called to be a contrast society, largely non-conformist and dissenting in relation to majority culture not motivated by a desire to honour God. Surely this is a basic Christian aspiration rooted in the biblical sources that conceive of the church as a chosen people and a holy nation, after Israel before it. The church is a social phenomenon and must inevitably, therefore, be a political entity properly understood. In continuity with Israel, its vocation is to be a witness, a sign of what it means to live under the rule of God.

What would be a proper understanding of such a political dimension? Inevitably, distinctions become necessary. Ask any number of retired or former ministers what they least miss about active ministry, and most would probably reply 'church politics'. By this, they mean the push and pull of human social interactions when they are soured by vested interest, unproductive conflict, the desire for dominance, or by manoeuvring for advantage. These are at their worst when they are given a theological rationale, though I am the first to stress that doctrinal issues are of great importance. I am also cynical enough to recognise that theological contests sometimes mask power struggles. No less than anywhere else, these dynamics belong to church life and within communities founded on trust, they can be acutely painful. A true Christian politics consists in learning how to deal with these negative factors constructively, but therein lies the challenge. In this discussion, we might also include the pursuit of national or party politics. To what extent should churches align themselves with political causes within the societies where they are set? I recall a comment by the former Chief Rabbi, Lord Sacks, that in his view, faith communities should be places where it is precisely possible to find shelter *from* the hostilities often evoked in political debate and to rehearse more basic human virtues such as love, fellowship, and mutual respect. I agree with this but also consider that it should be possible to find a common mind on humanitarian issues while having differing views as to how political strategies might address them. Some humanitarian concerns raise significant questions about how society is structured and, therefore, become political. 'But churches should be sparing and selective about how they align with these and aware of the complexity and wider implications of proposed solutions. In other words, there may be no straightforward identification with any one political perspective. There is value in maintaining critical distance. Which positions individual church members adopt for themselves belongs to the sphere of personal conscience. For a church community to come to a united mind might be something; else, and the transition from the convictions of a Christian community to what should govern a plural and largely non-Christian community is something else again. It is surely a Christian value to allow for differences of conviction.

In what sense, then, is the Christian church, or are Christian churches, political? We return to the notion that our calling is to be a distinctive social reality embodying a way of life consistent with the way of Christ. Churches cannot avoid 'politicalness' since they have to do with how we relate to one another. The values so embodied include the willingness to forgive, to lay aside hostility and division, to live out the life of mutual love, to serve and seek the well-being of others, to 'do justice, and to act kindly and to walk humbly with your God' Micah 6:8). There is such a thing as 'the politics of Jesus' not in the sense that Jesus involved himself in the power structures of his society but in that he gathered round him a community that would live according to an alternative expectation, that of the kingdom of God. I resonate with the perception that the practices of the community, its sacraments and ordinances, mould churches in particular ways and habituate their members to certain ways of thinking and living. Baptism signifies submission to the Lordship of Christ in distinction from any other pretended lord. The breaking of bread shapes our communion with God and with each other, with all its overtones of mutual equality and regard. What may be regarded as 'lesser' practices, such as the right hand of fellowship, the washing of feet, anointing for healing, the laying of hands for the impartation of God's blessing or for ordination, all shape the Christian community as a civilisation of mutual love in which forgiveness and the abolition in Christ of what divides us, humans is overcome.

The church then lives at variance with 'the world' that has different loyalties. Yet, there is no possibility of ever being unambiguously separated from it. The primary aspect of what I mean by 'impossible possibility' is that however 'saved' we consider ourselves to be, we are not saved enough. We continue to carry within ourselves the seeds of our own self-destruction. This is a theme I find repeatedly reiterated in the biblical story. The evidence is clear. It is regularly demonstrated by the repeated failure of the church to live up to its vocation. How can flawed human beings ever achieve the civilisation of love we aspire to?

A further aspect concerns our entanglement with a world and social structures that pull us away from the ideals we espouse. In the Anabaptist *Schleitheim Confession* of 1529, a distinction is made between the church's being inside 'the perfection of Christ' and the world that is outside that perfection. At first glance, this might seem highly dualistic, and I have acknowledged above that things within the church are far from perfect. Equally, outside the church, because of the combination of residual human goodness and common grace, the realm beyond the church is not without grace. An overly binary approach seems ill-judged, unreal, and sectarian. It is sometimes pointed out that the line between 'world' and church lies not between the two realms but within us all. The moral life is more complex than might be imagined. Yet Schleitheim is not without its insight. Within the realm of the church in which God's Spirit is savingly active, there is a magnetic pull towards righteousness, but the same could not be said of the 'world' beyond it. Were this not so it would seem hardly worthwhile belonging to the church. Yet Christian lives must be lived most of the time and for most intents and purposes beyond the church where rules and expectations and that magnetic pull are different. To avoid this, one would have, as Paul indicates, to 'leave the world altogether', which is neither possible nor desirable. Realism requires us to negotiate this divide, and there is no guarantee of perfection. Engagement with the political means involvement in the realm of the relative, not the absolute. This is a rather long-winded way of declaring myself not to be a pacifist in the Anabaptist-Mennonite tradition. There is legitimate Christian participation in the 'order of preservation', even in the use of coercion to curb and resist wrongdoing. If I read the New Testament aright, the 'state', whichever legitimate forms it takes, is a manifestation, though certainly an imperfect one, of divine wrath, which I have previously defined as God's implacable resistance to evil. In its proper function, it preserves from criminality and destruction, although indeed, it sometimes becomes a manifestation of both.

In the diversity of the church's theological traditions, each one settles upon a major idea that then determines the parameters of the espoused theology. For Roman Catholics, it becomes impossible to surrender the notion of a powerful and authoritative church to which, finally, obedience is due since it is, in effect, the continuing incarnation of Christ. Within this paradigm, there is room for exploration and diversity but there remain boundaries that should not be crossed. For Lutherans, the 'big idea' to which adherence is due is justification by faith. This is sometimes portrayed as 'the article by which the faith stands or falls'. Within Calvinism the parallel stress rests upon the sovereignty of God, which it is careful to prioritise. For evangelicals more conservative than myself, the big idea may be the supposed inerrancy of scripture, which acts as a touchstone as to 'who is in and who is out'. All of these 'big ideas' have the potential to become idolatrous. Quakers prize silent waiting upon God. Within contemporary Anabaptist-Mennonite thought, peace and non-violence are the defining big ideas which it is impossible to deny whilst continuing to be part of the tradition. To be sure, there is a powerful rationale for this which is to be respected. It is rooted in an understanding of the teaching and actions of Jesus in which he called his disciples to renounce revenge and violence and to interrupt the 'vicious cycle of recrimination'. This is crucially (an apt word) fulfilled in his endurance of the cross. Here, Christ absorbed the hostility projected towards him by corrupt religious, political, and popular powers and defeated them by not submitting to them. His victory consisted not least in this refusal and was vindicated as acceptable to God in the resurrection. This is behaviour that is pleasing to God and is redemptive; it changes situations, overcomes evil and can be considered as quintessentially Christian. When people respond to wrongdoing by refusing to repeat it and by rising above it, returning good for evil, they engage in redemptive action, overcoming evil with good. I have profound respect for this understanding and its outworking and most certainly embrace it as an important aspect of the saving power of the cross, though not its only one. Christians are to behave in this way, though if others are like me, it requires us to overcome some very primal instincts.

Even so, this strong doctrine, sometimes called non-resistance but, to my mind, better understood as non-violence, is vulnerable to criticism. I cannot understand that Jesus intended us never to resist an evil person, at the very least morally and perhaps in other ways. Most crucially, given its own terms of reference, I wonder whether the teaching and action of Jesus can be applied absolutely across the board to all circumstances. Those more inclined to a 'justified war' philosophy chip away at it by pointing to Jesus' forceful cleansing of the temple, driving out the moneychangers and their animals. They also recall that his followers were known to possess swords, presumably for self-defence against aggression, and that Jesus, admittedly somewhat ironically, hinted that they should keep their swords, the mood having turned against them. It is worth pointing out that the direction of Jesus' teaching is of a first-person character, what I might do if am abused, physically or verbally, where the advice not to retaliate amounts to not making a bad situation worse by responding in like manner. Refuse to perpetuate the cycle by exercising self-restraint. Yet does this offer clear guidance in the case of third-party situations where any of us might be under obligation to protect others? This is the famous, 'What would you do if?' dilemma and readily springs to mind. And what about the civil authorities who are obligated to care for strangers, widows and orphans? What I suspect Jesus intended is that the cause of the kingdom of God and that of human redemption cannot be constructively advanced by means of violence. This did not preclude that in other areas, for instance, in the preservation of the peace, there might be a necessary and legitimate use of force - I prefer the word 'force' since there is not a moral equivalence between the legitimate use of power to prevent evil and the kind of violence that perpetuates it. I consider that both Martin Luther King and Mahatma Gandhi understood this: positive social change is not brought about by violence, but this does not mean that either of them denied the use of force in other necessary areas. As noted, the Anabaptist tradition agrees with this but with the caveat that such force or mandated violence happens 'outside the perfection of Christ' and, therefore, should not be a realm in which Christians should participate. My own distinction between the 'order of redemption' and the 'order of preservation' allows for conscientious participation in both. This, therefore, questions whether absolute pacificism can coherently be the 'big idea' that determines our theology. It certainly has its place, but it is a grace and not a law. The instinct for peace and for peace-making is certainly part of the political contribution and strategy of the Christian church but can only be maintained as societies are preserved and stabilised by the order of preservation, which has the right of compulsion. The two orders should work together, but neither be intermingled with the other: the church should not seek to coerce, and the state should not clothe itself in religious garb to exalt itself.

To return to the concept of a controlling idea that underlies different theologies, I cannot escape the recognition that this is true of my own approach. I concede that 'freedom' looms large as a fundamental thought in my theology: the freedom of God, the freedom that is given in Christ, and the implications of this for aspirations to a free church in a free society. For freedom, Christ has set us free. I am content with this big idea but hopefully am self-critical enough not to exalt the idea in itself to an absolute or autonomous place. God is greater than all our thoughts.

Having touched on political existence and affirmed that the church should be part of a nonconforming and countercultural civilisation of love, however difficult its achievement might be, it is worth saying something about how I approach the political options presented in British culture. I have become something of a floating voter, having for most of my life leaned to the centre-left. At the same time I am a moderate social conservative on issues of personal morality such as temperance, sexual integrity and fidelity, simplicity of lifestyle, financial probity, honesty, and decency. I recognise there is a distinction to be navigated between the morality I might embrace for myself and the legislation that needs to be in place for a plural and morally complex society. In navigating this potential gulf, I find the axiom helpful, 'This is my faith and therefore *I* can't', and its contrast with, 'This is my faith and therefore *you* can't'. The former I count as a dissenting perspective but the latter as a dictatorial one. A good society allows people to live in harmony with their consciences and protects their right to do so. A healthy religion does not seek to impose its own value-set upon unwilling others but also resists having alien values opposed upon it in like manner. Between these two sides, there is a political and cultural space in which the moral consensus of a society can be debated and potentially agreed. In other words, there is a social conscience as well as an individual one. Unlike some of the rhetoric I encounter, I believe there is more common ground across society than is claimed. I would like to describe this as a 'common humanism' that can be shared by those of Christian faith, those of other faiths and those who claim to be of no-faith. It could be likened to a trade language that enables productive co-existence within societies. It is our duty to sustain and extend this consensus as much as we can and to subvert the 'culture wars' that might otherwise engulf us.

British political culture presents the electorate with various options. An alert and fair-minded voter, rather than a simply tribal one, might discern that there are authentic moral concerns that underlie the various political traditions. At the same time, each may be susceptible to pathological and unjust tendencies. Conservatives may, for instance, claim to be the party of personal responsibility, continuity, social and cultural evolution rather than revolution, free enterprise, and monetary and fiscal stability. In a pathological form, they may knowingly or unknowingly be the bulwark for privilege, vested interest, inequality, and resistance to legitimate change. Labour may be the vehicle for wealth distribution, economic and social equality and equity, elevation of the disadvantaged, internationalism, and freedom from oppression. Pathologically,

Labour might fall prey to class hatred, obstructive trade unionism and over-dependence on public welfare. It is less easy to caricature Liberal Democrats, but, as the name suggests, their strength must be in the areas of personal liberty and civil rights and in the nurturing of more perfect democratic structures. If there is a pathology here, it might be that of being neither one thing nor the other (if this is a pathology at all). In other words, the responsible citizen can find praiseworthy aspirations in most responsible political groupings. This would exclude those that specifically trade on bigotry and ill-feeling. In principle, there is nothing immoral about civic nationalism such as the aspiration towards a united Ireland or an independent Scotland, even where they may be regretted by others.

In the aspiration to be fair-minded, I acknowledge the positive values I have outlined. As a now-floating voter, I would make my relative judgements as to which ones most require attention at any juncture and who might best deliver them. If pressed to give a label to myself, it would be that of an 'ethical socialist'. I distinguish this from utopian socialism, that dreams of a better world but without a strategy of how to achieve it. Arguably this is not far distant from the vision of a world in which spears are turned into ploughshares and where the wolf lies down with the lamb. I have no optimism that humans will achieve such a world, which can only be given by God, but I do have hope that in the light of such a future, we might make our present world a bit better. This is known as 'meliorism'. I also distinguish my position from 'scientific socialism', as defined by

Marx, with its claim to have discovered a law of progress towards the perfected world through dialectical materialism. Whatever insights this has brought, I regard it as a pseudo-science, indeed, as 'the god that failed'. Where it has been attempted, it has more than failed. I cannot say the same about social democracy, which, to my mind, has added much to human flourishing where it achieves the balance between democratic consent, strong social institutions which help to share the risks inherent in human existence, the values of a mixed economy, and the maximisation of human freedoms, religious freedom being the most important of all. By 'ethical socialism', I refer to something less defined and more in the direction of values than policies. I mean by it (though others may see it differently), the recognition that human beings are of equal worth; that they stand on level ground before God both as sinners and those capable of redemption; that responsible hierarchies within societies, should not be based on birth but on worth and should reflect competence and ability; that power conferred can also be taken away when it is misused; that none of us are possessors of the earth since 'the earth is the Lord's in all its fullness' and we are simply stewards of it, and of the parts of it temporarily allocated to us; that we are part of the natural environment and our well-being depends on its care; that all people have their place (call them rights if you will, but also responsibilities) and that we are all better off as each person is enabled without undue restriction to bring their gifts, talents and abilities into the public sphere in an equality of opportunity; that we co-exist with other animals who may not have rights in the same way as human beings because they do not have corresponding responsibilities but onto whom humans might helpfully project rights; and that, all this considered, human beings have supreme responsibility under God to do what is right for each other, for their co-creatures and for the planet. I value the idea of human societies as 'commonwealth' in which all can share in the benefits of life on earth. I also value the idea of an 'equitable equilibrium' which sustains all, values hard work and creativity and rewards them, respects age and experience but disrespects and curbs greed and excess.

I acknowledge that the basic values I have outlined are widely shared within social and liberal democracies as the 'common humanism' to which we should aspire, though maybe in varying proportions. They could be regarded as bland or as the philosophical ramblings of a do-gooder. Nonetheless, as the substructure of our political life in society, they are of significant value and would be embraced at least notionally by the mainstream British political parties. The idea that religion and politics should not mix is correct when it warns against the desire to attain coercive power for religious purposes. But at the deeper level of undergirding values as to how to live together, religious faith should certainly have political implications. Paths diverge when it comes to fashioning a strategy for the application or maintenance of those values, and here we enter the territory of the party political, a territory that abounds with relative judgements and unintended consequences. I don't regard myself as competent to expand too greatly on these themes. They require closer knowledge and greater research than I have achieved. However, instinctively, I gravitate towards the value of a mixed economy in which both private investment and state support might harness the best efforts of all in the causes of stability and responsible growth.

It is important to distinguish between *society* and *state*. It is not correct to argue that we live in a secular society. British society is, rather, plural in nature, comprising elements that are secular, both actively and residually Christian, and religiously plural. The function of the state is both to preserve society from criminality and promote its well-being so that people may pursue their personal and corporate goals freely and constructively. By 'residually' Christian I mean that whether people choose to believe, British society and culture are profoundly shaped by their Christian heritage. To substantiate this claim, one need only indicate that both urban and rural landscapes are marked by cathedrals, parish churches, chapels and meeting houses that testify to a legacy of devotion. Given that many of these buildings are constantly frequented, it might be claimed that 'churchgoing' is still a feature of life on these islands. To these buildings many others may be added that testify to the presence of other religious traditions or, indeed, to newer manifestations of Christian faith. Such a diverse social landscape sheds light on what it means to describe the state as 'secular' state.

It is also questionable whether the British 'state' (the word covers those organs of society that have the power of compulsion) can be described as 'secular'. Given there is an established church in England and a 'national' church in Scotland, both enshrined in law and with a monarch as head of state who occupies certain civic and religious functions, the British state is not straightforwardly 'secular'. I am comfortable with the idea of a secular when understood as the alternative to a 'sacral' or religious state or a theocracy, and equally, provided the word 'secular' is properly understood. Paradoxically, it is itself a word with religious origins, as becomes clear when the Roman church refers to 'secular' priests as distinct from those who serve religious orders. Secularity has to do with this world rather than the world that is to come. It is concerned with temporal rather than eternal affairs. The necessary distinction is between a state that propagates or promotes an ideology that denies God and discriminates against believers, as has been the case with communist tyrannies, and one that holds the ring open for those of faith and safeguards their human rights within a framework of equality. A secular state, and in this respect, we could properly also speak of *society* as secular, is one that refuses to impose religious tests when it comes to gaining access to the 'goods' that society has to offer. Nobody is excluded or privileged for solely religious reasons. There are, therefore, different kinds of secularism as there are different kinds of Christianity. This can be characterised as the difference between being *hospitable* or *hostile, programmatic* or *procedural*. It is in the interests of Christians to support and preserve a hospitable state that preserves religious freedoms (which are enshrined in a series of codifications of human rights) and to hold states democratically accountable when they are denied. I hold this to be a fully Christian position that has, in part, grown out of the free church tradition. The Christian church has no interest in religion that is compelled since compulsory religion is not true religion. The notion that states should be religiously neutral does not mean that they are or ever could be value-free. The claim is that neutrality *is itself a value*, even a religious value, in that it signals the determination of the state to hold the ring open for people to negotiate their spiritual pathways through life. The preservation of such freedoms can only be guaranteed if we regard them as reciprocal. That is, we all have the same rights. I safeguard my own my supporting those of others. This holds true whether we agree with the beliefs of others or not. It follows from the Golden Rule expressed by both religious and non-religious traditions: 'Do as you would be done by'; or 'do not do to others what would be hateful to yourself'; or 'love your neighbour as yourself'.

Post Fifteen: Divine Judgement

I have not yet said everything about the idea of divine judgement, a strain in Christian thinking suppressed in much Christian thought, popular and serious, for fear of seeming narrow and negative. We are all familiar with the stereotype of the hard-line Christian who spits out vitriol and sees only the evil in people. This mirrors the charge against the Judeo-Christian representation of God as a 'psychotic delinquent'. How accurate this is must be a topic for debate. I don't enjoy those parts of scripture that, to our minds, come close to this, and there are a few. In fact, I am inclined to rank these as somewhat sub-Christian, insufficiently informed by the fuller vision of God to which the wider canon bears witness. Even so there is that which can be learnt even from such problematic passages. If they have a value, it is in the shock tactic of undermining the image of God as a laid-back Californian hippy who always says Yes and never calls anyone to account. This is an equal caricature of course, and a contemporary one at that. An appropriate articulation of the holy love of God is apparently difficult to achieve. It is unfortunate when preachers portray God as struggling between wrath and mercy, divided within between the need to punish and the will to forgive. It is yet worse when the cross of Christ is portrayed as the way in which God resolves his own dilemma, thus rendering the cross something that God needs to achieve forgiveness. Even worse is the pitting of the Son against the Father such that a loving Son reconciles a hostile Father. God is not divided either within God's own self or between Son and Father. Father and Son are one in essence and the way to the cross is an act of the one God, Father, Son, and Spirit for lost humankind. It is *for us and our salvation* that Christ has become incarnate. Having gotten this assertion out of the way, we still cannot avoid the recognition that this same God poses a threat to us. This may be understood at one level as the threat the infinite poses to the finite by reason of sheer size. A parallel might be the way in which the world of nature, the very reality on which we depend and of which we are integrally part, nonetheless threatens us once we step beyond certain boundaries. The boundless sea, the extremes of hot and cold, the dangers of exposure, and the sheer unimaginable size of the universe that can only be measured in light years all render us vulnerable to a power that engulfs us and could destroy us. We need protection from it. We might feel the same about God, and scripture does not lack a testimony to God as an almost impersonal power in whose presence we do not stand a chance. We think of Moses on Mount Sinai: the people are to be kept at a distance lest God breaks out upon them and annihilates them. In modern metaphor, it is as though God is a nuclear reactor. Divine holiness threatens to break out upon us and fatally contaminate us. We cannot see God and live. We cannot stand in God's presence because it is awesome, and we cannot bear it. This sense of what older generations might have thought of as the 'fear of the Lord' or a sense of dread as defined in Rudolf Otto's characterisation of the core of religious experience as the *mysterium tremendum et fascinans* is alarmingly absent in much contemporary worship. Yet this raw holiness that threatens to annihilate us is tempered in a Judeo-Christian understanding, and no doubt elsewhere, by belief in God's mercy and loving-kindness, by God's essential nature as love: 'Because of the Lord's great love we are not consumed, for his compassions never fail' (Lamentations 3:22 NIV).

These things can be said about finite human existence irrespective of sin. Human sinfulness intensifies the situation yet more as our disobedience towards God encounters divine reality. Raw holiness, God's sheer 'size', yields to God's purity, to ethical holiness: 'Your eyes are too pure to behold evil, and you cannot look on wrongdoing. Why do you look on the treacherous?' (Habakkuk 1:13). Some are embarrassed by the biblical witness to divine wrath, and 'there is no anger in God' (anger and love supposedly being incompatible), but I want to insist on the opposite. God is love, not wrath in essence, but that love is experienced as wrath by those who go against it. In Emil Brunner's words, God's wrath is the 'contrary wind of the divine will which he soon discovers who runs against it'. God's wrath is God's just and measured response to evil. God's wrath is not like petulant human manifestations but a form of God's love for the world. Ethical holiness accounts for God's implacable resistance to evil. God cannot cease to be God. God's love for the world accounts for God's unwillingness to surrender that world to evil. The good news is that just because of this, the world will not be surrendered to the evil that threatens it. Evil will finally be overcome. If there is a mystery here it is why this final reality is presently delayed, why God 'tolerates the treacherous'. Far from finding this divine resistance embarrassing, I rejoice in it as good news, even more so because this God who threatens us by being what God essentially is and cannot be other also mercifully seeks our redemption and restoration. God's wrath, therefore, is not God 'losing it', but God 'resisting the proud' while at the same time giving 'grace to the humble' (James 4:6). I consider this to be written into the moral fabric of the universe, the grain of how things are. Just as the love of God is made manifest in the providences and regularities of nature, in the rain that falls and the sun that shines, so the wrath of God means that evil and sin are turned back upon those who do wrong, that we reap what we sow, that the doing of evil unlocks a consequence that rebounds on the one who does it. I have a preference, therefore, for that idea of wrath that likens it to a law of cause and effect. But this is not simply impersonal since, finally, it is rooted in God's own being and is not remote from God or divorced from God's essence. It is *God's* wrath.

So, judgement is to be taken seriously. In this life, it is active but incomplete. Even now, we might discern how those who choose the way of disobedience tend to destroy themselves and others with them in a way that defies justice. Evil is a form of over-reach. Yet evil doers may seem to escape (and this injustice is the cause of some perplexity in the Old Testament). The two ways outlined in Psalm 1 are not always realised. One of the drivers in scripture towards belief in a world to come lies precisely here: for justice to be done one way or the other, either in justifying the righteous or condemning the wicked, life's timeline needs to be extended into a future reality, a life after life when realities will be faced definitively. Here, my mind has shifted. Along with many others of my evangelical ilk, I have believed that decisions made in this life are determinative for the life that is to come. In this, I have been shaped by the parable of the rich man and Lazarus as narrated by Jesus in Luke 16:19-31. In the life to come, their fortunes are reversed, with the rich man being in torment in Hades and Lazarus finding himself at Abraham's side. So, the typical evangelical infers that those who fail to give heed to the word of God in this life find themselves in torment in the next, whereas the humble are in paradise or the equivalent. The point of division is death, so it is vital to decide rightly before this point. It is believed that this is then confirmed by other biblical indicators. This holds as a major assumption for evangelicals, and probably others, who look with favour on the need for decision and even the idea of a death-bed conversion. I do not junk the underlying concern here since I do believe in the gravity of the decisions we make and in the seriousness of life itself. Life is not trivial. However, the extent to which we should deduce this from the parable is a moot matter. Parables usually illustrate a main point, which at this point might be thought to be the reversal of fortunes in the life to come.

Jesus has taken a well-known existing story and has fashioned it for his own ends along the lines just stated. Furthermore, no parable does justice to the whole truth. To be awkward, for instance, I could point out here that the parable makes no reference to or even hints of Christ's sacrificial death as the ground of our hope for a future life. In addition, the 'furniture' of the parable suggests it should not be taken wholly literally; specifically, the notion of being 'at Abraham's side', or in other translations being 'in Abraham's bosom', suggests interpretative caution. Is Jesus teaching secure doctrine or embellishing the parable as a parable? I suggest we should be careful how far we take its details even as we accept its warnings. In fact, there are two levels of meaning at least within it. One is the need already indicated to repent and believe to be secure in our personal salvation. The other is an expectation of the reversal of fortunes between the rich and the poor in the age to come. It is a statement about social justice, a theme prominent in 'Moses and the prophets', which is not to be ignored in this life or else. What is striking for my present purpose is the claim made by Abraham, 'And besides all this, between us and you a great chasm has been set in place so that those who want to go from here to you cannot, nor can anyone cross over from there to us' (v.26). This does appear to say that our fates after death are immutable and irrevocable, so get it right now! Fair warning given.

We do well to heed the warning. But is God so bound? And is it true that the chasm can never be crossed? I point out that there is one who has crossed the great chasm, and that is Christ himself who, according to the creed, descended into 'hell' and rose victoriously from death: 'For this reason, Christ died and returned to life so that he might be the Lord of both the dead and the living' (Romans 14:10). A careful reading of the New Testament indicates that we have not been well-served using the word 'hell' in translating the New Testament. The latter distinguishes between two realities: *Hades* and *Gehenna*, with Hades being the realm of the dead, perhaps an extension of the shadowy realm of Sheol in the Old Testament, and Gehenna, the realm of destruction referred to by Jesus in Matthew 5:22 and elsewhere – the worst thing that could ever be contemplated. In fact, Jesus makes more reference to Gehenna than anyone else, not least in his warning, 'Do not fear those who kill the body but cannot kill the soul; rather fear him who can destroy both soul and body in hell' (viz, Gehenna – Matthew 10:28). It is an abiding mystery that even in more recent versions, the translators regularly use the word 'hell' to indicate both Hades and Gehenna without distinction. This obscures the fact that Hades represents the place or realm where the dead await the final judgement and Gehenna what may follow on from that judgement in the destruction of the wicked. Fair enough, there may be a foretaste in Hades of what might await some in Gehenna, but the idea that death is immediately followed by heaven or hell neglects the possibility something important happens in between death and final judgement. What might that be?

The clue to me is in Hebrews 9:27-28: 'And just as it is appointed for mortals to die once, and after that the judgement, so Christ was offered once to bear the sins of many'. Typically, this is interpreted to mean that once we have died, we face the judgement of heaven or hell, and there is no altering this. The verse, however, is equally susceptible to the interpretation that once we die, we begin to face a process of sifting and sorting, judgement in the sense that the truth of our lives is made manifest. This is judgement understood as a process by which God enables the truth to emerge, one that is brought to finality in the last judgement. Such a process is sometimes termed 'probation' or seen as a 'portal' that precedes the conclusion. It is not to be confused with 'purgatory', but it is not unrelated to it. Purgatory applies to those who have been baptised into the fellowship of the church rather than those who exist outside it. The redeemed are made fit for the vision of God and so undergo, as the word suggests, a purification. Probation, by distinction, is the recognition that in this life, justice has not been fully done, and so, in myriad ways, the record needs to be set right. 'For Yahweh will see his people righted, he will take pity on his servants' (Deuteronomy 32:36 Jerusalem Bible).

There have always been questions about those who have apparently been excluded in this life from the hope of salvation: those who die in infancy (or even before it); those who die at a later age but so young as not to have the opportunity to hear or believe the gospel; those millions who have lived before Christ and yet outside Israel; those whom the gospel has never reached, or whom it has reached only a distorted form; those who have been subject to abuse by the very people who should represent or transmit the faith to them but who have become an understandable obstacle to that objective; those who by reason of mental incapacity have lacked the cognitive apparatus that faith requires; and so we could go on. These questions cannot be pushed on one side but must be accounted for, or at least acknowledged by those who believe in the unqualified goodness, justice, and compassion of God. It is common to say that all such persons will be judged 'according to the light that they have'. But even such a statement presupposes some kind of space within which judgement takes place. That such a space exists is indicated by Paul's words in Romans 2:14-16: 'When Gentiles, who do not possess the law, do instinctively what the law requires, these, though not having the law, are a law to themselves. They show that what the law requires is written on their hearts, to which their own conscience also bears witness, and their conflicting thoughts will accuse or perhaps excuse them on the day when, according to my gospel, God, through Jesus Christ, will judge the secret thoughts of all'. A 'day' here, as elsewhere in the Bible, is not a period of 24 hours but a time of confrontation and exposure. This reinforces the teaching of Jesus: 'For nothing is hidden that will not be disclosed, nor is anything secret that will not become known and come to light.' (Luke 8:17). Judgement is not first and foremost about punishment, though it may well lead to it and, when it happens, will be essentially self-imposed. Primarily it is about truth and transparency, about everything being seen for what is, about justice being done, wrongs being righted and every single one of us being called to account for our own actions: '(God) has fixed a day on which he will have the world judged in righteousness by a man whom he has appointed, and of this he has given assurance to all by raising him from the dead' (Acts 17:31). 'For all of us must appear before the judgement seat of Christ, so that each may receive recompense for what has been done in the body, whether good or evil' (2 Corinthians 5:10). 'For he will repay according to each one's deeds: to those who by patiently doing good seek for glory and honour and immortality, he will give eternal life; while for those who are self-seeking and who obey not the truth but wickedness, there will be wrath and fury' (Romans 2:8). Let no-one say, 'there is no anger in God': it just happens to be just, holy, righteous, measured, proportionate and at the service of love: 'for our God is a consuming fire' (Hebrews 12:29). The fire both destroys and purifies, and yet, as the Old Testament repeatedly declares in a way that becomes a major theme in its pages, God is slow to anger and abounding in steadfast love. The wrath of God is but for a moment, but God's favour is for life (Psalm 30:5). The divine mercy exceeds the divine wrath, and yet wrath is at the service of mercy in that it both resists and overcomes evil; it sets a limit to the damage evil might do and assures us that it will not finally triumph. That is good news, and it is to be set against the modern preference for a God of love over a God of justice as though there could be one without the other.

The parable of the rich man and Lazarus suggests that death is followed by judgement, but Hades is still not to be confused with Gehenna. So, how have I come to see the judgement of God that follows on from life? There is no doubt that the imagery of Hades and especially of Gehenna is frightening. In Hades the rich man was in torment. But the torment that counts, and which 'fire' symbolises, is surely that of the tormented conscience inflicted from within when faced with the holiness of God and the shortcomings of the creature. All that is hidden will one day be made manifest, and if accountability is meaningful, judgement must consist in our being faced up with the way each of us has lived our life. 'And before him, no creature is hidden, but all are naked and laid bare to the eyes of the one to whom we must render account' (Hebrews 4:13). It is claimed that when faced with imminent death, many people (those who survive the experience) report having gone through a life review, in a moment in time looking back on their lives. Similarly, I have heard it said (but have not confirmed it) that there is in the human brain (itself a remarkable organism) a mechanism that records and can recall everything we have ever done, like a scroll unrolling. To be faced with the truth of our lives, to see clearly the wrongs we have committed, the people we have hurt, the damage we have done both directly and indirectly, whether intentionally or accidentally, the corruptions in which we have been implicated, all this strikes me as a recipe for anguish and torment. Nor do I imagine that for all that God 'casts all our sins into the depths of the sea' (Micah 7:9) and 'remembers them no more' (Hebrews 8:12), that Christians will be exempt from the experience. The difference would be that the Christian has the wholesome assurance that he or she 'will not come under judgement' but has passed from death to life' (John 5:24). We might think, therefore, that as we pass through judgement, the anguish of failure is transformed into gratitude because of all we have unjustly done and from which we have been redeemed. 'We have an advocate with the Father' (1 John 2:1), one who in his life and death has made intercession for us because he is our Brother and continues so to do (Hebrews 2:11, 7:25).

If so much might be imagined for those who are 'in Christ', what about those who fall outside? I have already written enough to indicate that I entertain the widest hope that even beyond death, God in Christ will continue 'to seek out and to save the lost' (Luke 19:10). Although the scriptural evidence for this is contested, as we previously noted, I find it theologically necessary. A possible biblical foundation can be found in 1 Peter 4:6, 'For this reason the gospel was proclaimed even to the dead, so that, though they had been judged in the flesh as everyone is judged, they might live in the spirit as God does'. The debate here hinges on whether 'the dead' are those who are spiritually dead but still living or the actually dead yet still saveable. This second interpretation is feasible, and with one qualification, I find support for it in a commentary on this text by

How My Mind Has Changed (or not) - A Theological Memoir

Steven Kraftchick: 'Christ did not restrict the gospel message to those who were alive on earth, but announces the purposes of God even to the dead. Likewise, those who are outside the bounds of the community will one day hear of the truth of God's purposes and yield to them. In the interim, the church is called to a life of witness among those who have not yet comprehended the nature of God's purpose and reality'.[35] This is easier to live with than the belief that the great majority of human beings are destined for a 'Christless eternity'. I see no theological sense in this at all, not in the light of a God who is 'not willing for any to perish, but for all to come to repentance' (2 Peter 3:9). We should reckon with God's persistence as the God who wills to save. Where I demur from Kraftchick's statement is in the claim that the dead 'will yield' to the truth. Whether or not they will remains an open question if we believe love to be reciprocal and not coerced. Some might restrict the scriptural words only to 'the elect', those alone whom God has determined to save, but I am not among them. Both the justice and the love of God point towards a wider hope. While writing these words, there have been several cases of young children being brutalised, starved, and killed by parents or their parents' partners. Their short lives have been ones of such unrelieved and painful misery that I must stop myself thinking about it, or else I would fall into black despair. It is

---

[35] Steven J. Kraftchick, in Gail R. O'Day and David L. Peterson (editors), *Theological Bible Commentary*, (Louisville, Kentucky: Westminster John Knox Press, 2009) p. 457.

easy to ignore the questions this raises, but I utterly reject any notion that because even such children supposedly share (according to some) in the guilt and condemnation of Adam, they are consigned to hell. Here is another point of cognitive dissonance: how are such lives held accountable for sin when what they need above all is to be healed by the unconditional love of God? The demands of the justice and love of God point in this direction. Even if, exegetically, we are unable to point to unambiguous texts that explicitly resolve the issue, theologically we are capable of a response in the light of the God who is 'good to all, and his compassion is over all that he has made' (Psalm 145:9). If it is possible, following certain schemes of theology, to believe that God saves whomever he chooses to save, then I have no hesitation in broadening my horizons about the scope of salvation. This helps me to live and to love. It does not make me a complacent universalist. I acknowledge 'the mystery of iniquity', the irrationality of declining the love and grace of God, who is the quintessence of goodness. I cannot exclude the possibility that even given the truth made manifest in judgement, and even in the face of God's persistence in seeking the lost, there could be those who, out of hatred of the light, resist it to their own destruction. I am repeating myself, so I obviously care about this.

So, I have indicated my belief that the trajectory of salvation has necessarily, for reasons of both justice and compassion, to stretch beyond this earthly life. Some exegetical substance and theological justification can be given to this conviction. I have also made two axioms clear: there is no salvation apart from Christ, and there is no salvation without repentance. So, there is no complacency here such that neither Christ nor repentance matter. My position is sometimes characterised as belief in 'post-mortem evangelism', but I prefer to think of it as rooted in the fact that God, as revealed in Christ, wills to save and takes no pleasure in the death of anyone. God is *against us* in our rebellious or slothful state but is so for the sake of being *for us* and for our redemption. Moreover, God is persistent in pursuing this goal, and I see no reason why the death of human beings should be an insuperable object to it. True enough, this may be the case for those who have embedded themselves in a state of final resistance to God. But this is surely not everyone.

However, we must face the challenge not so much of Hades as of Gehenna: the place of final destruction. To be sure, all the language is imagery, and we need not think literally of a place so much as condition or reality. In taking up the great debate between Calvinism and Arminianism (though truth to tell, I see the latter in many respects as both historically and theologically a form of the former; certainly within the spectrum of Reformed theology), the distinction between the two centres round the view in the former that those who are finally impenitent are so because God has willed it to be so, in this way displaying God's holiness and glory in condemning the wicked. In Arminianism, the finally impenitent are such because, although God wills to save them, they resist every attempt of God to do so. The twin foci of the ellipse are, therefore, either the sovereign will of God or the recalcitrant will of mortals. It is generally agreed that there is no via media between these two, although I have indicated my view that Karl Barth's doctrine of election does, in fact, do this. Some Calvinists (e.g., Charles Hodge) believe that the number who are finally lost will be 'inconsiderable' when compared to the saved. So, Calvinism can prove, in the event, more optimistic and hopeful than Arminianism, which shares with it a radical view of human evil and inability. I have also pointed to 'hypothetical universalism'. I rest in the belief that however it works out, the Lord of all the earth will do what is right, and no-one will be able to fault the final outcome. I decline to close the universalist circle, and thankfully, all this vastly exceeds my paygrade. This said, I can envisage a situation in which those who persistently resist God's will to save dig themselves into a position, either in this age or the age to come, where they render themselves incapable of a positive response to God's grace and refuse to come to repentance. Perhaps this also means that they become 'post-human', having deprived themselves of the qualities that made them human in the first place. This is where 'Gehenna' becomes not the only option but the merciful one.

Where I do not hover between opinions is in the belief that Gehenna is a place of destruction, not of everlasting torment.[36] At

---

[36] For a recent review of the scriptural evidence see, Paul Marston, *Hellfire and Destruction: What Does the Bible Really Say about Hell?* (Eugene, Oregon: Wipf & Stock, 2023).

this point, I diverge from and have always diverged from, what some regard as a defining evangelical belief. I am glad to do so. Since there is no evangelical magisterium that has the authority to decide who is 'in or out' of the evangelical constituency, I can't say that the prospect causes me any anxiety. The position I do embrace and have advocated in various places is that of 'conditional immortality': this is the belief that the human 'soul' is not inherently immortal, incapable of dying, but can be destroyed, as Jesus affirmed in 'Gehenna'. To me, this is so plainly the teaching of scripture that I have tired of demonstrating it. God alone has immortality. Immortality is not something inherent but a gift, something with which we will one day be clothed. So, the argument that in eternity, our never-dying souls must live somewhere, either in heaven or hell, falls to the ground. There is no equivalence between life and death; they stand opposed to each other. The immortality of the soul is a Greek rather than a Hebrew construct. To be fair, for some, it is simply a way of saying that the soul (the inner reality of the human being that cannot simply be reduced to the physical organism, however much it depends upon it) does not die with the body but can exist apart from it. Much of what I have said would be meaningless without such a belief. The question is rather whether such a personal reality must necessarily endure for ever without qualification. Again, I would distinguish conditional immortality, in turn, from what I think is intended by 'annihilationism'. If this means that those lost to God simply cease to be without being faced with judgement and the reality of their condition, then it is not my view. I strongly believe that the truth must be out, that everything must be seen for what it really is in the eyes of God, that no mysteries other than the mystery of God's own self can be left unresolved. I think this can be called 'universal history'. Conditional immortality sets no timetable for this. Human souls that are finally impenitent, whether they be many or few, may endure for as long as it takes for justice to be done, a day or a thousand years or more. Being faced with the truth is indeed a kind of torment, and there are those who have caused such harm to others that the reckoning ought not to be momentary. But there will be a just and merciful end. Equally, there are those who have been history's undeserving victims for whom only a complete healing and restoration can be considered just. To believe otherwise would be intolerable.

The notion of eternal torment, an everlasting process that can never be moderated or attenuated, strikes me as deeply inhumane and so sub-Christian. In fact, I suspect that those who advocate it either do not really mean it or have not much thought about what it implies. As a symbol, it might do service in pointing up the horror of rejecting God, but when confronted as a literal reality, it is surely unacceptable. I can imagine few worse fates than that of burning to death. I imagine someone being trapped in a car that is on fire and unable to escape, the stuff of nightmares. In human terms, there would come the point where death would follow, and the agony would end. But eternal torment posits the situation where such a fate would never end, not after a day, or a year, or a millennium or a millennium of millenniums. The burning, the agony, the screaming would go on, allegedly to the glory of God and at the hands of One said to be merciful and kind. No way. The fallacy is in misinterpreting texts and, sometimes, the apocalyptic imagery that they entail. Supremely, it is in substituting the word 'everlasting' for the word 'eternal'. The word eternal is qualitative rather than quantitative, the life of the age to come in which we face the reality of things. Life may last forever, but death does not. Death and Hades are themselves destined for destruction (Revelation 20:14).

There is another point I might make here, though I do so tentatively. I have declared myself unsympathetic to the notion of inherited guilt that has loomed large in some doctrines of original sin since the time of Augustine. The idea is that irrespective of the evil deeds each of us may have committed, we have all been implicated in the sin of Adam, that the guilt for this sin is imputed to us on the grounds that we were 'in Adam' and so his guilt became ours, whether we be young or old, infants or responsible adults, and consequently liable to eternal torment unless we are saved. This is clearly a difficult doctrine to contemplate, even for those who hold it (which I do not). Because it is problematic, attempts are made to mitigate it. Some claim or have claimed in the past (the doctrine seems to have gone out of fashion) that the baptism of infants clears the debt, so to speak, and delivers those who receive it from the guilt of original sin, leaving them to account before God for those sins they themselves commit. This is then a justification of the practice of infant baptism. So, to be baptised as early as possible after birth becomes a matter of urgency. Such a mechanical rather than relational view of salvation is, to me, a distortion of what salvation is. Others mitigate the doctrine by speaking of 'elect infants', which leaves open the question of non-elect infants being lost. Yet others believe that election applies to all premature infant deaths, only those being allowed by God to die if they are elect anyway. Another way of approaching the issue would be to consider the ways in which Christ has died for the elect and yet also for the whole of humanity. A tension is created here by those biblical texts, already referred to, that suggest, on the one hand, that Christ has died for all and on the other for the elect only - the 'general' versus 'particular' debate. So, it might be held that Christ has indeed died for all to clear all of the pollution of original sin and guilt. The value of his death as the Son of God outweighs the debt of original guilt, and Christ, having suffered the torment of punishment on the cross, delivers all from the supposed eternal torment of Gehenna. This then leaves each person accountable for their own sin. If they resist the grace of God, they perish. They face judgement but then cease to be. God has mercifully delivered us all from eternal torment, though not from final judgement. Though I do not myself embrace this train of argument, I do think it is sufficient to hammer another nail in the concept of everlasting torment.

Post Sixteen: World, Flesh, Devil

This takes me to reflect further on some of the negative presuppositions that underlie the positive Christian hope of salvation. To be saved implies that there is something to be saved from, and the message of good news has no meaning apart from a prior or consequent analysis of what needs to be remedied. I say 'consequent' here to acknowledge the insight that the depth of what is wrong can best be understood precisely from God's action to set it right. So, an analysis of human sin might be attempted by reference to the early chapters of Genesis that describe the fall. But it might better be undertaken by considering how it is that Christ fulfilled what it means to be truly human and then allowing his light to expose the degree to which we 'fall short of the glory of God' that is revealed in him. After all, God has fixed a day when we shall be judged by Christ Jesus, that is, by him as the exemplar of righteousness. It does seem to be that contemporary advocates of the Christian faith are reluctant to name what is wrong for fear of being characterised as world-denying 'Jeremiahs'. I can sympathise with this, but also believe that cogent and intelligent analysis of human corruption alongside continuing affirmation of what it means to be made 'in the image of God' should strengthen the church's prophetic witness. The absence of such analysis is a weakness in secular humanism. There is no shortage of voices that are happy to condemn humans for their 'speciesism' just as there are others anxious to assert the uniqueness of the *humanum* within creation. Yet it is hard to sound the right chords in the right way. And despite our corruption, human beings remain undeservedly 'graced' by God.

Christian analysis of what is wrong traditionally divides into three categories: the world, the flesh, and the devil and relates the saving work of Christ to each category. Perhaps enough has been said above about the 'flesh', the fallen human condition whereby we are estranged from the ground of our being in God and consequently lost both to God and ourselves. To adapt the saying, we are 'turned in upon ourselves' (*curvatus in se*), and we live in enmity towards God and so under the wrath and displeasure of God. Our own hostility towards God encounters God's implacable resistance (my definition of divine wrath), the 'contrary wind of the divine will', so forfeiting the dynamic that leads to complete human flourishing. From Reinhold Niebuhr, I have derived the idea that human sin has its origin in anxiety. Being caught between heaven and earth, between animal, organic existence and yearnings for the transcendent, human beings experience a state of anxiety. They seek to resolve this in two ways. The first is to immerse themselves in the lower impulses of their nature, in their sensual appetites and lusts, and so to smother or ignore anxiety. Perhaps the existentialists would have seen this as 'inauthentic existence', a flight from the harder questions of human life to extinguish them. The second strategy is to overcome anxiety and personal crises by exercising power over others and maintaining that power at all costs through violence, exploitation, and corruption. The analysis holds for both individuals and groups in the form of tribes, nations, and empires. This is a cogent naming of what is meant by the word 'sin'. It is intensified by contemplation of the way in which Christ succumbs to neither strategy but lives as an authentic human being in communion with the Father and in command of his own appetites and as one who did not seek to gain or exercise power over others but to live and die as one who serves.

In all events, using more biblical language, human beings, in their estrangement from God, can be described as 'by nature children of wrath' (Ephesians 2:3), which I take to mean that we live collectively and individually in a state of conscious and unconscious hostility towards God our creator. There is a dynamic that draws us away from God. This could equally be thought of as a condition of disregard or slothfulness towards God, a condition that 'falls short of the glory of God'. The Apostles' Creed identifies 'the forgiveness of sins' as a primary benefit in this life from trust in God. This must have a degree of primacy as the first step in the benefits contained in being reconciled to God: regeneration, conversion, sanctification, and enlightenment. We need to seek God for mercy through the atoning work of Christ and lay aside all enmity towards God. Ephesians 2:1-10 is a primary passage for all evangelicals, and I am surprised to find it less quoted in the present than in former times. It is a paradigm statement of the gospel. Personal salvation, repentance towards God and faith in our Lord Jesus Christ expressed in baptism are foundations for the life of the believer.

Once upon a time, this might have been considered a sufficient evangelical analysis of the human condition. It is indeed crucial for personal faith and for public proclamation. Yet it contains a possible trap, and that comes into play when we consider the dimension of 'the world' contained in our trilogy of the 'world, the flesh and the devil'. The trap consists in so concentrating on personal salvation that we neglect the need for salvation or liberation from 'the powers' that constrain and define fallen corporate existence. I was alerted to this dimension through the work of the Mennonite theologian John Howard Yoder, and it further pushed me in the direction of thinking of the church of God as socially and sociologically significant as the realm of corporate salvation, the church as a present sign of the coming kingdom (after all, a political term), even if an imperfect one. Amid the fallen powers orientated towards themselves and their self-interest, there is a community, or a series of communities, which, for all their faults, seek to be orientated towards God, to be holy. It then becomes impossible to envisage personal salvation as the be-all and end-all of God's saving works or to see churches, so to speak, only as a series of service stations on the motorway that leads to eternal life – there to support us on the way but significant in themselves only, to change the metaphor, as 'useful boats to fish from'. Rather, how churches have their existence, the ways they live their lives and manage their affairs, are to be embodiments of the life of Christ and signs of the coming kingdom. Salvation is corporate as well as personal. All of this is expressed in Ephesians 2, building on chapter 1. To extend Yoder's insights further (in collaboration with others), my thinking shifted from understanding 'principalities and powers' in wholly 'spiritual' terms as demonic realities that corrupt human life to seeing them as a way of referring to human sociological realities, the political, cultural, structural, corporate dimensions that grow out of human social existence and are both necessary for our lives and oppressive of them precisely because they are fallen. This became a way in for me to understand how the Christian life together in community can itself be 'political', not in the sense of aping worldly or power politics but as an experiment in forging the 'civilisation of love'. I say 'experiment' because its realisation is so difficult and partial, and churches are themselves always under the pressure to conform to the ways of the 'world'. They are scarcely free from the temptation of their members to control, compete and dominate. All of this helps towards an analysis of 'the world'. This is not a reference to the world as the creation that God has made and loves but to corporate human existence organised without regard to God and in estrangement from him. I found Walter Wink's work on 'the powers' extremely helpful here in identifying 'the powers' as created, fallen and to be redeemed. By this, he meant firstly that human life is meant to be lived communally, and so enabling structures emerge from that existence and are intended to be supportive, just and enriching. Yet, human fallenness means that such powers are themselves fallen and, instead of liberating and supporting, have come to be oppressive and destructive even while continuing to be necessary. Then again, the work of Christ has a corporate dimension in that through his obedience to the Father and refusal to submit to the powers, he has triumphed over them, as revealed in the resurrection and the ascension. He refuses to be beguiled or intimated by them, and this is a victory. Consequently, the powers are capable of redemption, of attaining in a degree to God's 'original' intention for them as a foretaste of their full restoration in the kingdom that is to come. In the interim, God's churches are called to live as free communities embodying the 'civilisation of love' as best they are able, not falling prey to the powers or conforming to them in their godlessness but discerning in them that which belongs to their created essence and holding forth hope for their eventual redemption. If personal salvation operates at the 'micro' level of individual lives and is essential to the Christian enterprise, there is also the 'macro' level of corporate witness and impact of calling the powers to serve the good and humane ends of human (and indeed earthly) thriving. A further insightful moment for me was in learning about German Baptist congregations under the Third Reich. In so far as these churches confined themselves to preaching personal salvation, they represented no threat to Hitler's Germany. Equally, in so far as they were allowed to do so by 'the powers,' they considered the emerging Third Reich as no threat to themselves, even possibly as a support. Consequently, lacking an analysis of social existence, they failed to see or to resist the catastrophe that was emerging around them and, in effect, became complicit in it (as, of course, did many others). In effect, these 'free' churches were not free at all but were in thrall to the powers. The lesson needs to be learnt and constant vigilance maintained. Is the mistake being repeated? Absolutely.

The analysis of the 'principalities and powers' as, at least in part, a reference to the social structures of human existence functions for me as a way to understand the church as a dissenting, nonconforming community set amid the powers and seeking to form the civilisation of love. In this sense, the church is inevitably political, but in the sense of a 'contrast society' rather than one assimilated to the powers. Walter Wink enabled me to see that the powers are 'created, fallen and to be redeemed', and in this way, along with others, rehabilitated the New Testament emphases as a way to understand the challenge to Christian witness. Much of this has found its way into my PhD research and whatever modest contribution I may have made to contemporary thought, especially thinking about 'Baptist identity' (as we came to call it).

But Wink went further than this in rehabilitating language about demons and the devil. He saw such language as capturing an important dimension greatly neglected in both Christian thinking and secular thought: that is, a spiritual dimension whereby human institutions constellate what he called 'interiority'. Because the whole is always greater than the sum of the parts, any institution develops a spiritual character that can be wholesome or oppressive and shapes those persons who are part of it. This is not to say that an 'interiority' is, in itself, something, an ontologically existent entity of some kind. It is only the product, the effervescence if you will, of the human beings that underlie it. Yet, having no substance of itself, it nonetheless is a reality. This can be called 'nonontological realism'. In its turn, this train of thought has led me to make connections with the longstanding tradition in Christian thought, which has come to see evil not as something that exists as part of God's creation but as *deprivation,* the *absence of the good, privatio boni.* The thought goes back at least to Augustine and even further to Neo-Platonism. Evil is emptiness, not something but nothing, yet a powerful nothing. It is not difficult to conceive of how it works. For instance, a vacuum is a sheer emptiness, not something but the absence of anything. Yet it can be immensely powerful in its capacity to suck things into itself. Darkness is not something discrete, but the absence of light, and we are familiar with it daily. Most notably, death, the final enemy, is the absence of life, and we all live in its shadow and go in fear of it. In the New Testament, it is regarded as a power and is personified as though it were an agent. In a sense, it is. But not as an ontological being – we are back to 'nonontological realism', a power that does not discreetly exist in itself but is an undoubted reality that impinges upon us in no uncertain terms.

This train of thought has pushed me in the most speculative direction of my theological pilgrimage, and that concerns the very nature of evil. Beyond the personal and the structural dimensions of the sinful and God-resistant human condition, there is a further dimension. It is the dimension of evil as a dominating force, a reality devoid of all goodness that can only deny, distort, contradict and destroy discrete. I learnt from Karl Barth to make a distinction here between 'the Shadow' and 'Nothingness' (*das Nichtige*). He saw the Shadow as a way of speaking of the inevitable obstacles to human flourishing faced by every creature. Following Irenaeus, we might say, therefore, that God designed the world not as a perfected paradise but as a place of tough decisions, hard choices, and difficult experiences. Life would consequently be a sort of training ground, a 'vale of soul-making', in which we might become morally responsible individuals such as we would never have become if we had known only happiness. Although hard and problematic, these experiences do not count as 'evil', which is to be distinguished conceptually from them. Following a German folktale, those who have no shadow do not exist. A shadow is inevitable for persons who exist, and so it is with life. Life is hard, and so it is intended to be for the sake of growth in character and sheer resilience. It is also the point where God's love can be 'poured into our hearts' (Romans 5:1-5). Beyond the Shadow, and different from it, there is Nothingness or evil. Evil requires malice. It is this that the New Testament conceived as the devil, satan, the prince of this world, the 'power at work in the sons of disobedience', and that Jesus Christ came to destroy. It is a failing of modern Christianity when and if its analysis of what's wrong confines itself only to personal and structural sinfulness. We travel some way to a fuller understanding if we agree with Walter Wink that 'satan' is a way of capturing the totality of human fallenness, the 'spirit' that is constellated when human depravity is at its peak. Yet, in my view, we need to travel somewhat further.

Even in a secular environment, unbelieving people feel the need to fall back on the religious language of 'evil' to describe the things they see and to express, sometimes, what they even feel in their souls. It is questionable whether their philosophy allows them language which is such a concession to religious perspectives. This evil power is what Barth referred to with the idea of Nothingness. He insisted, in a bit of a tongue twister, 'Das Nichtige ist nicht Nichts': Nothingness is not nothing. The reality of intentional and unqualified malice is what the language of the devil and satan seeks to capture; there are few linguistic alternatives to which we can resort. When Jesus set free the 'Gerasene demoniac', the demons are said to have begged him not to send them back to the 'abyss' (Luke 8:26-31, 31). Likewise, in the highly apocalyptic, and to me horrific, language of Revelation, there is a reference to the 'bottomless pit' (9:11). However we parse these words, they surely point to a negative reality of sheer emptiness and the negation of the good, the stuff of nightmares. This, too, is that from which we have been redeemed by the grace of God and without which no representation of the gospel is complete. Evil is a power, not just an idea.

So, where does evil come from? How are we to come to terms with it? I have struggled in my writings to answer these questions and that struggle has not come to an end. It is possible that we simply reach a dead-end. After all, it is surely in the nature of evil to be irrational and so incapable of reasoned analysis. Were it to be so rendered, it might not be as evil as we imagine. There is a place for saying that evil is absurd, that it serves no good purpose, and that in a universe that has its origin in the Logos of God, it is futile to search for anything logical about it. Evil is simply absurd, and we can go no further. It is there, but to ask how it is there may be futile. This would be parallel to the atheist's attitude to the existence of a universe: it is simply there, and there is no point in asking how or why. Powerful though this approach might be, it is hard in either case to leave off questioning. The majority Christian response, historically speaking, appeals to an 'angelic catastrophe' whereby, in some pretemporal existence, a proportion of the angelic host under the leadership of Lucifer rebelled against God and precipitated themselves and the ensuing creation into disaster. I can trace this back to Origen, and it may have Jewish antecedents. This proposal might account for the fact that evil predates the emergence of humankind, explaining both the presence of the serpent ('that ancient serpent' - Revelation 12:9) in the Garden of Eden as the agent of temptation. It may also account for the fact that has come increasingly to light, of pain, waste and suffering in the natural world. Although I can cope with the mythological tenor of this idea (how might we speak of it other than with 'mythic' ideas?) I have long since found it unconvincing on solely scriptural grounds. I fail to find any such doctrine present there, and most of the adduced 'proof texts' are distinctly tenuous. Other things count against it. If the devil and his angels are fallen creatures with an underlying but created ontology, is it not necessary that there should be some provision for their reconciliation and redemption, as Origen notoriously speculated? Yet, no such provision is suggested in scripture. Furthermore, when it comes to the redemption of the world, Christ did not become an angel but a human being, indicating that the seat of the problem of alienation lies in humanity, not in the angelic sphere. I believe Karl Barth to be right in rejecting this ancient idea in that granting the evil powers an ontological status, even a personhood, is to dignify them beyond measure. Our theological constructs need to demote them, not promote them. The idea of a 'personal devil', which has found its way even into some church confessions of faith, is problematic. If personhood is an aspect of being made in the image of God, I am not prepared to concede that the devil (whatever we mean by that) was ever or can ever in any sense be granted personhood. The most that can be said is that the evil power is a parody of personhood, assuming an appearance that is deceptive, being at most a kind of artificiality. Rather than *believing* in the devil, I choose to *disbelieve* in the devil, to *renounce* the devil as the appropriate response now and always to irreducible evil. Barth's warning that when it comes to the demons, we should only cast them 'a short sharp glance' lest we ourselves 'become a little demonic' belongs to the wisest words ever written.

The concept of a pre-mundane angelic catastrophe does have certain strengths. It is a kind of explanation of the inexplicable. It has a 'concrete' nature in that it focuses and directs attention. Consequently it makes the kind of theological proposal I shall shortly take up seem abstract and deficient. Most importantly, it portrays evil not as a direct creation of God, thus distancing the good God from culpability for evil, but as an aberration within the created sphere. Evil is not, therefore, part of the good creation but a distortion within it, a misuse, for instance, of human, or possibly angelic, freedom and agency. It is, therefore, limited in scope, potentially limited in duration rather than a power rivalling God eternally as truly dualistic religions, such as Zoroastrianism, imply. There is certainly a dualism of good and evil, but it is a temporary one which is destined to end with the overcoming of evil by the good. These are helpful elements I wish to preserve and incorporate in an alternative statement. Yet, while doffing my cap to these, I am clear about the need to avoid granting ontological dignity to evil. Rather, it is parasitical, feeding off the good, negative in denying the positive, and discreative in opposing the creative.

So, I must come to the 'realism' in non-ontological realism. It is possible in proposing my alternative statement to imagine I am thinking of evil as mere delusion. Whereas it must contain elements of delusion I assert strongly that evil is real. Though I and others find it necessary to use 'mythic' language in speaking of evil, it is the language that is mythic, not the reality. We are, after all, speaking of that which lies beyond our immediate sense perceptions and even beyond our rational analysis. The reality of evil is clear to me both in my pastoral, personal experience and in the facts of social and political existence. The statement by John F. Kennedy that 'all man's problems are created by man, and all can be solved by man' verges to my mind on the nonsensical. The fact is that we are beset by problems we are unable to solve, most of our own corporate making and many others, because there are powers at work that exceed our comprehension and certainly our control. How may we speak then of powers that are nonontological but frighteningly real? I can only attempt this by deploying language that is mythic and doing so in a way that is 'as if'. So, in what follows, I cannot offer firm doctrine but only constructs of the imagination that operate 'as if'.

For instance, as a first reflection, it is 'as if' when God ordered the world out of the primaeval chaos, God left the task unfinished so that the universe continued to be threatened by that chaos, always with the possibility that it might be overcome by it. One way of understanding human stewardship of the earth, the 'image of God' that implies a kind of dominion within creation paralleling that of the creator, is to see that we are called to be co-workers with God in bringing creation to its fulfilment in ultimate harmony. The 'Fall', therefore, consists of our forsaking this vocation and falling prey to the chaos and compounding creation's incompleteness. In that God pronounced the creation 'very good', this might be understood not as creation's being perfect but its being a suitable arena within which this project of divine-human cooperation might take place. In the Garden narrative of Genesis 3, the serpent precedes human beings and is already present as a tempting agent. This certainly would fit the narrative of an angelic catastrophe and give it substance. Yet I am inclined to see it as a diminished and altered variation on the Babylonian myth of a primaeval conflict between the creator and the sea-serpent (Isaiah 51:9) that appears in varying if reduced guises in the Bible. At points, these ancient writings employ remnants of Semitic mythology when it refers to the chaos monsters of Leviathan (Psalm 74:14 and five other references), Rahab (Psalm 89:10) and Behemoth (Job 40:15). Similar ideas are taken up in the symbolism of Daniel and Revelation. These monsters of land and sea can indeed refer to natural creatures, but the language echoes those myths that refer to God overcoming the chaos in the act of creation. True to its common method of putting ancient mythologies in their place and subjecting them to a superior creation narrative, the serpent is a much-reduced symbol of the original chaos out of which creation was ordered. In place of ordered obedience to God, Adam and Eve, representing us all, fall prey to the chaos, and this constitutes their sin. They divert from the divine purpose. Although this is sometimes characterised as 'free will', it is rather an abuse rather than a use of freedom, a precipitation into bondage and disorder, as Genesis 3 portrays. The rest, as they say, is history.

I find a difficulty in my own train of thought when I ask the question, chaos may be chaotic, but is it evil? If I understand scripture rightly, God first creates what is 'formless and void' and then orders it (one could say 'justifies it') to give us and other creatures a habitable world. If everything that God creates is good, even the chaos cannot be evil as such. What is evil is the *turn* to 'the dark side', from God's order to its opposite in disorder that human beings in their origins have made and that we continue to compound by our own choices. Such an analysis places the origins of evil squarely on the shoulders of humanity. A similar argument could be made for the construct of a primaeval fall of angels if those who hold to it choose to do so. A problematic aspect of this belief is accounting for how such supposedly perfect and spiritual beings (if such they are) could ever turn to the 'dark side'. An answer could be that even they are preceded by the 'chaos', and this opens the possibility of such dislocation. I have indicated in previous comments that I do not follow this thought for three reasons: Firstly, I find little to suggest it in scripture, despite the texts commonly adduced. If it exists at all, it is on the margins of the biblical revelation, such as in Jude and 2 Peter. Secondly, the fact that the Redeemer embraces a human nature in Christ indicates that this is where the problem originates and how it may be resolved, as Christ turns towards the divine will and refuses its opposite. Thirdly, there is no hint in scripture that the devil and his angels will be redeemed and restored, which would seem to me to be necessary if they are created beings since 'The LORD is good to all, and his compassion is over all that he has made' (Psalm 145:9). God cares for everything created. As indicated, this problem is relieved if evil (satan, the devil) is not a divine creation but is *privatio boni*, non-ontological (but real) negativity.

To add to my tally of 'as ifs' at this point, there are two further approaches that are worth including. I have pondered much Karl Barth's idea of *Das Nichtige*, Nothingness. He is to be credited with exploring this theme and going where others do not, and his influence on my own reflections should be evident. As I understand him, he argues that in the act of creation, for the sake of having a world to which God says 'Yes', there is an implied 'No'. In affirming the world that God does want, he has passed by the world that God does not want. And yet even the world God does not want necessarily has 'existence' in virtue of God's powerful word. In this way, God is proclaimed as the good creator who calls into being out of nothing a good creation suitable for the divine purpose. But God is not the creator of evil. God has, therefore, not created evil, but in creating what is good, the possibility of evil arises as the opposite of what has been created. I have not been able to follow Barth closely at this point as it rather suggests that in intending to do one thing, God cannot help doing another. However, what seems inevitable is the conclusion that in creating a good world, the *possibility* of its opposite also arises. That possibility then waits to be *actualised*, and this is what has happened and continually happens. This is the nature of evil, to do intentionally and collectively that which God does not will, but the possibility of which arises simply because it is not possible to have a good world without its conceivable opposite.

Another 'as if' that emerges here is one to which Jürgen Moltmann draws attention and derives from the thought of Isaac Luria, a Kabbalistic Jewish theologian. It is the concept of the *zimzum*, the self-imposed withdrawal of God into God's own self for the sake of creation. God, who fills all things, must freely withdraw into God's own self to create a space in which creation that is not God may exist. Because of such a withdrawal, the resultant space is 'godless', an emptiness over against which the creation exists, though the creation is consequently threatened by non-being. This might account for the fact that all life has its being in 'survival mode' and struggles to exist against a background, or abyss, of possible extinction. When the divine purpose is fulfilled, God will freely 'derestrict' himself and once more fill all things, being all in all to everything and necessarily banishing what is godless and sheer negation. Inevitably, we are still here in the arena of 'mythic' thought, but it is difficult to see how, if we are to think at all at this level, it could be different. I am reminded of the fact that even hard-core science verges on the mythic and the mystical when it seeks to account for what presses our imaginations to the limit. It is not my intention to hold tenaciously to any of these constructs, but I do regard them as pointers to possible ways of understanding that might become more fully available to us in due course. In the meantime, it is possible both to claim again that the 'mystery of iniquity' may not be wholly susceptible to rational analysis but that its reality is a matter of experienced fact.

I seem then to have come to the position where instead of seeing 'evil' as a force that precedes human beings and their actions (as with the angelic catastrophe idea), I am concluding that it is the other way round, even if the possibility of its existence must necessarily precede its actualisation: the power of evil is a product of collective human alienation from God. It is a negating force that emerges out of corporate human existence, and so it grows as the human population grows and is always present wherever those humans are to be found. To reiterate: the *possibility* of evil does indeed precede human beings, although its *actualisation* is a consequence of human choices and actions. Whether this is coherent, I leave others to judge, and I am all too aware of its tentative nature. But in my defence, I am not here promulgating a doctrine so much as engaging in speculative 'as if' thinking. Perhaps this is a way of saying that I have reached my limit. And that would be fine.

To elaborate further, I am struck by a reference made by Barth to the ancient tale of the Sorcerer's Apprentice as developed by Goethe. The eponymous and unfortunate apprentice unleashes powers that prove to be beyond his control:

> In the sudden or gradual movement with which man breaks free from God, he revolutionizes the natural forces that are co-ordinated with him . . . It is he who is at the helm, who pulls the levers, who presses the knobs. Nevertheless, they automatically or autonomously rumble and work and roll and roar and clatter outside him, without him, past him and over him. He finds that he himself is subject to their law, which he has foreseen, and to their power, which he has released. Turning aside from God, he is himself displaced, that is, jerked out of his proper position in relation to these forces into one that is unworthy of him. Still his slaves, they now confront him as robots which he himself must serve, and not without being forced to fear their possible pranks.

The rationale here is that by foolish actions powers are unleashed that assume control and become beyond the power of the apprentice to retrieve. In the same way, both the original and the present acts of disobedience of humanity create a situation whereby that which we are intended to master begins to master us and does so in a way that is 'robotic', that is, exercising power mindlessly and without regard to human feeling. If the 'powers' are those variegated institutions, structures, and possibilities that human beings were intended to build for themselves as a peaceable home in which they may thrive, they have become all too often a prison in which they are ensnared, the sources of oppression, injustice and crime. This captures the analysis of the 'powers' that I have previously described. But beyond this, which is bad enough, further powers are unleashed that, in my analysis, have the character of 'pure' malice as they move towards a state of unadulterated malevolence and godlessness. This power becomes everything that God is not. It becomes sheer and unredeemable negation, that about which no good or qualifying word is to be spoken. And it exists purely parasitically, feeding upon the creation as a negative force. It is no accident that in contemporary literature, we are fascinated by figures that embody these traits, whether this be Sauron in *Lord of the Rings* or Voldemort and the Dementors in the Harry Potter series. They distort, destroy, and suck the life out of their prey. They are the stuff of our nightmares, of the night terrors that afflict us. They are agents of nothingness. It is also not surprising that although Christians have identified the 'sins of the flesh', the concupiscence that seems to accompany embodied existence, they have also held that the worst range of sins consists in those that are more 'spiritual' in nature, the sins of pride, arrogance, envy, covetousness, malice, hatred, and the like. The portrayal of evil as a spiritual force that we name satan, the devil or demons seeks to capture this 'higher' (though actually lower) dimension.

Being led in my thoughts to places that surprise even myself and seeing no good reason to turn away from them, I do, however, return to more traditional categories. I do not count myself among those who simply ignore the New Testament language about evil forces, the language of devil and demons, or who are embarrassed by it such that they want to 'demythologise' it (though in truth, I have engaged in my own form of demythologising). Even as I seek to dethrone these powers, to insist, for instance, that the devil is not a person (egregious blasphemy!) but a non-person and a destroyer of personhood or that evil powers have no ontology (which would be to grant them excessive dignity), I affirm, along with Barth as it happens, that the power of Nothingness can *take form* within human experience. And we need language to identify and resist those forms. The 'tweak' in my thinking is that the form they take is a masquerade and that the language of the New Testament employs personification to name and, therefore, resist and cast out the powers behind the masquerade. Almost irresistibly, having arrived at a non-ontological analysis, I still find myself employing the language of agency: there is seemingly a stratagem. Am I once more verging on cognitive dissonance? Probably. The powers of darkness are intending and doing something, or at least apparently so. To my mind, this is a 'seeming' along the lines of the kind of 'teleological functionalism' that leads us to look for some kind of purpose in forces that are essentially chaotic rather than structured. I recall here the ways in which some atheistic proponents of evolution insist that any appearance of 'design' in nature is an illusion, that the reality is happenstance or even accident, that there is no intentional or purposeful drive in the evolutionary impulse. The watchmaker is blind or non-existent. As I see it, the polarity of good and evil, of God and the devil, requires that whereas God is deeply personal and profoundly intentional, evil is precisely the opposite. There is no false equivalence here. The suggestion that if we abolish the devil, we must abolish God also assumes that the devil and God exist on the same plane, whereas the reality is that of total contradiction. If there is an opposition between what is called 'conspiracy' or 'cock-up' theories of history, I am decidedly part of the Cock-up Tendency. Conspiracy theories are very enticing but, for the most part, exist within the constructs of the human brain (though not always!), and by and large, they are pathological. In preference to the idea that the devil is a conspiracy theory writ large, I choose the idea that evil exists as negation, and it is we human beings who grant it form, that if there is a logic or a conspiracy, we are the ones who supply it because of our inherent tendency to look for patterns and teleologies. And herein lies one of my most contestable suggestions.

Nigel G. Wright

Post Seventeen: Wrestling with Demons

I am still in the realm of 'as if'. I have been propelled along the path of thinking about the nature of evil because, in the very first year of my ministry, I was thrown somewhat surprisingly into situations of 'deliverance' or exorcism. I look back on those situations now with a degree of puzzlement as to what was really going on. I can only say that whatever the final answer to this question, what I encountered was straight out of the pages of the New Testament and bore striking parallels to the ministry of Jesus, who was, despite all attempts to ignore or suppress the fact, an exorcist. He cast out demons and set people free from what I now prefer to call 'evil influences'. I am not inclined to avoid this as an embarrassing fact or to engage in reductionism, explaining it away as a failure to understand the nature of mental illness. Things are more complicated than that. Certainly, both sociological and psychological factors are always in play, but even when these have been fully exposed, there are residual elements that require other paradigms of understanding. There are phenomena that come into the category of 'possession', and my own experience and that of many others confirm this fact. The problem is how to understand it. We are here on the borders of psychological medicine, and certainly, with time, we have understood more about the complexities of the human psyche. This has been underlined to me as I have observed and personally experienced what are sometimes thought of as 'revivalist' phenomena, certainly ones that exceed our expectations of 'normal' human behaviours. This has been part and parcel of the charismatic movements of the latter part of the twentieth century, paralleling my lifetime. At stake, there is a fuller understanding of what it means to be human, what happens within us at the communal level in the 'collective unconscious', and whether there are 'psychic' depths to us all which, as we penetrate them more deeply, reveal that human beings are bound together at subliminal levels that are always in operation and can be tapped into more directly under certain circumstances. There are resonances here with hypnotism, mysticism, extra-sensory perceptions, visionary or near-death experiences, bereavement visions and parapsychology. Whereas much of this remains unexplored or only partially explored, I have no doubt that we are talking of something real rather than merely illusory. It is a constant and established realm of human experience and requires thoughtful attention. Religious and spiritual experience is, therefore, an authentic dimension of what it means to be human. There is that in the 'secular gaze' of materialistic ideologies that wishes to overlook it and dismiss it, or in the last resort to label it fraudulent, but this is surely unscientific. It presents itself to us and, therefore, is worthy of investigation. Even if such investigation concludes that there is nothing 'transcendent' in these experiences, as would certainly be the case for some investigators, a fuller understanding of our humanity could still emerge productively. So, I welcome the suggestion that is made from time to time that we are on the verge of a paradigm shift analogous to the many that have preceded us, expanding and enriching our vision of reality.

I go further than this in arguing that ruling out authenticity from the beginning, as some reductionists do, represents a form of ideological prejudice contrary to the spirit of open-minded scientific enquiry. Science is an outstanding methodology but fails itself when it becomes an ideology outside of which nothing else counts as truth. I have benefitted greatly over the years from the writings of Jonathan Sacks, former Chief Rabbi of the United Kingdom and Commonwealth. He has written, 'You do not have to be religious to have a sense at the sheer improbability of things. James Le Fanu, in *Why Us?* argues that we are about to undergo a paradigm in scientific understanding. The complexities of the genome, the emergence of the first molecular life forms, the origins of Homo sapiens and our prodigiously enlarged brain: all these and more are too subtle to be accounted for on reductive, materialist, Darwinian science'.[37] Over the years, science has penetrated both into the distance of the universe and has shown it to contain something like a billion galaxies, each with a hundred billion stars. At the same time, in a parallel and equally awesome way, it has penetrated the depths of things and shown the universe to be composed of smaller and smaller elements only discernible with the most sophisticated of instruments or by conjecture. Creation is no longer understood as a

---

[37] Jonathan Sacks, *The Great Partnership: God, Science and the Search for Meaning* (London: Hodder and Stoughton, 2011), p.270.

machine but as an organism and energy. Every moment, millions of neutrinos, themselves a million times smaller than an electron, pass through our bodies. It makes sense to me that even deeper still are realities that border on the mystical and the spiritual, not (yet?) detectable by scientific means and yet determinative of life. To call all this 'psychic' makes it sound spooky, but spooky it probably is.

It makes further sense to me that if in the animal creation we find what has been termed 'Supernature',[38] uncanny abilities beyond our comprehension though not our recognition, the same should be writ large in human beings, creation's most developed if also most problematic creatures. It is possible to believe that these things are true without deriving the theistic conclusion. Yet, on the one hand, they serve to expose the hollowness of naturalism and materialism and, on the other, make the God hypothesis more possible. They also make credible the fact that in each human being and in humanity collectively, there are psychic depths deeper than the conscious mind, deeper than the subconscious and deeper yet than what Carl Jung identified as the racial unconscious, a reservoir of shared psychic connectedness in which together we participate. It is in this realm that we become vulnerable to influences that go beyond our individuality and that are categorised by terms such as 'communal hysteria', 'social contagion', 'psychic epidemics' and 'pseudo-reality'. Such phenomena tend not to last long before they burn

---

[38] Lyall Watson, *Supernature: The Natural History of the Supernatural* (London: Hodder and Stoughton, 1973).

themselves out or are exposed as falsities. Sadly, sometimes they become harmful frenzies such as panics about 'satanic ritual abuse', or therapists routinely diagnosing childhood sexual abuse, or fashions for uncovering repressed memories, or even witch hunts. Most dangerously, they can produce the kinds of hysterical inter-ethnic massacres that tragically took place in Rwanda. My point here is that phenomena of this kind draw upon the psychic corporate depths of humanity and that such depths are an unruly mystery to us. I have never forgotten a poster I once saw that read, 'Just because you're paranoid, it doesn't mean to say they're not out to get you'. What I took from it was that although there may be states of mind that are pathological, once these have been recognised and dismissed, there may yet be a core of truth or reality beneath them. Honesty also requires me to add that revival phenomena in Christian history have something of the same character, hopefully, but not always of a more positive nature. The latter quarter of the twentieth century witnessed both the revivalism of the 'Third Wave' and then of the 'Toronto Blessing' that had very much the same contagious character. These two were a mixed bag, the full spiritual value of which has yet to be determined, however exciting they may have been for participants.

I have found very little theological analysis of what the New Testament is describing when it portrays Jesus as an exorcist. I don't mean by this that there are no books, scholarly and otherwise, that deal with the subject – there are. There are also writings about parallel phenomena in other contexts than the New Testament, religious and cultural. Much of it is dubious and requires careful handling. I refer instead to work that seeks to answer the question, what reality lies behind the language of evil spirits and the demonic? One suggested answer is that demons are departed, ancestral human spirits that, for some reason, do not have the freedom to leave this world behind. The proposed remedy is to release them from their earth-bound existence, perhaps by means of a requiem mass in which they are called to mind. I am not persuaded about this, but nor am I prepared simply to dismiss the idea of 'land-locked' spirits. Who knows? Perhaps the most common assumption (rather than analytical argument) is that demons are fallen angels, numbered among those who fell with Lucifer in the aforementioned 'angelic catastrophe'. This, too, I find unconvincing, given that the demons I think I have encountered were trivial, if also destructive. I am sure 'they' would like to imagine they were fallen angels and to present themselves as such. I have rejected any idea that the demonic realm is an ordered hierarchy of evil powers and regard it instead as essentially chaotic, though assuming whatever form might seem to give it credibility. If there is any semblance of a demonic hierarchy (as some analyses have traditionally wanted to claim), I would attribute this to deception. If, in the absence of biblical data, we are working with 'inside information', how can we trust what we think we are being told? It should be clear from my previous claims that I don't regard evil as having ontology or substance but as being negation, parasite, and emptiness and not something 'in itself'.

I have never come across any analysis that I find adequate, and the one I am about to advance might be equally lacking. I make no great claims for it other than that it is an attempt to understand. To put the matter in rather crude terms, I offer the thought that rather than demons being degraded angelic 'stuff', which follows from the idea of an angelic catastrophe or perversion, demons are a form of degraded 'psychic' stuff. In other words, they exist in the realm of human psychic existence in its state of corporate and individual alienation from the ground of being in God. I build to this point by means of several observations. The first is that, as already hinted, there is a 'psychic' realm in the depths of human beings. We live lives that are conscious, subconscious, or unconscious and, at a yet greater depth, psychic. It is in the psychic realm, above all, that many of our spiritual and religious impulses reside, and it is a realm that we are only just beginning to understand. There is, therefore, a quality of religious or mystic experience that is universally common to humankind and, from a Christian perspective, is not necessarily aligned with the will and purpose of God precisely because we are alienated. On the other hand, neither is it totally without openness to the divine. Secondly, as we go deeper into what it means to be human, we find ourselves to be bound together with others and entangled with the whole of humanity and, indeed, with the universe. This is the realm of the 'archetypes', shared instincts, images, and patterns that are universally, if unconsciously, shared and probably owe their origins to early experiences during the evolution of the race.

I advance an analogy at this point drawn from the virtual realm. In the worldwide web, there is a 'conscious' realm in which information is open, available, and accessible. At a further level, there is the 'deep web' where information may be concealed and hidden. This is not necessarily a bad thing since people have a right to privacy in areas such as their bank accounts and personal details. At a yet deeper and more sinister level, there is the 'dark web' that is deliberately hidden and contains what is criminal, corrupt, and malicious. It veers towards evil and is entered by and large by those of evil intent. It is like the bilge of an ancient ship containing unwholesome and festering corruption. The analogy consists of understanding what 'lies beneath' in our corporate, fallen existence and what becomes unfortunately possible and perhaps inevitable because of this. If we take the triad of the world, the flesh and the devil, this realm is an amalgam of all three: the downward pull of fallen human nature, the structural drag of the 'lordless powers', and the powerful dynamic of evil that is personified in the mythic language of the devil. In this realm of corrupted and complex human existence, we are to locate the demons. Rather than exist as external powers over and above human beings, they emerge from within, and from them, we need to be delivered, cleansed, and healed. It is no accident that people are sometimes described as 'wrestling with their demons'.

Let me pivot the discussion at this point and refer to what is discussed in the realm of psychology (and here, I speak self-evidently as a non-professional). It appears that we humans are capable of 'splitting off' aspects of our personalities under certain circumstances. All of us who are 'normal' can be aware that we exist as a multiplicity of selves, which, most of the time, are unified into a single and functional self. Yet we can tap into different aspects of our personalities and can express, for instance, agreeable, cooperative, or hostile selves (or more) by turn and in the face of different pressures. On the basis that mental illness is, in the main, an exaggerated and extreme expression of what we 'normally' are, it occurs that at times, parts of ourselves become 'split off', denied by our conscious selves and manifested as autonomous 'selves' within the one person. This can be referred to in its more extreme forms as 'multiple personality disorder' and has as its remedy (assuming it is a disorder, which some people might deny) the process of acknowledging and owning those parts of our personality that knowingly or otherwise we have suppressed and reintegrating them into our functional selves. If tapped into, these flows of internal energy might bear some resemblance to what in the New Testament and other religious traditions, is considered 'demon possession'. I make no claim here other than that these phenomena are explicable in terms of standard human psychology and should be so treated.

Yet I also think that in the depths of the human personal and collective psyche (of which I have given a tentative account above using the analogy of the 'dark web'), these split-off selves can become malicious and unambiguously destructive to the degree that they tend in the direction of 'nothingness' or 'non-being'. At this point, they draw parasitically on the human psyche. Perhaps we might imagine them as elements of the psyche that have become malignant or cancerous and need to be cauterised. In other words, they do not exist discretely of themselves but as 'hypostases of nothingness'. This is a term I learnt from Karl Barth, and it is found in the record of informal conversations known as his *Table Talk*.[39] I take it to mean that there are forces within us that are negative in nature but draw substance as non-ontological entities from the human psyche. They suck the life from us, take hold and destroy. It is appropriate to speak of the need for deliverance from them. This line of thought can account for why exorcism is not an illusory practice of diseased minds but a matter of fact. At the same time, it indicates that phenomena such as 'multiple personality disorder' in which the self can be expressed as a variety of selves within one body can be mistaken for 'demonisation', and great caution needs to be exercised to avoid unhealthy diagnoses of complex conditions. If within each of us, there are denied, unintegrated or mildly 'split-off'

---

[39] *Karl Barth's Table Talk*, edited by John D. Godsey (Richmond, Virginia: John Knox Press), p.72.

dynamics at work, these might be mistakenly and unhelpfully identified as 'spirits' or demons.

It is possible to speak of someone having a 'spirit of pride' or a 'spirit of criticism' and of meaning by that something that belongs to the corrupted self but not to the demonic realm. As already said, even in common parlance we talk about people 'wrestling with their demons'. To my mind, this accounts for why some deliverance practitioners find demons everywhere and others consider them very rare. The former mistake locked in sinful attitudes or pathologies for demons. Fair enough. People still need to be cleansed of them and delivered, but this is not full-blown possession. Human beings are psychologically, morally, and psychically complex, and this should never be forgotten. I make a connection here with an aspect of the 'psychic' that is perhaps more empirically verifiable, or at least observable, and that is the phenomenon described as 'poltergeist'. This is alleged to involve the projection of unruly psychic energy into the environment, causing kinetic turbulence and disruption. It is sometimes associated with adolescence and the management of troubled subconscious emotions. Experience confirms that prayer and counselling can bring peace to what some would understand as a disruptive spirit. I would rather interpret it along the lines I have suggested as an unsettling psychic event or events. However, there may also be more to it than this. I have a friend who likened those who see demons everywhere to 'one-club golfers': it's the only game they know how to play. As with any other such limited account of complex matters, this is not good or wise pastoral practice. A better framework might be to see the need for ministry in this regard as a 'cleaning-up operation' rather than exorcism, as it could be more measured in tone than exorcisms are imagined to be. In the 1980s, Lyall Watson wrote a book entitled *Beyond Supernature: A New Natural History of the Supernatural*[40], which, apart from an interesting sub-title, included chapters cataloguing phenomena of the most bizarre and uncanny kind, including miracles, possession and poltergeists, way beyond the conventional scientific mores of physics. He concluded, 'I know the problem well, having found myself on many occasions torn between intellectual and emotional certainty. Knowing at one level that something was impossible, that it could never happen, and yet convinced at another that it had. Finding resolution of the conflict only in a growing suspicion that the model may be incomplete'. Once more, Hamlet's words are justified, 'There are more things in heaven and earth, O Horatio than are dreamt of in your philosophy'.[41]

Let me stress again that all I have attempted to say in this section is tentative and in the nature of 'as if'. If someone could come up with something better, I would be delighted. I am 'feeling out of sight for the ends of being'. However, what I have proposed enables me to think of evil, unclean spirits or demons as parasitical intrusions of negative powers into human experience. It is

---

[40] (London: Hodder &. Stoughton, 1986). Chapters 6, 7 and 8. The quotation is from p.188.
[41] William Shakespeare, *Hamlet*, 1b. 166.

appropriate to drive them out, but only when the space they leave behind is filled with the wholesome and life-giving presence of God can we be sure they will not recur, precisely as Jesus warned. This enables me once more to claim that the demons are real but are not ontological. They exist only in negation. They do not belong to God's good creation. They have no legitimate existence. They cannot be redeemed because they do not exist other than as sheer emptiness. This also allows for something more to be said about 'satan' or 'the devil'. This, too is parasitical on human existence, personal and social. It is the dynamic that is summoned into being when we human beings prefer the absence of God to the presence of God. It is not personal but anti-personal, and in its negative energy, it becomes a kind of agent, the kind that confronted Jesus in his temptations. In this way, and in the demons, evil takes form and can be named and renounced. So, we do not 'believe' in the devil but disbelieve or believe 'against' as an act of renunciation for Christ's sake. For the sake of the one in whom we do truly believe, we stand against the powers of evil, whatever form they assume.

The Christian confidence is that in his death and resurrection, Jesus Christ has gained the victory over sin, death, and the devil. The victory was gained in and through Christ's work, and so is a matter of historical record. But it is evident to all that it is not yet completed. The reason many Jewish believers find the messiahship of Jesus hard to accept is because the world remains so unredeemed: a messiah who fails to redeem the world and to put things right cannot, on this account, truly be the Messiah of Israel. The battle continues to rage. The Christian response is to claim that Jesus is the

Messiah who comes twice. In his first coming, he opened the door of salvation to all who believe, and in his second coming this same Jesus will consummate that which he rendered possible in his first coming. Christians of the present, therefore, are caught between a great memory and a great hope, a fact upon which they insist each time they celebrate the Lord's Supper. They remember the saving work of Christ in history, and they look forward to 'the marriage supper of the Lamb' when every knee shall bow and confess him to be Lord. This future perspective of hope and expectation is something that came into focus for me largely through the work of Jürgen Moltmann, and I have found it deeply enriching. Faith is determined as much by what will be as what has been.

Post Eighteen: Realising the End

Approaching faith with a future perspective does put many things in a new light. I have referred to the way in which the concept of 'the true church' might be better perceived if understood in future terms. In place of fighting over which of our existing denominations is the 'true' one, we do better to acknowledge that whatever we have gotten right, we are all still deeply flawed. The true church is something *we will be* only when, as pictured in Revelation 7, we are at last gathered before the throne of God and of the Lamb. For the present time, we are *in via*, on our way, travelling towards the future, and hopefully doing so together. A future perspective demands that we look forward, not just back, and as such, functions as a critical principle. It exposes how far we still fall short. The future does, after all, have a kind of priority: the past can never become the future, but the future can become the past. Sadly, Christian thinking has often become mired in attempts to predict and to do so by treating scripture as though it were a jigsaw puzzle to be pieced together in the most ingenious of ways. This is a default to treating the Bible as a magic text. At root, here is a mistaking of biblical apocalyptic and imagery. What is visionary and imaginative is taken as though it were a literal depiction of things to come. I was greatly helped in this area by Adrio Kŏnig's book *The Eclipse of Christ in*

Eschatology[42]. He rightly maintains that literalistic attempts to predict the end are, in effect, bypassing Christ and constructing schemes that are inadequately informed by Christology. Jesus and his work become a moment in an imaginative scheme of world history rather than its core. Christ is eclipsed. His constructive alternative requires us to think of the 'end' not as history's full stop but as the realisation of creation's goal. This is a shift from a negative reading of scripture that sees the 'end' as the cessation of all we know and love in this world to a positive reading that sees it as the fulfilment of everything for which creation, and we within it, were called into being in the first place. Even the Book of Revelation, so often a happy hunting ground for fantasists, is not about the end of the world but about the end of evil within it, and so the triumph of God's sovereignty. Accordingly, the end, God's goal and purpose, has been realised first of all in Christ *for us*; in the church, it is being realised *in us*, and as we move towards the future it is being realised *with us*. I find echoes here of Philip J. Rosato's understanding of the Trinity: God the Father is the Creator; Christ the Son is the Re-creator; and the Holy Spirit is the Trans-creator. Both schemes appeal to me not only because of their three-fold schemes. My own predilection for 'Christological concentration' in the doing of theology also draws me to these patterns of thought.

---

[42] The Eclipse of Christ in Eschatology: Toward a Christ-Centered Approach (Grand Rapids: Eerdmans, 1989).

To elaborate further on König, just as creation is said to exist 'through Christ and for Christ' (Colossians 1:16), so the realisation of creation's purpose is definitively achieved in him. I have pondered what the theological meaning of creation's coming into being 'through' Christ might be. I have concluded that God's intention for creation is that it may share in the quality of communion with the creator that we see exemplified in Jesus. Christ is, therefore, the 'firstborn of all creation' (Colossians 1:15) in that it is in him and through him that this is supremely accomplished: creation at peace with God in a communion of love. This was supremely realised *for us* in the person and humanity of Jesus the Christ in a way that enables its communication first to all humankind and then to all creation. Creation is and always has been destined through him to share in the 'liberty of the children of God', even if it must 'groan as if in the pains of childbirth' until it comes to pass (Romans 8). Christ is the very image of God, and so what is accomplished in him is *for us*: it begins with him and is mediated through him to us in the church so that the 'end' is realised *in us,* and we become progressively conformed to his image. This new creation in Christ is being accomplished as we are transformed into his likeness. All of this is then set within the eschatological goal that is being realised *with us*. Again, it is 'as if' the unfinished work of creation has been awaiting the 'revelation of the children of God' so that we may be fellow workers with God in perfecting the yet incomplete creation. If, in the beginning, the creation was declared to be both good and then very good, this is not to say that it was already perfected. Rather, creatures follow the commands of God to 'bring forth' and to engage in the project of creation, working with the creator to realise creation's potential and to perfect what has been made. Jesus himself referred to the 'renewal of all things' (Matthew 19:28) and envisaged such a future. This suggests that those theologians are correct who have suggested that, even apart from the facts of sin and disobedience, Christ would have become incarnate to bring the creation to its promised end. As it is, because of sin, the incarnation has taken the particular form it has, but it is to be seen as much God's creative work as a re-creative one. There is an intriguing interplay here: God's work of creation is a saving work in that it keeps chaos at bay, and God's redemptive work is creative in that it achieves God's purpose for creation. There is, therefore, a profound futurist cast to the gospel, and this is entirely in accord with the sense of destiny that is intrinsic to the biblical narrative as understood from a Christian perspective: history is going somewhere. The horizon is ever before us until the work is done and completed in the new heaven and new earth in which the righteous dwell. This vision thrills and motivates, not least because it is all-embracing. It spells the restoration of 'all things'. I have moved in my theological pilgrimage away from the theology that views the rest of creation apart from human beings as peripheral to salvation. Not at all. All things are embraced by this vision: all creatures, great and small, the physical universe itself, the past, the present and the future. The declaration 'Behold I am making all things new' (Revelation 21:5) must accordingly be held to have maximum value. Yes, there are biblical passages that speak of creation being 'rolled up' and 'dissolved with fire', and I cannot discount these (2 Peter 3:10). I see them, however, as preliminary to the renewed heaven and earth, as referring to the purging of creation from evil and imperfection on its way to the redeemed and glorious future in which it will be unambiguously the 'theatre of God's glory'. I acknowledge that these things remain in the realm of vision, the imaginable future, not to be reduced to the merely literal. They stretch our imaginations and push us to the limits because they deal with 'what no eye has seen'. Even so, their magnetic pull can be felt in the present. Such a hope also allows us to envisage the incorporation into the new creation of human cultural achievements, particularly, as Jonathan Wilson points out when we think of the 'heavenly city': 'This is striking because we do not readily think of creation in relation to the built environment. And when we think of "city," we think of human work, not God's work. In this image, then, we are shown that God redeems what we have done with this world and incorporates it into the new creation as God's gift to us'.[43]

This Christologically informed approach to eschatology is infinitely superior to the literalistic and sometimes fanciful theorising that has often prevailed in the more sectarian and wilder

---

[43] Jonathan R. Wilson, *God's Good World: Reclaiming the Doctrine of Creation* (Grand Rapids: Baker Academic, 2013), p.135.

reaches of Christianity. Since they have proven universally mistaken, it is also a safeguard against them. This is not to despise the imagery in which things unimaginable are brought down to earth - how otherwise could we approach them? Scripture is not a cryptogram to be penetrated by the particularly ingenious. The operative word here is 'imagery'. At this point, I, too, am engaging in an element of 'demythologising'. I certainly wish to uncover the existential value of the imagery, the ways in which the images shape our devotion and our living. But the existential has an ontological reference. The realities of God at work in Christ and the Spirit cannot just be dissolved into human language about existential states of the human adventure. This would be to 'speak of man in a loud voice', and that is not enough. There is an objective ontological reality to which the existential is an appropriate response. The objective is real, so I am not a 'non-realist' by any stretch of the imagination. Scripture's apocalyptic imagery needs to be rendered into theological ideas. This is particularly the case when we speak of the second coming of Christ and the ways in which the New Testament employs the language of imminence: Christ is coming soon. In the judgement of some scholars, Jesus and the writers of the New Testament, including Paul, expected that the period between the first and second comings would be short. This impression can certainly be gained but can also be overplayed. The New Testament arguably 'telescopes' the events of the end so that the whole of history post-resurrection is seen as the 'latter days', the days lived in recollection of the first coming and expectation of the next. The telescoping compresses the resurrection, the ascension, Pentecost, and the mission of the church, and then the fall of Jerusalem and all those subsequent events, such as 'wars and rumours of wars', that cause our hearts to fail and to anticipate the final crises of human history. The time gaps between them all are foreshortened to increase the sense of urgency. This is the nature of apocalyptic and it heightens the significance of the events described. Similar rhetorical devices are employed today as warnings of catastrophe, as in the challenge of climate change – possibly the largest corporate threat humanity has ever faced. Even as humans have abandoned a biblical apocalyptic, they have (in my lifetime) created new ones to challenge us, such as race war, the nuclear threat, epidemics, and world hunger and now climate change and ultimate disaster. It seems we cannot live without some form of 'catastrophism', secular and religious, to keep us on our toes (and this is not to deny the reality of the identified threats). But I remain unconvinced that the first disciples were totally wedded to an early coming of the end. There are indeed suggestions, even in the teaching of Jesus, as we now have them, about the possibility of delay. Some would suggest that these are later textual insertions once hope of a 'soon' return was disappointed, another sign of the 'cognitive dissonance' intrinsic to the Christian faith. Shorn of unhelpful literalism, however, what is of ultimate importance is impressed upon us by the idea that Christ is coming soon. Life should be lived on this basis.

Each day may be our last, so no opportunity should be lost to do good. Existentially, therefore, Christians live their lives on two levels: the level of immediate accountability to God in the light of God's coming kingdom and that of sober realism in recognition of the 'not yet' of that kingdom's coming. These two perspectives held together can leave us in a good place, keeping us on our spiritual toes.

Traditionally, the 'Four Last Things' of eschatology have been identified as Heaven, Hell, Death, and Judgement, and this is certainly a helpful way of foregrounding subjects worthy of further thought. I prefer to think there is only one Last Thing, and that is our final encounter with the God who will one day be all in all. If it is 'as if' God who fills all things has 'retracted' God's own self to make space for an independent yet still entirely dependent creation that is the object of God's love, so it will be the case that this same God will one day 'derestrict' God's own self and once more fill all things. There is no way of avoiding a final encounter in this human pilgrimage with the One who is the Ultimate Reality. That encounter will precipitate the realities of heaven or hell, eternal life or death, purifying judgement, and rectifying justice. There is no escaping these realities. It is a weak form of Christianity that seeks to deny or ignore them. Just as it is through many tribulations that we are to enter the kingdom of God, so it is through encounter with the divine nature that we become inheritors of the world to come. Yet, having affirmed this 'strong' position, I do not make too hasty assumptions about what lies beyond these last encounters, that is, about the ultimate that lies even beyond the ultimate. This, to me, is a mystery. But it is a safe mystery. There are the best of biblical reasons to believe that through and beyond judgement, we may entertain a maximum degree of hope for creation and humanity within it. We should not downplay the reality of Gehenna, the possibility of 'perdition', of the final and eternal loss of God. But beyond that there is the highest of hopes about what God's promised end will bring.

A strange aspect of Christian belief is that we are more inclined to talk about the negative aspects of eschatology than the positive, that is, about 'hell' rather than 'heaven'. Perhaps this is because we are afraid of giving way to sentimentality or being criticised for 'pie in the sky when you die'. Equally strange is the persistence of vague heavenly beliefs, even in the secular mind. When a child loses a parent or any other close loved one, it is almost irresistible to talk of that person 'going to heaven' rather than facing up to the fact of oblivion. I have lost count of the occasions I have heard people refer to the departed 'looking down on us now'. Is this just a way of appealing to our memories of those we have loved, or is it an example of 'implicit religion', the intuition that there is something beyond death? Equally, it is very common to speak of people being 're-united' in death. In a sense, they are in that they are united in being dead; but is there any more to it than this, the idea of a happy reunion with the departed? Part of me would like to believe this, meeting again with those we have 'loved and lost', and I take seriously those 'near-death' experiences which could point in this direction. Even if these are illusory, some trick of the expiring brain, they are very comforting. There is a point here: even if it is only oblivion that awaits us, to *believe* that there is more, that we will indeed be re-united, might ease our dying, and that is no mean thing for us poor humans. Conversely, I can understand how the expectation of oblivion might be comforting: there is nothing to fear because there is nothing anyway, no judgement, no accounting for our actions, no holy God to confront: when you're dead, you're dead, so enjoy life while it lasts, eat, drink and be merry. Yes, dying might be difficult, but morphine or Dignitas might help. Let's just hope it happens quickly. I believe more than this, but I remain cautious of describing what awaits us in imagined detail and prefer to say simply, 'for me to live is Christ, and to die is gain'. What more than this I anticipate is directed towards the resurrection and the new heaven and new earth in which righteousness dwells; in other words, it is a corporate and holistic hope for nothing less than all things.

Post Nineteen: The God of Jesus Christ

I come at this point, perhaps belatedly, to speak more precisely about God. One question is how to begin to do this, given that God is in every sense beyond human speech and even human imagination. I find it undeniable that there is something inchoate in the depths of all people that might be termed in some sense 'God' or 'divine'. I find this indicated in that from the beginning of the emergence of the race, there is an instinct for 'religion' in some form. There are no human groupings for whom this is not true, though, absolutely, these instincts take a multitude of often contradictory forms, some of them less than wholesome. Even atheists are known to pray in extreme situations, though no doubt this is typically denied or only reluctantly confessed. We find it hard to be wholly 'secular' despite our best efforts, and in fact, that proportion of humanity that claims to be so is a minority usually located in the sections of society most distanced from the realities of nature. I once had a conversation with a fellow of Manchester Business School who pointed out to me that the shape of my own beliefs was the consequence of the context in which I was set. Had I been born into an Islamic society, I would have been a Muslim, not a Christian. This is a perfect example of the 'genetic fallacy', the notion that by identifying the origin of a belief, you undermine its validity. It is a form of 'reductionism' or 'nothing-buttery'. I pointed out to him that the same could be said of himself, that had he been born in an Islamic society, he probably would not have been an atheist. He thought this was a good 'debating point'. I thought it was fatal to his argument – at least in that form. I could have claimed that his own atheism was simply the consequence of inhabiting a deeply secular world and worldview and was 'nothing-but' the product of these. Atheists sometimes claim a privilege for themselves and their beliefs, that they are not subject to the same objections that apply to the rest of us. The appropriate response is 'you too'. Whatever their origin, beliefs of all kinds should be tested for their validity by whatever means are appropriate. The pervasive nature of religious belief leads me to the conclusion that you cannot be wholly and healthily human without a religious dimension or an appropriate equivalent, a belief in something that goes beyond the merely material, that relates itself to value and not only fact, to meaning and not just to stuff. About these, and if we retain a degree of modesty and self-criticism, we can have honourable and respectful discussions. The question then is, what qualifies as such?

For the Christian, there is such a thing as 'true religion'. This refers to both belief and behaviour, things held to be true and behaviour congruent with those beliefs. I once discussed this with a Reform rabbi who insisted that Judaism is not concerned with beliefs but with practices. This suggests that you can have practices that are not rooted in particular ways of construing the world. I have heard others making a similar point – what you do is more important than what you believe. I am quite happy to accept that belief and behaviour are mutually impactful and can be in conflict – if your actions deny what you claim to believe, then you don't really believe what you claim – but find it incoherent to say that you can have one without the other. To believe that the world is a certain way leads, at least logically, to actions that are congruent with such belief. Our belief 'system' requires both that those beliefs be internally consistent and that we can live with them. The decent atheist, to my mind, who believes that the world is purposeless and meaningless, that there is no objective value or morality to be considered, actually and blessedly finds it hard to live out such beliefs in action. This suggests that, since it is hard to live with such beliefs, they are inadequate. If it is replied that it is up to us to create our own meaning (which in many ways we certainly do), the counter-response is that some people find meaning in that which is cruel, destructive, and plainly evil, and the rest of us revolt from it. We do this because there is an even higher meaning that judges our own choices and theirs and is held to be objective. Then, we are back to the rumour of God. There must be a solid foundation for 'the good', and here we are at least veering in the direction of 'God'.

I put the word 'God' in quotation marks because I recognise it to be a 'floating signifier'. It can and does mean different things to different people. Paul is instructive when he says, 'there are many gods and many lords' and then goes on to say, 'yet for us there is one God, the Father, from whom are all things and for whom we exist, and one Lord, Jesus Christ, through whom are all things and through whom we exist' (1 Corinthians 8:5). I particularly like the 'for us' in this sentence because by it, and as both a Jew and a Christian, Paul distinguishes one vision of God from the rest of the field. Whatever instinct towards God is shared among humans, there are divergent pathways that can be taken. In these verses, Paul assuredly does not mean that alternative gods and lords do exist but that human beings fabricate and imagine them and make them the object of their 'ultimate concern' (Tillich); they exist as projections of the religious instinct. They might have good or bad features, and once posited, they possess their own kind of power. But they are not God in the way that Christians think of God, and, with Paul, we distinguish ourselves from them. It has been said that 'God created us in his own image, and we have been returning the compliment ever since'. This still happens as we insist on projecting onto 'God' whatever ideologies currently suit us or seem important to us. I cannot exempt myself from this temptation, but I try to be alert to it.

It is a major challenge to think of God through the lens of revelation, that which arises out of Israel's prophetic experience, and which comes 'for us' to concentrated fulfilment in the person of Jesus Christ, the Word of God: 'Whoever has seen me has seen the Father' (John 14:9). This must inevitably be in the form of a hermeneutical circle. We approach revelation with a set of pre-understandings. We assume some version of the word 'God', and this assumption needs to be tested, purified, and reformed in the light of Christ, our teacher, so passing through the 'narrow

Christological defile' that will lead us to the truth. It is no exaggeration to say that through Christ, we undergo a revolution in our understanding. This happens not so much as we know God through Christ but as we come to be known *by* God through him and enter the experience of the divine life, glory, and communion. Monotheism has come under criticism in more recent years because of its potential alignment with oppressive social systems. This reflects the modern tendency to see everything through the lends of oppressive power rather than gracious love. It is deeply appropriate to speak of a single will undergirding all reality and giving unity to its people, inviting the allegiance of every mind and heart. I am persuaded, following the historian of thought John Gray, that even those atheisms that deny the reality of God do, for the most part, still follow the patterns of thought that monotheism instils within us. Monotheism is a hard act to shed. Where it is fully and completely overcome, I shudder to think what the nihilistic consequences might be. As already argued, to be left to construct meaning simply on our own leaves the door entirely open to the worst of possible alternatives. In similar ways, polytheism can simply not be a wholesome and generous diversity but the fracturing of human existence into warring and destructive tribalism.

The heart of the Christian faith is the conviction that the one God has revealed God's own self in history through the story of Israel and its fulfilment in Jesus Christ and in the gift of the Holy Spirit to the church. It is in this Trinitarian history of God that the Christian vision of God is made known. The vision of the unity of God arises out of biblical Judaism as modified and re-envisioned through the risen Christ. This vision is rooted in experience, not speculation. At no point does the Bible set out to prove the existence of God. This is because confession of the reality of God is not a product of philosophical argument but of revelation and encounter. This does not deny the role of stringent argument in explicating and defending such a belief once arrived at. But it is to claim that belief in God, especially of God as triune, is derived from the fact that God breaches the boundary between heaven and earth, between the visible and the invisible worlds to come to us. 'I will be your God, and you will be my people'. The story of scripture is the story of God with us and God for us. Against this, philosophical debate remains cold and uninspiring. A large part of me identifies with the claim that for many Christians, 'your God is too small'. When God is imagined as simply a very much larger version of ourselves, we are in grave danger of blasphemy or triviality. There is truth in the belief that God cannot be spoken of directly but only indirectly, by means of negation rather than affirmation. God is the mystery of the world and exceeds our descriptive or imaginative capacities: 'O the depths of the riches and wisdom and knowledge of God! How unsearchable are his judgements and inscrutable his ways!' (Romans 11:33). The 'apophatic' approach to God that questions the capacity of our language to 'capture' God is surely right. We can know God truly, but we can never truly know what it is *to be God*. I can understand, therefore, the revolt against 'localised' and excessively anthropological thought forms that risk diminishing God to levels we can grasp and perhaps even control. I appreciate the logic of thought advanced by John Hick that sees all the religions as circulating around a central reality that he first described as 'God', and then fearing that even this might be too Christian, as 'the Real'. If this is an attempt to transcend a restrictive localism, I grasp it. Unfortunately, it leaves us nowhere, or more precisely, lost in an abstraction that cannot do anything for us. It is unappealing to most religious traditions that have more character to them than such abstract and obscure ideas allow. The construction leaves us with something vague, uninspiring, and essentially unknowable, rendering God a 'giant ineffable Whatsit'. It is hard to find the warmth of love in this. It is impersonal and cries out for something more. This leads me back, therefore, to the language of revelation, the narrative of encounter with God, the God who meets is in a particular history and self-revelation and so becomes apprehensible to us. Whatever its dangers of making God too small, too anthropological, the prophetic word enables us to relate to the One who, even in revelation, remains a mystery to us. We are known by this God who made us, loves us, and comes to us. I severely doubt whether Hick's concept of 'the Real' finds any extensive acceptance in the particular religious traditions because it exists apart from them all. An impersonal abstraction cannot be love because love is an activity of persons towards persons. The reality of revelation takes time to apprehend and even longer to understand, hence the several centuries of Christian history and debate that preceded the formulations of the Nicene-Constantinopolitan Creed, to which I firmly adhere. Life in the resurrection power of Christ was clearly a reality from the church's beginning, but finding the words to express it of necessity took time. It troubles me not at all that formulating appropriate understandings of Christ and the Spirit and then fashioning the word 'Trinity' to encapsulate the history of the one God's self-revelation as Father, Son, and Spirit involved the corralling of a non-scriptural word (Trinity). What I do question is the extent to which the historical drama into which Christians enter when they come in Christ to participate in the life of God can be turned into an esoteric debate about the inner life of God. This threatens to become an area of abstract metaphysical reasoning that drifts away from the biblical narrative. It is more secure to celebrate the fact that in the self-donation of the one God in a three-fold movement of Father, Son and Spirit, as witnessed by scripture, it is the very life of God we experience. Through Christ, we have access to the Father by one Spirit.

If this offends 'reason', then so be it. Reason is the handmaid to revelation, not an autonomous power that can stand in judgement over it. Its task is not to dictate to God what God must be but to attend to God's self-revelation and follow it where it leads. Religion within the limits of reason alone can only be a form of hubris that ascribes to the powers of human intelligence more than they can bear, in the theological realm more than any other. I like the words of the rabbi who said something like, 'I don't want to believe in a God I can understand since that would make me God'. Yet, it does not stretch my imagination too far that there should be in God a 'differentiated unity', a unity that internally contains distinction. This is surely true of the very basic phenomenon of space, which is one but is formed by height, length, and breadth. Something can be one and yet three at the same time. In another way, it is true of light, which, when passed through a prism, breaks down beautifully and astonishingly into the colours of the spectrum. Who would have imagined this did we not know the reality of its happening? Admittedly the latter example would serve my argument more conveniently were there not seven colours but only three! But it does serve to demonstrate that a unity can be internally differentiated. This is what we see in the reality of revelation. Karl Barth derived this from the very idea of revelation in distinguishing between the Revealed (the Father), the Revelation (the Son) and Revealedness (the Spirit). As well as satisfying my appreciation of three-fold arguments, it provided, and provides a coherent structure for a creedal or confessional statement (as for example the 'Apostles Creed') and for a systematic theology. This is because it conforms to the Christian experience of revelation, illumination, and salvation. A crucial insight I gained from my early study of Barth's theology, and which still guides me, is that the way God has revealed God's own self in history is the way in which God is 'antecedently within himself'. Hence, God's triunity is not God assuming three different 'masks' for the sake of revelation in time but the way God is in God's own self in eternity. The 'economic Trinity' reveals the 'ontological Trinity'. This is an inescapable conclusion if we believe that God has truly revealed God's own self and not just assumed a temporary appearance for the sake of convenience. To assert the latter is to say that there is no such thing as revelation; God is simply hidden. The church has consequently always been right to reject 'Modalistic Monarchianism' and unitarianism. The vision and the reality are richer.

What I do find more problematic intellectually is giving an account of how the 'threeness' of God is a threeness of persons, not just dimensions. One difficulty is that the doctrine becomes misconstrued as a conjunction of three 'individuals' and so veers towards tritheism, as both Judaism and Islam point out critically. Conversely, the unity of God can sound like there is a divine substance out of which Father, Son and Spirit extrude, leaving us with more of a Quaternity than a Trinity. It is surely better to see the Father as the 'fount and origin' of deity, but then the temptation to conceive the Son as a subordinate deity and the Spirit as a third begins, at least in some minds, to jeopardise the equality of the persons. Questions like this lead to metaphysical speculation about God's inner life, about which I am cautious. I think I have understood Karl Barth correctly in believing that the expression of God as both fount of deity and also second and third should not be thought to jeopardise the equality of the persons in essential deity. It is in the freedom of God to be second and so to express the divine humility which is common to the three persons. I am inclined towards theological modesty at this point and to refer again to the idea that though we may know God, we can never know what it is to be God. What we can do, however, is share existentially and ontologically in the life of God though Christ into which we are drawn by the Spirit and in which, at each point, we are truly participating in God who is one. We don't meet with different 'gods' but with the God who is one at each point, with one will, purpose and consciousness. As indicated, the formula that through Christ we have access to the Father through one Spirit is one I find satisfying as an expression of participating in God's life. We have been made to share in the divine nature. I do not deny the importance of the trinitarian debates, which have concerned themselves with the ideas of an 'eternally begotten' Son or a Spirit who 'proceeds from the Father' but see them as attempts to make much out of little. I can also see sense in claiming that it is the Son who constitutes the Father's eternal being as Father (which therefore enhances the Son's status as one who 'constitutes' the Father's deity). To this, I can further appreciate the enhancement of the Spirit's status as one who, following the reasoning that proceeds from the economic to the ontological, sees the Son as 'eternally begotten of the Father through the Spirit'. But neither can I escape the feeling that we may be getting above ourselves. The existential reality to which I return is that worship is owed to the Father, Son and Holy Spirit, and it is from this that our theological formulas are to be derived. It is well recognised that in this, we employ the category of 'persons' because we have to say something rather than nothing. But I am also confident that without some such language, we cannot speak of God as love. The personhood of the 'three-personed' God is, to my mind crucial to the faith and to the belief that it is in this that our ultimate destiny lies. Unlike, for instance, Buddhism, which seeks the negation or absorption of the self into a higher state that takes us beyond the dissatisfactions of personal (and so suffering) existence, Christians look forward to becoming truly and fully personal in a divinely graced community of unsullied togetherness. Perhaps this is what attaining to the 'image of God' finally means.

There is a point at which discussion of God's essential and eternal deity becomes very important, despite my cautionary words. Many years ago, I was somewhat drawn to the movement known as Restorationism. During my interest, I attended a seminar at Bradford 'House Church' led by one of the foremost early teachers in that movement, Alan Vincent. Alan took up a theme that was very current in the early movement (1970s-80s) and that concerned 'superordination' and 'subordination' (or submission). In its defence, this impetus was a reaction to a perceived lack of order and discipline within the church and was intended to remedy it. The logic was that within God's own being, there was an order in which the Father was over the Son and both Son and Spirit owed submission to the Father. The appeal was made to Christology, the way in which, in his earthly existence, the Son gave obedience to the Father, an obedience that was an insight into the eternal and prior relationship of the Father and the Son in the eternal Trinity. The further logic then followed that in the marriage relationship, wives should submit to their husbands and in the churches members should submit to their elders. Elders, in turn, should submit to 'apostles', that is, recognised external figures resembling (though the connection was not made) bishops, who in turn functioned collegially in a form of mutual accountability to other apostles. All those who were considered superordinate were, of course, male. Quite rightly, this schema was considered by many to be problematic for various reasons. I was among those who criticised it, particularly in my early book, *The Radical Kingdom*. Its claim was that it gave substance to the Lordship of Christ, conceived of as a series of 'delegated authorities'. Though I could see that the intention was to fashion orderly churches and to develop patterns of accountability across the board, what seemed to me to be wrong was its fixation with power and its exercise. In the event there were examples of the misuse of power by people placed in positions of authority who had neither the wisdom nor the maturity to make it work humanely. It buttressed patriarchy and turned the church into a power structure over and beyond anything else. Again, in its defence, this was to do little more than what some much more traditional church structures have done for a long time, notably the

Roman Catholic church with is hierarchical patterns of 'sacred power'. My observation is that those Restorationist churches which have survived have attenuated their original ideology, partly as the original and influential leaders have died or diverted into other pathways. I acknowledge that my own ecclesiology has been shaped by these early engagements, both in the learning of some points and the rejection of others. However, the fundamental mistake was to conceive of the Trinity in hierarchical terms as super- or subordination, which gave rise to the justification of a hierarchical church. Above all and in distinction, the divine Trinity and the church that participates in the divine life should be understood as a community of mutually self-giving love immersed in the power of love, not the love of power.

Unlike others, however, I do not have a knee-jerk reaction whenever the idea of hierarchy emerges, as though it were one of those words out of *The Devil's Own Dictionary*. Hierarchies, in some forms are justifiable and necessary, not to say intrinsic. I do not share the instinctive anarchism that I see in some others. However, the crucial and entirely theologically healthy shift is towards understanding the Trinity as primarily the communion of love, not a pattern of power, and authority is the authority of love. Biblically, especially following the Gospel of John, the persons of the Trinity indwell each other in a way that should lead us to prioritise mutuality and self-giving relationship in freedom. If there is a pattern for the churches and for human life in general, this is it.

There is a kind of ideological programme that deliberately sets out to find a legitimating model for democratic social existence and fashions its doctrine of God in its own image. I am critical of this method since, through it, we make God what we want or need God to be. However, to participate in the life of God is to share in relationships that exert a gravitational pull and draw us (or at least me) towards communal images of the church rather than hierarchical ones and, within society at large, democratic rather than authoritarian forms of society. I am suspicious of the temptation, even my own, to create God in our own image and make God serve our purposes rather than the other way round. I identify within the relational doctrine of God not a hierarchy but a sense of order. The Father is the fount and origin of deity; the Son is eternally begotten of the Father, and the Father is also the source of the eternal Spirit, as the creeds affirm. None of this points to an origin of the Son and Spirit in time since they are, as God, eternal. Yet there is an order or internal economy of a triune kind, and this does not jeopardise the equality of the persons. Equality and subordination are not mutually antagonistic when at the service of love. The same should be said of order within the churches and society. There are such things as hierarchies of competence and of responsibility that enable life to function, and they are to be welcomed and supported for this reason. They are not inimical to equality in so far as they are accountable and are embedded in a theological culture of service and a civilisation of love. To pretend that there is no validity in 'power' is nonsense. The challenge is to ensure that all power is at the service of love.

I realise that in the discussion above, I have not entirely encompassed the *mysterium tremendum et fascinans* identified by Rudolf Otto in his seminal work, *The Idea of the Holy*. Christian as he was, Otto nonetheless was able to identify an experience that is widely shared by those of religious inclination, that of being awed and overwhelmed by a transcendent power to which we owe reverence and honour. At the same time, we are drawn to this power because it attracts and delights us. This surely is at the heart of the worship of God and is far from being confined to Christians. It is true to say that even those who are not theists may know the experience. Otto's insight resonates forcefully with scripture; Isaiah 6 narrates Isaiah's vision in the temple of the Lord 'high and lifted up' and of the angelic host singing, 'holy, holy, holy'. He is struck dumb and with a sense of being a 'man of unclean lips', before then being cleansed and commissioned as a prophet. Most significantly, in Luke 10:21, we have a rare glimpse into Jesus himself at worship when he 'rejoiced in the Holy Spirit and said, I thank you, Father, Lord of Heaven and earth'. This is a beautiful expression of both the transcendent and the immanent, of the God who is way beyond us, yet as Father is wonderfully close. The sense of transcendent majesty makes most sense to those who find within it inklings of the meaning of things, the idea of a coherent purpose that grants added depth to the material creation in all its immensity, and most of all, the notion that we might actually be wanted and loved by the benevolent power that is behind all powers.

Cynics who have contempt for the Christian faith sometimes characterise our God as the 'Invisible Magic Friend'. More thoughtfully, it has been said that the 'new American religion' is a 'moralistic therapeutic deism'. God is thought of as one who provides therapeutic benefits to adherents without the need for repentance from sin and a call to live as servants of a divine Sovereign. The criticisms come all too close, and I certainly sometimes feel we are in danger of trivialising God. Perhaps even the picture I have painted above of the triune divine communion in which we share has its dangers, presenting God as a kind of comfortable 'wrap around deity'. Once more, we hop from to foot lest in saying one thing, we leave another unsaid. The God of Abraham, Isaac and Jacob, who is also the Father of our Lord Jesus Christ, is infinitely above us, the 'immortal, invisible God only wise'. To this end, images both of height and depth are entirely appropriate in casting our vision of God. I am cautious about speaking of God as a 'being', even as the 'supreme Being', since this can sound as though God happens to be one being among others and of the same order, only bigger. To think of God so is to come near to idolatry, the antidote to which is to affirm unambiguously that God is not within the system but external to it, the source of all its beings and the giver of being itself. This is the assertion of monotheism, and we owe it to our biblical Jewish heritage. Learning to speak properly of God is a challenge. I find help here in the 'Credo' of Jonathan Sacks: 'I believe that the idea that the universe was created in love by the God of love who asks us to create in love is the noblest hypothesis ever to have lifted the human mind'.[44] Equally helpful to me are words by Rowan Williams: 'The God I believe in is not an object inside the universe, not a being among others, but an energy and action of love and intelligence that saturates everything, that is the source of everything, that sustains everything moment by moment, that is always in the depth of every situation capable of turning things around and making a difference precisely because this God is not just part of the system but the context of it all.'[45] Here, we are at least tending in the right direction.

Do I know these things to be true? This depends on how we understand knowledge. I am happy to say that I believe them probably to be true. In this age, absolute knowledge escapes us and all knowledge, even of material things, is provisional, always subject to revision. There is a kind of knowing that Christians call 'assurance', an inner welling up of spiritual affirmation inspired by the Spirit. I certainly experience this periodically. When Jane Fonda became a Christian, she expressed it nicely: 'I felt a presence, a reverence humming within me. It was and is difficult to articulate.' This is different from objective certainty. Yet, there can be confidence that we are on the right track and that hope will not disappoint us. Objectively speaking, the truth of God awaits eschatological verification, and consequently, present faith always has the feeling of risk.

---

[44] Sacks, *The Great Partnership*, p.288.
[45] In a conversation with Gay Byrne in 2015.

Post Twenty: Faith, The Faith, and Other Faiths

I move on to some reflections on the position of the Christian faith in relation to other faith traditions. This has been very much a concern in recent decades and, throughout my lifetime, has been extensively explored. I find the discussion enjoyable rather than fraught. The questions have become more acute as engagement with other religions has become inevitable, and they are less easy to characterise as ignorance and delusion. I begin my version with certain broad-brush statements that general though they may be, are bound to shape, possibly even determine, my overall conclusions. I have already aired various understandings to which I hold fast firmly. The first is that God has created, cares for and wills the salvation of all people. Unlike some therefore, I am not anxious to close the door on salvation for others, particularly when I believe myself to be 'in the fold' of those who are confident of God's grace. It is distasteful to me to believe in my own salvation while intellectually giving reasons why others must be excluded. I do indeed hold open the possibility of final loss, as I have clarified; but if this happens, it is clear that this is against every effort of the God of love to rescue people from themselves. Nobody is lost by accident or because they happen to be in the wrong place or time, but only by dint of finally resist the grace of God made known in Christ both in this world and in worlds to come. I have explained, therefore, that for reasons of justice and in the light of God's will to save, the arc of salvation cannot be confined to this life but must reach beyond it. Death need not be a boundary beyond which people cannot be saved. One of the many tensions in the Christian faith, another 'cognitive dissonance', is that between the very particularity of Christ's incarnation and work and the universality of the need for salvation, the so-called 'scandal of particularity'. In affirming incarnation, the Christian faith is certainly particular, just as is Judaism in locating God's revelation in a given people's history. But according to John, 'God did not send the Son into the world to condemn the world, but in order that the world might be saved through him' (3:17). We are forbidden, therefore, to see the means of God's salvation as in itself an obstruction to God's will to save. Given that many have not known and cannot know of Christ ('those who have never heard'), or if they do hear, only hear a distorted version of the gospel, how do we come to terms with the fact that billions of those whom God loves and wills to save lie or have lain beyond the 'sound of the gospel'? I make the seemingly 'exclusive' affirmations that there is no salvation apart from Christ and that there is no salvation apart from repentance. I have, therefore, to reconcile these statements with the universality of God's love and grace and the hope for final salvation.

As it happens, I don't find this too difficult. For a start, I believe that in his saving work, Christ has 'made intercession for sinners' (Isaiah 53 et al.), and this is all-inclusive: nobody is excluded from this intercession since all are sinners. This is the definitive expression of the will of God. I find it inconceivable that this intercession should go unheeded. It is, after all, Christ who interceded, the Christ who is God's only and beloved Son and in whose name, when we pray, we are assured that 'it will be done for you'. Furthermore, the glorified Lord 'always lives to make intercession for them' (Hebrews 7:25). I grant that this verse may be understood in more restrictive ways, but it can equally have wider application. Our prayers may be defective since our wills are not wholly aligned to the will of God; but this cannot be said about God's Son. All humanity is to be viewed from this point of orientation. Christ's work is sufficient for the salvation of all since his work is God's work for us. This is true whether a person knows of that work or not. It is safe to believe that when someone prays for me, I am likely to benefit even when I do not know prayer has been offered. Yet it is the purpose of God that all *should* know and should be placed in a position to respond to God with repentance and faith. Response to the message is plainly not universally possible for reasons that have been partly identified: some (very many) die too soon to be capable of knowledge and response. Others are never presented with the gospel or are mentally incapable of acknowledging it, and so on. Two propositions might follow from this: The God who wills salvation may be understood to be at work beyond the boundaries of the covenanted communities of Judaism and the Christian church. These acts of God have sometimes been characterised as 'uncovenanted mercies'. It is surely inevitable that we think of God at work throughout the world and in all corners of humankind, even if we only conceive this in terms of providence and preservation or even of general revelation. The proposition here goes beyond this in asserting the possibility and reality of salvation, not just preservation. God has 'other peoples', and this is a theme that can be well-established from scripture. My second proposition, already aired in what I have written above, is that God's search for the lost reaches beyond death and is not to be confined to this life only. This is the outcome of God's universal love and God's universal justice that are destined to put all things right.

Having asserted that salvation comes through Christ alone and through his intercession for sinners, I also affirmed that it does not come without repentance and faith. Grace is not cheap, and neither does it evade the challenge of reception. Salvation reaches its goal as it is realised through the Spirit in the gift of personal faith, either in this life or the next. In some sense, therefore, even in another life beyond this one, God's grace has to be received, and human beings remain responsible for its reception. Certain texts, as well as my understanding of the universal divine intentions in salvation, point in this direction. One such is Romans 2:6-11: 'For (God) will repay according to each one's deeds; to those who by patiently doing good seek for glory and honour and immortality, he will give eternal life; while for those who are self-seeking and who obey not the truth but wickedness, there will be wrath and fury. There will be anguish and distress for everyone who does evil, the Jew first and also the Greek, but glory and honour and peace for everyone who does good, the Jew first and also the Greek. For God shows no partiality'. Also significant is the conversion of Cornelius and his household, recorded in Acts 10. Cornelius is described (before his conversion) as an 'upright and God-fearing man' (v.22), and once the Spirit is conferred, Peter declares (v.34): 'I truly understand that God shows no partiality, but in every nation, anyone who fears him and does what is right is acceptable to him'. I could draw attention to other texts, but these suffice to make my point that there is 'salvation' outside the walls of the church, in the sense that there are those who are of good standing with God and will be vindicated at the final judgement. The old dictum 'outside the church, there is no salvation' might be better re-phrased as 'outside salvation, there is no church' (as Moltmann has suggested). Salvation is wider than the confessing church. Granted that this might lead us to reconsider what is meant by 'salvation', these texts question whether the easy equation 'all who are in the church are saved; all who are outside the church are damned' is too simple to fit reality, or even the biblical testimony. Paul indicates this possibility when he writes, 'When Gentiles, who do not possess the law, do instinctively what the law requires, these, though not having the law, are a law into themselves. They show that what the law requires is written on their hearts to which their own conscience bears witness; and their conflicting thoughts will accuse or perhaps excuse them when, according to my gospel, God, through Jesus Christ, will judge the secret thoughts of all' (Romans 2:14-16). Pauls' words here fall, at the very least, into the category of 'studied agnosticism' but perhaps point to more. I also find an interesting nuance in John 1:10-13, '(The Word) was in the world, and the world came into being through him. He came to what was his own, and his own people did not accept him. But to all who received him, who believed in his name, he gave the right to become children of God'. If 'coming to his own' means coming in incarnation to the people of Israel (as I suggest is the typical assumption), the alternatives of rejection or reception are firmly placed within the historical narrative of Israel and the church. The verses, alternatively, are capable of the interpretation that 'coming to his own' means coming to the world he has made in grace in a wider sense than incarnation and not being received, except by some who, therefore, become children of God. Incarnation is, therefore, an intensification of what is always happening: God coming to people through the pre-existent Word by whom all things have been made. Incarnation represents the furthest point to which God has come. This widens the discussion to suggest that in the world of humanity at large, Christ is seeking those who are lost and being both rejected and received (if only by some). The Israel-church account is, therefore, an instance of what Father, Son and Spirit are about synchronically and diachronically throughout the world. This is a much more expansive vision of what we might hope for and of how we should understand 'salvation'. Present salvation in the church is not wholly defined by the binary, forensic outcome of heaven or hell; the focus is rather on the transfer from 'the kingdom of darkness to the kingdom of God's beloved Son'. It is about becoming a participant in the messianic community, of which the sign is the gift of the Holy Spirit. This is eternal life. Those who are presently outside this kingdom are indeed lost in that they are estranged from what should be theirs. But this is not to say that they are not and will not be acceptable to God in the final judgement when the secrets of all hearts are discovered. It might be believed that, like Cornelius, they would recognise the fulfilment of the gospel in Christ when they learn of it. Or it may be that we need to suspend judgement, as surely we do in the light of what Paul says about Israel in Romans 9-11, pending a future resolution of what is currently problematic to us. I have no difficulty in living with such ambiguities, not least because I believe in a God who is righteous and does and will do, what is right. I can live productively with the cognitive dissonance. I like the words of H. Richard Niebuhr: 'Men are generally right in what they affirm and wrong in what they deny.'

In any case, it is, to my mind, undeniable that there are righteous and good people in abundance outside the church, both in other religious traditions and outside them. I hope for them. I have known some of them. I can acknowledge that there are good things to be learnt in those traditions and can attribute them to the gracious God who has not given up on humanity, resisting its evil implacably though God may. Yet I am not a 'pluralist' as are those who believe that all paths lead up the mountain in the same direction. This underplays the differences between the religions in that those other paths offer different things and have different aims, which are not identical. It is a kind of imperialism to insist they all result in the same thing. In other words, pluralism is not pluralist enough because it skates over the differing aims of those religions. There is greater integrity in recognising the starkness of this fact and allowing difference to be difference. It is, in fact, disrespectful to argue that, after all, despite the differences, they all offer the same thing, against what they claim. This does not lead me to consign all other religions to heathen darkness. I do not believe that we are saved by religion. I do not even believe that we are saved by the Christian religion, which, speaking in historical terms, I acknowledge contains a mixture of truth and error, like the other religions. Rather, 'salvation is of the Lord'. If Christian faith properly understood makes it clear that we do not find our way to God, but God makes a way to us, supremely in Christ, then I fully believe that God makes God's own gracious way to others not because and by means of other religions but largely despite them. They are not a final barrier to God's power to save. Scripture itself bears witness to what some have called the 'noble pagan' or the righteous Gentile and contains more than enough to point in the direction of a generous and inclusive hope for salvation.[46] But let me reassert there is no salvation except through Christ and with repentance. In his life, atoning death and resurrection, he has become an exemplary human who allows us to believe that humanity can be redeemed. He stands in the gap and continues to intercede for us. Yes, this is a deeply Christian perspective, and it is one that I do not seek to hide or mitigate in dialogue with others for the sake of politeness. I am content if those others are equally up front about their own claims to superiority, which is the actual reality of things. After all, we all make such claims: even the pluralist is claiming to understand things others do not and to have a better perspective. The more important point is whether our theologies allow us to hope for each other even beyond the disagreements.

A key debate in this discussion surrounds John 14:6, 'Jesus said to them, "I am the way, and the truth, and the life. No one comes to the Father except through me"'. This amply sets out the crucial and exclusive place of Jesus within the purpose of redemption. Its particularity is not to be evaded. But as with other verses it is capable of an expansive meaning. For some, it implies that conscious and deliberate confession of Christ is essential for salvation. But it might be read the other way round: where among human beings we find truth, and spiritual life and knowledge of the Father, wherever this

---

[46] I have found Gerald O'Collins, SJ, a pleasingly Protestant Jesuit theologian, helpful on this and on other matters: *Salvation for All: God's Other Peoples* (Oxford: OUP, 2008).

may be, it is there because Christ has already been present and active, even if unknown by name. Even more acutely, because Christ is the way, the truth, and the life, he alone, and no one else, has the right and authority to decide on people's destiny in this life or any other.

If what I write is coherent it accentuates the question of what is meant by salvation. There is the hope for final salvation, which, if what I have outlined is true, will be known when the secrets of all hearts are known. I expect this to exceed expectations. But what is it that Christians claim for themselves when they give testimony to having been made alive or saved in the present? I have puzzled here as to what those who live under the new covenant have as a possession which was not true of those under the old. By extension, what do they have that goes beyond the righteous among the Gentiles? My answer is Pentecost. In the outpouring of the Spirit, the future has entered the present. The church is, therefore, the messianic community in which the power of the eschatological age, the world to come, becomes a present reality, creating as it does so a new humanity in which the barriers of the old age are transcended in a new spiritual community that is unique. To be saved is to 'have tasted the heavenly gift, and have shared in the Holy Spirit, and have tasted the goodness of the word of God, and the powers of the age to come' (Hebrews 6:4-5). This is no mean gift, and it is in advance of what had previously been known. When Cornelius, 'a devout man who feared God with all his household (Acts 10:2), heard the gospel, believed it, and received the Holy Spirit, he entered salvation in its eschatological form. When the gospel is preached, it is not only to awaken the depraved to the possibility of new life but also to bring the Spirit to those who already fear God but have not entered the full possession of the messianic fulfilment in Christ.

I enter a relevant note here about the relationship between the Christian faith and Judaism. It is beyond doubt that the Christian faith has emerged from biblical Judaism and extends its understanding of God. Denying this fact is a primary heresy such as was advanced by Marcion, the first heresy to be positively rejected (though Gnosticism came a close second). Marcion believed that the god of the Old Testament was not the same as the God of the New. Similar things continue to be said or implied in mistaken and disparaging references to 'the God of the Old Testament'. I have no doubt that there is something profoundly creative about synthesising the multiple images of God that appear across the biblical writings. But, the assertion that there is one God known in both dispensations is crucial for a Christian vision of God. Contemporary Judaism is not a parent to Christianity since it, too, has descended from the same sources, although with significantly different horizons. Christians and Jews are like cousins. And paradoxically, it is Christianity rather than Judaism that has carried forward some of the ancient sources and our understanding of 'Second Temple Judaism', such as the division into the parties of Pharisees, and Sadducees. Whereas Judaism preserved itself after the destruction of the Temple in AD70 by doubling-down on the rabbinic traditions of the interpretation and application of the Torah, Christians found the fulfilment of the covenant expectations embodied in Jesus as Messiah rather than in a text. This led in time to a parting of the ways, sometimes tragically with bad blood and grievance, as is evident in some of the New Testament accounts that are reckoned as anti-Jewish. To balance this out, I consider the pain and distress the early believers in Jesus must have experienced in finding themselves rejected by Jewish communities. The responsibility is on both sides. On the one hand, Jewish communities would have found themselves threatened by the Christian strategy of 'to the Jew first and then to the Gentile'. No pastor today likes it when church members are drawn away to some other sect that comes into town! On the other hand, to be thrust out of Judaism would have exposed the early Christians to social and political dangers. After a millennia-long and unhappy continuation of these early hostilities, a degree of rapprochement has begun to emerge post-Holocaust with statements of regret and repentance by Christians for anti-Judaism and for anti-Semitism, and on the Jewish side with a greater appreciation of Jesus of Nazareth as a son of Israel. On both parts, the Jewishness of Jesus has come much more into focus. Fundamental differences remain and are unlikely to be overcome, although Christians will cling to what Paul holds open in Romans 9-11. What Jews fear is the possible erasure of Jewish identity potentially implied for them in 'replacement theory' and 'supersessionism'. In respectable theological circles, these are now regarded as unacceptable. I have struggled to disentangle the issues at stake here. I find it easier to dismiss replacement theory if this means that with the advent of Christianity, the people of Israel no longer count in the divine purpose. It is clear to me that this cannot be the case given the hope of a final restoration and joining of Jews and Gentiles in the Messiah that Paul envisions in Romans 9-11. For it to happen, the Jewish people are to be preserved and, indeed, have been preserved against all the odds to the present day. I regard this preservation of the people as theologically significant. Some have even regarded it as a proof of the existence of God. Others understand the return to the land and the founding of the state of Israel as a fulfilment of prophecy. It is striking that there are resonances in this belief in the ancient scriptures upon which it is possible to draw. I do not follow this train of thought myself, but do believe the state of Israel can be understood as a 'sign of the sign'. I mean by this that the continuing existence of the Jewish people, wherever they are scattered, is the real sign of the purpose and covenant faithfulness of the God of Israel. The state of Israel is a sign that the *people* continue to exist and to await their destiny without itself being a direct fulfilment of prophecy. And all of this should be set in the context of a hope for all the nations, not just Israel alone. Israel will not be excluded from the favour God wills to show to all the nations. Christians are internationalists. I reject, therefore, the idea that Israel, the people of the Abrahamic covenant, can be replaced. I see rather that Israel's destiny is one that is open to all the nations.

How does this impact supersessionism? I have more difficulty grasping this. It is clear to me that in Christ something new has come into being and that this takes us beyond ancient Israel's religion in both belief and practice. In its self-understanding, the Christian faith goes beyond biblical Judaism. What has come to be in the Christian church is the fulfilment of exactly those hopes and expectations that are contained in Israel's scriptures. To deny this is surely to deny Christianity and reduce it to a species of reformed Judaism. But there is much to be gained from positive, constructive conversation between Christians and Jews.

Nigel G. Wright

Post Twenty-One: The Obedience of Faith

It has long struck me that there is a confusion of terms associated with the entry into faith. Frequently used is the language of 'becoming a Christian', which, though understandable given that followers of Christ are Christians, may have the effect of confusing a cultural condition with the essence of faith. A messianic Jewish believer, for instance, might want to avoid the term if it is held to imply adopting a Gentile identity in preference to a Jewish one. I do know some who no longer call themselves Christians for this reason, although they continue to be devout believers in Jesus as Saviour. The language of 'being saved' seems to be out of favour, possibly because it is too punctiliar and does not stress the ongoing dimension of 'I am being saved', and the future one of 'I will be saved'. There is also the objective reality that we were actually 'saved' two thousand years ago. Perhaps there is also a reluctance in line with the above discussion to restrict the circle of the saved prematurely. I have always valued the language of 'conversion' since it stresses the fact of turning to God initially and then of being turned to God existentially (appropriate in the case of those who can't point to a day or hour when this began), The language of 'being born again' is also out of favour, perhaps because of over-use at certain points of recent history and the American overtones it has gathered to itself. All these terms can be biblically supported, of course. A more objective term that is, perhaps, coming back into favour is simply to refer to having been baptised, which is the sign of entry into the faith. It is said that in resisting doubts and hesitations, Luther used to find a place to stand by saying, 'I have been baptised'. But this has its dangers in that it could underplay active, personal faith in favour of formal ritual. I have noted that in some parts of the world, especially in Eastern Europe, the preference is to refer to the time when a person 'repented'. Similarly it would be possible to speak of having become a disciple, though the danger here would be in overlooking the regenerating grace of God that makes discipleship a possibility.

Almost never does anyone refer to being 'justified'. This may be because it is perceived as a forensic rather than a relational term. Yet its suppression might still be thought strange given the prominence of this term in the theology of the apostle Paul, in its revitalisation by the Reformer Martin Luther, and in the very identity of Protestant and evangelical Christianity. I hear less preaching these days on texts such as, 'For by grace you have been saved through faith, and this is not your own doing; it is the gift of God – not the result of works, so that no one may boast' (Ephesians 2:8-9). To a degree, our understanding of justification has been questioned in recent scholarship through the 'new interpretation of Paul'. This aims to rescue the doctrine from its forensic Lutheran framework of salvation by grace through faith rather than by acquired merit. In this perspective, Luther was reading scripture through the lens of his own struggle with medieval Catholicism which stressed the acquisition of merit as the path to acceptance by God. Luther allegedly read the Old Testament as teaching the acquisition of merit through the law in contrast with the gospel, which proclaimed salvation through grace by faith alone. To my mind the new perspective is correct at two points. The first is that the question Paul (rather than Luther) was wrestling with was not only 'how can I be saved from condemnation?' but 'who belongs to the people of God and on what basis?' Is it based on outward markers such as circumcision (the 'law') or on the inward transformation through faith in Christ? Faith in Christ vastly expands who may be considered to belong to the people of God, a cause deeply important for Paul. (The whole discussion is complicated by the several ways in which Paul uses the word 'law'). The second point where the new perspective hits the mark is that the Old Testament does not teach salvation by works but is at one with the New Testament in teaching salvation by grace through faith. If works of obedience come in, it is in maintaining the undeserved covenant God has freely made with Israel and walking in obedience to it. Communion with God is maintained by the obedience of faith, as it is in the New Testament. I do not see, therefore, that the 'new perspective' abolishes the fact that salvation comes by grace through faith. Hebrew scripture expressly denies that divine election is based upon anything other than divine affection and purpose (Deuteronomy 7:7-11). If I have an objection to how the doctrine of justification has been shaped in the tradition, it is that its articulation has taken an overly forensic or legal form. This is not inappropriate if the intention is to stress the stability and security of our relationship with God: these are safeguarded, so to speak, on a legal and unshakable basis. The inner reality of justification, however, is relational rather than forensic. It has to do with being accepted by God in forgiveness as God's own beloved children. In this regard, I have found the formula used by Paul Tillich very helpful: 'Justification means accepting that I am accepted by God even while continuing to find myself unacceptable'.

I do believe that there needs to be some re-engineering of the doctrine of justification by faith. One aspect of it is to incorporate the insights of the 'new perspective' while not losing the traditional importance of the doctrine for evangelical theology. Indeed, while I fully welcome any renewed emphasis on Christian discipleship, it does concern me to a degree that this might place the emphasis on human effort rather than the abundance of God's grace that precedes it (another of those areas where we need to hop from one foot to the other to maintain the proper tension). The greater concern, however, is that justification can be, and certainly has been, construed as cheap grace. Some memories come to mind. I once watched a dramatic sketch in which several candidates for heaven turned up at St Peter's door with a claim to be allowed in. The first several candidates were all able to point to their records of right living and honourable deeds but were turned away emphatically because they didn't have the right faith credentials. A final candidate had lived poorly and without righteousness, but having at some point towards the end of their life confessed Jesus as Lord, they were enthusiastically welcomed in. I was dubious about the morality of this presentation, not because I failed to believe in God's willingness to forgive the repentant sinner but because I could not see that right living and honourable deeds could be so easily dismissed in favour of what sounded like cheap grace. More reflection was called for, not least on Matthew 25 and much that is found in the teaching of Jesus. It is not saying 'Lord, Lord' that matters but doing the will of God. A second memory is of a discussion about closer ecumenical relations with Catholics in which a participant denied that Roman Catholics could be 'saved' because 'they did not believe in justification by faith'. This struck me as convoluted precisely because it is not believing in the doctrine that is supposed to save but faith in Christ to which it points: you can have faith in Christ without articulating a doctrine of justification by faith. Paradoxically, therefore, the statement is a denial of the meaning of the doctrine. A third cluster of memories concerns individuals blatantly living in non-Christian ways who nonetheless assured me that this was fine since 'once saved, always saved'. I would beg to disagree. Whatever Luther meant by 'the courage to sin boldly', it wasn't that. Antinomianism is a corruption both of the doctrine of justification by faith and of the perseverance of the saints. It is not a recipe for complacency or false assurance, and nothing in the New Testament can properly be interpreted in that direction.

Justification by faith goes very much deeper than the cheap idea that if I once make 'a decision for Christ,' I have an insurance policy that will guarantee a place in heaven. It points to a structural, an ontological change in a person's life. A person turns to God in such a way as to renounce reliance upon self and to trust in Christ as the one who can transform and reconstruct a life. Although it may be theologically valuable to distinguish between justification and sanctification for the sake of understanding, the structural change of conversion permits no separation in practice between the two. A transformed life leads to a holy life. Faith requires an intellectual content of belief but is essentially a kind of resonance with God, a structural alignment of a life in all its dimensions to God through Christ, who is the one who mediates such resonance. Thankfulness for the gracious gift of salvation leads to a 'eucharistic' lifestyle. This is why it is possible to acknowledge the possibility and reality of God's saving activity beyond the covenanted peoples of Israel and the church. Evangelicals are quick to discount 'works righteousness', and properly so. Yet much in the New Testament emphasises not how we believe but what we do and whether our lives are aligned to the will of God. This is true in Matthew 25, where the emphasis is doing the right thing even without knowing that in so doing, we were serving the Lord. It is true of Jesus' assertion that not those who say 'Lord, Lord' will be saved but those who do the Father's will. It is also true of Paul's designation of 'the obedience of faith' (Romans 1:5; 16:26), a term that interestingly both opens and ends his classic articulation of justification. The point is that faith does not equal 'believism' but means coming into alignment with the being and ways of God, otherwise known as righteousness. If this is to be the ultimate goal of creation, then present salvation is the bringing of our lives into alignment with God, the 'obedience of faith'. Faith properly understood is a reorientation of one's life towards God and so faith and works cannot be separated. To have faith in this way leads to a life restructured towards righteousness. Faith is a form of obedience, and its proclamation is a summons to surrender one's life to God and to become aligned to God's own righteousness, to resonate with God, and truly to be children of God. And it is appropriate to believe that throughout the world, embedded in varieties of culture and belief, there are those whose lives are indeed aligned with the life of God. This is not to say that this is salvation through acquired merit or by good works. It is not works-righteousness aimed at accruing merit. It does indicate that wherever there are those who seek for 'God and immortality' it is because the prevenient grace of God that brings them to this point is the cause. God 'has not left himself without a witness in doing good – giving you rains from heaven and fruitful seasons and filling you with food and your hearts with joy' (Acts 14:17). 'Every generous act of giving, with every perfect gift, is from above, coming down from the Father of lights' (James 1:17). If there is goodness anywhere or in anything it is because God has not abandoned the world he has made but our lives are undeservedly graced. 'The Lord is good to all, and his compassion is over all that he has made' (Psalm 145:9). For these reasons, I am more hopeful than many about the scope of salvation and am not surprised when I find signs of genuine faith in unexpected places. Nor do I overlook the prophetic hopes for a final ingathering of the nations: 'On that day Israel will be the third with Egypt and Assyria, a blessing in the midst of the earth, whom the LORD of hosts has blessed, saying, "Blessed be Egypt my people, and Assyria the work of my hands, and Israel my heritage"' (Isaiah 19:24-25). Stephen L. Cook, commenting on the Book of Ezekiel, is correct to write that, 'Here, as elsewhere in biblical literature, God's eschatological ideal for humanity is the inclusion of all willing nations and peoples into the reign of God'.[47] The idea that justification by faith has to do with the Godward structuring of our lives leads me to take seriously the criticisms of some concepts of justification by both Anabaptists and Roman Catholics. For the former, *Nachfolge Christi* is what counts supremely, following Christ on the way to the cross. This is contrasted with the cost-free nominalism of much conventional Christianity. From the Roman perspective, faith is manifested in incorporation into the sacramental life of the church, which sustains the faithful throughout life, and justification before God is the outcome of this way of life. I grasp the points being made: faith cannot be sundered from discipleship, nor should it be understood to exist independently of the corporate Christian community that is at the centre of God's purposes. Grasping these points helps to avoid turning justification by faith into something it was never intended to be.

---

[47] S.L. Cook in Gail R. O'Day and David L. Peterson, eds, *Theological Bible Commentary* (Louisville, Kentucky: WJK, 2009), p. 255.

Before leaving this discussion, I should pick up again the 'once saved, always saved' issue and express an opinion about it. The expression is a much-cheapened version of what is better called 'eternal security'. It largely derives from the Calvinist doctrine of 'the perseverance of the saints', which, in fact, does not permit the kind of complacency that I have already criticised. The doctrine is not that once a 'decision has been made for Christ', heaven is forever guaranteed. This is the kind of teaching that co-opts something important for self-interest, a not-infrequent tendency in religious thinking. Rather, in the Calvinist scheme, the doctrine asserts that those who are elect of God, whose sins have been covered by the atonement, will be known to be elect by the fact that they persevere in faith. Those who fall away demonstrate that this was never truly the case. Precious little comfort here then for the 'backslidden'! To my mind, the question of whether it is finally possible to fall away is not clearly answered in the New Testament, at least not in the same way that the question is posed. I see pastoral value in this. Because there is a mixture of promise and warning, there is enough to give hope and comfort to those who are faithful but not enough to allow complacency in the disobedient. Not every question can be resolved before its due time, and this is one of them. Each of us is called to endure to the end, to go on continually aligning our lives with the will of God, resisting all temptation to diverge.

Post Twenty-Two: The Moral Vision

Before I complete this piece of work, I will return to my understanding of the Bible and how it is to be understood and interpreted. However, that project might come more effectively into focus if I first address one of the moral and ethical issues that have achieved relevance in the later part of the twentieth century and the early part of the present one. I think here of issues such as abortion, human sexuality, and gender self-ID. For the sake of space. I restrict my discussion to that of human sexuality.

By many who see themselves as 'progressives', the Bible, and those who adhere to it, are routinely regarded as retrogressive and obstructive of legitimate and humane progress. They are on 'the wrong side of history'. However, change does not necessarily mean progress, and what is deemed progressive can sometimes be mistaken. Having grown up in Manchester, I am aware that after World War II, 'the planners' thought that civic progress consisted of demolishing large parts of the city, including its iconic town hall, to replace them with modern and visionary schemes for a new cityscape. The destruction of the past and of many communities would have been the price. Fortunately, they only partially got their way, and I am left with deep suspicion of the word 'progressive'. Of the many changes in my lifetime, the revolution in sexual attitudes has been amongst the most pronounced. I recall the surprise I felt when 'gay marriage' was first mooted politically. I fondly imagined this would prove unpopular, but opinion polls very swiftly proved me wrong. Increasingly, traditional Christian assumptions have come to be seen as outmoded and their advocacy 'controversial'. Contemporary culture appears to be in tension between a desire to celebrate sex unambiguously and an increased awareness of how it can become transgressive. We have become aware of the shockingly widespread sexual abuse of children, not least in arenas that would once have been regarded as safe spaces, including churches. Yet this is only part of it. The sexual liberation of women in the 1960s turns out to have been as much about the freedom of men to exploit women as to empower them. If it is in sexual expression that human beings can be at their most loving, it is also true that precisely they can be at their most corrupt: rape, incest, adultery, pornography, exposure, promiscuity, predation, and bestiality all being testimony to the fact alongside the abuse of children already highlighted. To be fair, there are attempts to state an appropriate modern ethic, and these include an insistence on the need for consent and on there being an equality of power relations between partners. No argument with either of these, but there must be more. Sexual energies are immensely powerful and need to be disciplined and channelled in constructive ways, ways that traditional Christian aspirations to chastity and fidelity have sought to instil. If these are now characterised as prudish and unmodern, as 'straight and narrow', there are good reasons for defending them rather than retreating from them. I am not about to apologise for them. Of all the issues that clamour to be addressed, homosexuality is the one I choose to discuss here.

Traditional Christian morality has argued that proper sexual expression requires fidelity within marriage and abstinence outside of it. Marriage is the context in which sex is at its safest. It provides the most basic and considered form of consent to sexual relations. Whereas there would still be among many a strong sense that adultery and promiscuity are a violation of the marriage bond for those who have chosen to marry ('cheating' is frowned upon still), for the rest, the traditional Christian perspective has come to seem increasingly old-fashioned and impossible, even controversial. If once it was sexual minorities that felt themselves outside popular approval, today it is those who hold to stricter disciplines who are regarded as beyond the pale. The reasons for this are many and various but surely include the availability of contraception, the loss of social sanctions that once prevailed in working-class communities in particular but no longer, and, probably, the impact of pornography as now a mainstream phenomenon. Things which once were thought perverse, or deviant have come to be thought acceptable such that the 'normalisation of what is not normal' now prevails. Legislation has kept pace with this and probably reached its height in the redefinition of marriage, away from a contract between one man and one woman to one between two people irrespective of sex or gender. Even a short time ago, this would have been unthinkable, but a major shift has taken place in the early years of this millennium that stands in stark contrast to traditional Christian thinking as for centuries defined by the marriage service of the *Book of Common Prayer*. There is a challenge here to the Christian churches, one which provokes major disagreement and, in some cases, schism. Is this change to be resisted in faithfulness to scripture and tradition or, given that it is hard to resist and could be held to make its own legitimate claims, should the churches seek to minister to it by accommodating it, re-defining their own marriage doctrine, or offering to bless same-sex-civil unions? At the time of writing this is dividing churches and denominations across the Western world. For some, this would seem an appropriate way of responding to societal change with compassion, and there is a logic to that: if marriage is a benefit and a blessing, why should it be withheld from same-sex couples who are unable or unwilling to forge opposite-sex relationships? After all, those who wish to enter permanent commitments on the model of marriage are surely at the responsible end of any same-sex spectrum and should be supported? The appeal is made to the hugely significant doctrine of love and the right to love (and so marry) whom you wish to love. Powerful stuff. And secular states do well to recognise the diversities of viewpoints in their populations. To others, it is to bless what God has not blessed, and that comes near to blasphemy. By what authority do we do this? Do we know better than the God who, according to scripture, instituted marriage as between male and female? Crucially, this injunction was reiterated by Jesus himself. Churches that solemnise same-sex marriages claim to be following Jesus. But how can this be if they explicitly go against what he taught?

I have twice published material on this topic, and in general, though my mind may have changed marginally, I continue to stand by what I have previously written. In the first article I wrote, I borrowed the typology that divides Christian responses into four: rejecting-punitive, rejecting-compassionate, conditional-acceptance and full-acceptance. I have thought of myself as oscillating between the second and third of these options while regarding the fourth, the acceptance of same-sex sexual relations as fully equal to heterosexual ones, as potentially disastrous, at least within the church. The issues are complex and have biblical, traditional, medical, legal, missional, and pastoral dimensions. So, I now also distinguish in my mind between welcoming, accepting and affirming responses. It is entirely right for churches to *welcome* people of all kinds and conditions who seek to explore or enter faith in Jesus Christ as Lord. In this regard, 'inclusion', one of today's characteristic social values, is entirely right. People should not be regarded as 'types' but as persons. Martin Luther King had it exactly right when he looked forward to the day when people would not be judged by the colour of their skin but on the content of their character. He was speaking first about racial or ethnic differences, but the principle is rightly extended to any properties that are given rather than chosen. People are what they are. Yet, even as it *includes* people as people, the Christian faith *excludes* certain forms of belief and behaviour deemed immoral or inappropriate. Not everything is acceptable within it, either by way of doctrine or morality. Inclusion is 'in Christ' (Galatians 3:28), and 'in Christ' is a defining and critical principle. At this point, any faith-community distinguishes itself from a secular society. A liberal, secular society imposes no religious test, and this is as it should be (though it has other tests to apply). But paradoxically, its intention to be inclusive is exactly what enables it to foster communities that *do* apply tests for the sake of preserving their identity. This is true across the board and not uniquely of the religious – of political parties, for instance. Christian communities practise a form of exclusion since they require repentance, faith and normatively baptism for full membership. It is hard to imagine churches that are not, in principle, welcoming and inclusive in the sense that they fully desire for others to share their faith, whoever and whatever they may be. Churches that are not so are failing badly and are probably doomed to go out of existence. Then, beyond welcoming, there is the value of *acceptance*. Since we are not alike, there is the acceptance of difference, even if this is within a broadly shared way of believing and living. Time and time again, I notice that personal and pastoral engagement in good faith with real people makes hard-line dogmatism difficult. Pastoral and ideological engagements happen on different levels. Where differences are deemed to be substantial they may lead to divergence into different ways of 'being church'. This is already the case in our division into denominations. Yet most churches have diversity within themselves and practise high levels of personal acceptance. Surely, this is good, the kind of thing that Paul commends in Romans 14. For myself, I accept not only differences of preference but also of conscience. What some persons may consider morally right for themselves, others may deem contrary to conscience. Paul is pointing to this tension in Romans 14:22-23: 'The faith that you have as your own conviction before God...for whatever does not proceed from faith is sin'. He is surely indicating the integrity of having personal convictions within the community of faith while not requiring others to share those convictions, the right, in other words, of personal judgement. Those of same-sex orientation may have sincere convictions about what is possible for them. Others may take different views, but a degree of acceptance of each other should be possible in good faith and within certain limits (for instance, it ought not to be possible to accept behaviours for Christians who are 'gay' which are also not acceptable from those who are 'straight'). Accordingly, I am an 'accepting evangelical' and can offer calibrated responses to those of same-sex attraction rather than blanket ones, provided I am not required to endorse that in which I do not believe. It should be noticed that the Bible nowhere forbids such loving relationships between those of the same sex, including life-long bonded partnerships. Aggressive campaigning either way makes nuance more difficult. So, this comes to the word *affirmation*, and I regard it as the most sensitive. I can accept the freedom of others to live according to their conscience, but I am not able to affirm practices that would go against my own conscience. This is not to say I cannot affirm *people* struggling to do what is right. But I may not be able to affirm *practices* that I deem unwise, unhelpful, or even sinful. The rubber hits the road for me if I am asked as a minister to bless formally or liturgically a same-sex relationship or marriage. Most of the time, it is possible to 'live and let live' and even to pray with people on a personal level, but personal conscience becomes a material factor concerning what is prayed. The same would be true of the shared conscience of a congregation.

In fact, I question here the value of the world 'sin'. Although I generally hold to a robust doctrine of human sin and depravity and believe the nature of sin should be more carefully understood, in the present discussion, I find it unhelpful since it can act as a 'thought terminator' in what should be a sensitive encounter. Perhaps the words 'appropriate' or 'wise' might be more constructive. The problem for people like me is that the fourth option I have recorded above, 'full equality', indicates more than I am prepared to concede. Problematically, although many might be content to be part of churches where the convictions are mixed, those gay Christians who argue for the 'full inclusion' of gay people within the life of the church are unlikely to be satisfied and might continue to feel excluded unless 'full equality' is granted. Full equality would regard all forms of gay sex as being equal to heterosexual sex. Thus, anal intercourse is on a par with vaginal intercourse, and gay marriage is of equal standing as other-sex marriage (note the preference for 'equal marriage' rather than 'gay marriage'). These are things I cannot in good conscience concede, given that human bodies are structured for reproduction and that humanity perpetuates itself by heterosexual means. This does not leave same-sex relationships without value, but it does mean they do not have the *same* value in evolutionary terms as heterosexual relationships. I cannot avoid the conclusion, therefore, of heteronormativity from both theological and evolutionary perspectives. This sets me outside the ideology that has emerged in recent years, according to which everything is equal to everything else and that provided there is consent and equality of power, any form of sexual activity is permissible).

It has come as a surprise to me, and even a disillusionment, how even within the churches, this ideology is coming to be accepted. I take the legalisation of gay marriage as an example. Before this legislation was enacted in the UK, the churches were unanimous in opposing it, apart from small and unrepresentative groups such as the Unitarians and the Quakers. After the legislation, there is taking place a process of gradual assimilation, with some churches formally redefining what is meant by 'marriage'. Not surprisingly, this is leading widely to schism and division. So, positions once held firmly across the board are now being revised, suggesting to some minds at least a lack of moral principle and courage. Consequently, it becomes less easy to speak of a clear collective mind on the subject. The shift is towards 'this is where I stand on the issue', to the 'I think' rather than 'Christians think'. For some outside the churches, this suggests that, as usual, the churches are catching up with progressive thinking, 'getting with the programme' at last and deciding to be 'on the right side of history'. Those resisting are seen as moral retardants rather than progressives. This revisionist trend is visible even among evangelicals. To some within the churches, this is a sign of moral and theological weakness, a betrayal of scripture, tradition, and reason.

Speaking for myself, therefore, on a 'here I stand basis', I can see that some degree of accommodation is inevitable for pastoral and missional reasons. In the past, churches have resisted the liberalisation of divorce laws. I have regularly noticed that many of those who have come to faith under my own ministry have previously been divorced and, in some cases, had remarried. It is not always possible to unpick the past. Conversion has involved accepting people where they are, avoiding judgementalism and proclaiming forgiveness and new beginnings. Principled pragmatism has been the order of the day. The position towards divorce has, therefore, become less absolute. I can now envisage situations in which people of same-sex orientation who are married according to law come to faith in Christ, seek baptism and ask for church membership according to the Baptist pattern. Following the principle of 'acceptance', and perhaps in the light of Paul's advice, 'Let each of you remain in the condition in which you were called' (Romans 7:20), I would certainly not expect them to 'unmarry', and even less so if there were children involved, as increasingly might be the case. For the rest, I would seek to walk with such converts pastorally and to work out the implications of their newfound faith. It is clear from this act of imagination that even for one such as I who wish to maintain traditional positions, a degree of accommodation to prevailing conditions is inevitable and responsible. Involved in this is the entirely proper tension between moral and pastoral theology, holding fast to a moral vision while applying it to less-than-ideal circumstances and always with an eye to redemption.

The 'red line' that prevails for me is the endorsement of anal intercourse. My reading of scripture (to which I shall come) is that it is precisely this that scripture rejects rather than the fact of loving relationships between people. Here, we enter an area of which it is difficult to speak, and which is characteristically approached by euphemism rather than plain speaking. To address the matter directly may be thought of as offensive or as the reduction of loving relationships to their lowest form. Of course, what people choose to do in the privacy of their own bedrooms and with whom they choose to do it is no business of mine, and I don't wish it to be. This does not prevent ethical, in-principle discussion of the issue. The private issue would become my *de facto* business if I were asked to give approval either explicitly or implicitly, as I would be if I presided over or blessed a same-sex marriage. Marriage is a conjugal relationship that involves the union of bodies in a way that a civil partnership does not *necessarily* do (though, of course, it may, in fact). I found little difficulty in supporting legislation towards civil partnerships since it seemed that if two people wished to share their lives faithfully rather than, say, live promiscuously, the responsible thing on their part was to put that on a legal basis and gain the relevant rights and advantages. In advance of current legislation, I would also propose that legal partnerships should be extended to people related to each other since any rules of consanguinity do not apply. If asked why, therefore, I would refuse to 'bless' a same-sex conjugal relationship, my answer would be, 'for the same reason I would not perform a circumcision or a bar mitzvah', namely, I don't have a theology for it. It is a civil arrangement, not a theological one. Whether or not the state acknowledges the fact, by going beyond civil partnerships and creating gay or 'equal' marriage, it has given its endorsement to anal intercourse as a practice on a level with vaginal intercourse and, for this Christian and citizen, at least, this is beyond what I endorse or give consent to. In this regard I remain a dissenter or nonconformist and decline to join in. Fortunately, the law allows this, but I regard the increasing assimilation of the churches to this altered definition of marriage as a crisis of obedience that is bound to create division. It fits into the category of the fourth possible Christian response, which I have already identified as 'disastrous' because it represents unfaithfulness and is bound to divide the body of Christ. To balance out what would now be seen as a controversial position, let me add that I am totally at ease with civil partnerships as a way of granting a same-sex couple all the legal protections and advantages otherwise conferred by marriage. I can do this because of my own form of 'intersectionality' as both a civic liberal and a committed Christian. Politically, I happily grant equality of rights, as I suppose is probably the case with others who have 'come out' against gay marriage, not because they wish to deny others their rights but because they have a different definition of marriage.

The objection, then, is to anal intercourse. It is, in fact, surprising how little the Bible has to say about homosexual activity. It knows and says nothing at all about homosexuality as a condition. Revisionists who wish to reinterpret scripture make this point, and it is a fair one. The argument is that the Bible does not address the question of same-sex orientation as we have come to understand it more fully. That we have sexual 'orientations' is a recent understanding originating, as I understand it, in the late nineteenth century and is never so much as touched upon in the Bible in these terms. That it becomes necessary to reframe biblical teaching in the light of advanced knowledge is a valid point. This is attempted by striking down the small number of prohibitive biblical texts, 'the clobber texts', and declaring the Bible either neutral or positive about more nuanced concepts of loving same-sex relations that are stable, monogamous, and faithful. Certainly, there is a very large moral gap between such relationships and promiscuous lifestyles. It is credibly argued that the narratives about Sodom and Gomorrah (from which the word 'sodomy' is derived) are about gang rape and so clearly morally reprehensible, whatever one's point of view, though it is male gang rape that is in question. More difficult are the two references in Leviticus, which revisionists rule out of court because of the highly contextual nature of that book (Leviticus 18:22-23, 20:13-16). Can we be bound by prescriptions that go back several thousand years and belong to cultural and religious mindsets that we struggle to understand, and some of which we already reject? Colloquially, if we can eat prawns (also forbidden by 11:24), why can't we have gay sex? Simply striking these verses down, however, is, to my mind, problematic. There are moral teachings in the book we might well discard, but others we would do so at our peril, such as the verse that enjoins is to love our neighbour or to show loving hospitality to strangers (19:34). Both the prohibitive verses are immediately followed by a rejection of bestiality. Does this go, too? Clearly, there is a hermeneutical task of deciding what falls away and what is carried forward into a Christian morality, a process known as 'sublation'. I regard with misgiving attempts to re-exegete the scriptures to make them say something they plainly do not say. I find myself in accord with the historian Diarmaid MacCulloch, himself a self-identifying gay man and 'critical friend' of Christianity, who regards homosexuality as today's 'chosen battleground' that threatens to divide the churches. This is certainly true, though I am less sure that it is 'chosen'. He goes on, 'Despite much well-intentioned theological fancy footwork to the contrary; it is difficult to see the Bible as expressing anything else but disapproval of homosexual activity, let alone any conception of a homosexual identity. The only alternatives are either to try to cleave to patterns of life and assumptions set out in the Bible or to say that in this, as in much else, the Bible is simply wrong.'[48] If it came to it, I would sooner admit, with MacCulloch, that the Bible is wrong than try to make it say or endorse something it does not.

Biblical interpretation poses many challenges. I baulk at seeing the Bible as a problem we must get round rather than as a light that illuminates our path. MacCulloch is undoubtedly an outstanding and admirable historian whom I like greatly. But, I am less confident about his ability to interpret the Bible. My point here is that though there is nothing there about homosexual *orientation*, the relevant scriptural verses are not about who we are but what we do. That men are enjoined 'not to lie with a man as with a woman' is clearly, to my mind, at least, a prohibition on anal intercourse. To say this is wrong is itself wrong since it is, at the very least, a defensible point of view from several aspects, not least that of hygiene and the transmission of disease. The criminalisation of anal intercourse goes back to the reign of Henry VIII and the panic spreading across Europe surrounding syphilis, then known as the 'French disease'. In our own times, similar panics have arisen in relation to HIV and AIDS. Panics are unfortunate, but the substantive issues are not trivial, nor are they simply prejudice. In identifying anal intercourse

---

[48] *Reformation: Europe's House Divided 1490-1700,* (London: Allen Lane, 2003) pp.707-8).

as the primary concern in Leviticus, I am following the rabbinic scholar Daniel Boyarin as summarised by Richard B. Hays in his *The Moral Vision of the New Testament*.[49] Whereas some regard this as an unfortunate, not to say reprehensible, prohibition on a legitimate sexual expression, to me, it coheres from theological, rational, medical, aesthetic, and ethical points of view. I cannot get over the persuasion that anal intercourse is, in turn, unnatural, abnormal, unhygienic, abusive, humiliating, and violent. It is these factors that have constituted, and continue to do so, the deep revulsion against the act that has been so widely in evidence across many cultures and religious instincts. This prohibition can apply to sexual activity, whether between men and men or men and women, so, in that sense, there is an 'equality' to it. If I am to be told that this is 'homophobia' (that most convenient and bullying of words), then I confess to it; generally, it seems to me to be simply heterosexuality or even simply 'decency'. Neither do I believe that

---

[49] *The Moral Vision of the New Testament: A Contemporary Introduction to New Testament Ethics* (Edinburgh: T&T Clark Ltd, 1996). In footnote 6 on page 404 he summarises as follows: 'In a recent article, Daniel Boyarin (1995) argues convincingly that these Levitical prohibitions were understood in later rabbinic tradition to pertain to male homosexual intercourse in which anal penetration occurs. Other forms of male same-sex erotic activity would have been understood in this interpretive tradition as forms of masturbation, which was still frowned upon but subject to much less severe sanctions. Boyarin, noting that the Leviticus passages prohibit a specific act but say nothing about sexual "orientation", goes on to contend that the rabbis had no category corresponding to the modern idea of "homosexuality"'. The article in question is 'Are there any Jews in the "history of sexuality"?', *Journal of the History of Sexuality*, 5:333-355.

anyone has the right to dictate to anybody else what their sexual aversions ought to be. It follows that I would equally disapprove of the practice in the case of men and women and for the same reasons.

Legislation in Britain has now shifted from criminalising anal intercourse to, in effect, sanctioning it through gay marriage. An objection to my position might well be that it focuses disproportionately and possibly unfairly upon one possible, though not necessary, aspect of male same-sex relationships to the neglect of 'weightier matters of the law', such as loving partnership and support. I take the point and fully desire to value these qualities on the grounds that it is generally not good for anyone to be on their own. But given that two-thirds of sexually active male homosexuals are believed to engage in the act, and in the light of my characterisation above, I fail to see how anal intercourse can be an objectively loving act. This is a crunch point and is an evaluation over which there is likely to be a binary response. How many can explicitly say that it is blessed by God rather than speak in more euphemistic terms? I find myself in agreement here with the Roman Catholic teaching, offensive to many in the LGBT community, that it is 'objectively disordered'. It is so from a Christian point of view that sees male-female relations as normative; but the same can be said of an evolutionary, biological perspective that is determined by the need for the race to reproduce if it is to survive. Whereas the vagina is adapted (could we say 'designed'?) to receive the erect male penis, the same cannot be said of the colon. This is why I have claimed that rectal intercourse is a violent act. The anus is a *sphincter* that permits material to exit but not to enter, unlike the vagina, which is a *valve* 'designed' (or evolved) to allow both. Neither does the depositing of semen in the colon match reproductive reality. The arguments (that are difficult to articulate in normal discussion) can be countered by blurring the meaning of what is considered 'natural'. On this basis, if something can be done using any part of the human body, then it counts as 'natural'; this might apply to a penis/phallus penetrating the colon. Whether it is good for the colon is a different matter. My preferred reading of what is 'natural' is to consider what purpose parts of the body have evolved for and what their biological functions are. On this basis, I conclude anal intercourse to be both unnatural and abnormal. Furthermore, in Christian scripture and tradition, marriage has been viewed as a symbol of Christ's love for the church: Christ loved the church and gave himself for it. He is the bridegroom; the church is the bride, and sexual union symbolises their communion. To transfer this imagery to two men having intercourse through the rectum does not work, and it is hardly surprising that many find it offensive in the extreme. Not surprisingly, these considerations are not often discussed in polite Christian society! But surely they are there in the background.

More remains to be said. How does what I have so far explored relate to same-sex relations between women? Clearly, anal intercourse does not apply (though I am informed that there are forms of anal intercourse that some women, straight or gay, engage in). Whereas I have no desire to endorse same-sex sexual activity between women, neither can I regard it in the same way as the above. For a start, as a straight man, I do not find it repulsive in the same way as sex between men, so I do not have the same visceral reaction against it. Furthermore, it does not, in so far as I can imagine, involve what I have described as violence. Most of all, in my interpretation, it finds no place either by means of prohibition or endorsement in scripture. I have been surprised to find that the text in Romans 1:26-7, 'Their women exchanged natural intercourse for unnatural', is commonly taken as a reference to lesbianism. It appears to me, however (following sociologist Rodney Stark),[50] to be much more likely a reference, once more, to anal intercourse engaged in as a prophylactic against conception. In a world where options for contraception were limited and probably restricted otherwise to *coitus interruptus*, anal intercourse in the ancient world was feasible, and one of which Paul clearly disapproved. I am inclined to be more sympathetic to two women in partnership, and my own heterosexuality feeds into this: I can fully understand why a woman may not want to share her bed with a man.

I have stated my position and have indeed staked out some red lines. It troubles me not at all that this might be considered out of

---

[50] Rodney Stark, *The Rise of Christianity: How the obscure, marginal Jesus movement became the dominant religious force in the Western world in a few centuries* (San Franciso: HarperCollins, 1997), pp. 121-26.

joint with current trends. The argument that Christians and others should assimilate to culture and 'get with the programme' strikes me as the worst of all possible arguments and counter-productive for those who believe themselves called by both scripture and their own nonconformist, dissenting tradition to resist the moral drift of their society. There is a significant divide in modern religion between those who believe that there is an objective moral order which we are called to embrace and obey and those who believe we are at liberty to shape the moral order according to taste. I belong to the former, and it is summed up in the acknowledgement of the Lordship of Christ. More important to me than the kind of biblical exegesis that seeks to strike down prohibitive texts is the positive vision of marriage between a man and a woman that is rooted in the creation narratives and unambiguously reiterated by Jesus. It is the positive vision of wholesome, productive, consensual, and 'equal' marriage (in the sense that the partners are equal) that is fundamental to society and the context for the happy raising of healthy children. By contrast, there is nothing in the scriptural tradition that endorses same-sex sexual relations or even trends in that direction. To be sure, for those for whom homophile relations seem to be the best or only option (and I will come on to this), drawing upon a Christian understanding of marriage as stable, exclusive, and faithful has much to say: but this is a secondary form of exegesis, not a primary one.

I change tack here to explore some of the arguments that are followed in current debates and to show, I hope, that I do feel the moral force of them. The primary one that cannot be denied is that people do not choose to be gay, at least not in all cases. It is widely argued that sexuality can be fluid, even that all people are to some measure 'bi-sexual'. This does suggest that there is a measure of choice involved at least some of the time for some people. I have found the distinction between sexuality as 'constituted' and as 'constructed' helpful. It touches on the debate as to whether homosexual orientation is already formed in the womb or, shaped psycho-dynamically by early experience, or both in complex interaction. As I understand it, the debate has come to tend in the direction of the first of these, and this means that being gay is not a choice but belongs to those things which are simply given and belong to the hand that life deals to us. If this is so, it must surely shape our moral judgements. People should not be penalised for that which they cannot help, any more than should be the case in being male or female, ethnically different, left- or right-handed or in any other ways that we are given to be unavoidably different. However, I resist the idea that 'God made me this way'. This neglects the degree to which we are shaped by natural processes in a world where even nature is fallen. The same argument could be used and probably has been, to justify other conditions, such as paedophilia, that all right-thinking people, gay or straight, would consider deviant. There is no shortage of people who are born with disabilities and physical defects. Sympathy is required of us, not condemnation. Are we to say that God made them this way or that the natural world can malfunction? Human beings are fallen and corrupted, including those who are 'straight'. We cannot, therefore, accept that our human natures, as we have inherited them, are unconditionally as God intends them to be. All this said, if it is given to any person by nature to be gay, the question must be asked how that person should be supported in living a righteous life in the sight of God. Dietrich Bonhoeffer spoke of a 'penultimate' ethic by which, in our fallen rather than perfected world, we all learn to live as best we can with what we are given.

It is not my purpose here to propose an ethic for anybody outside the Christian community: as Paul said, what have I to do with judging outsiders? My first concern should be to explore sympathetically but not condescendingly with those who are Christian and gay what the options are that lie before them and to allow them to make discriminations in good conscience. Gay Christians, like any other believers, are under an obligation to be righteous, and so the debate becomes, what does it mean as a same-sex attracted person to live righteously? If non-Christians choose to draw anything from this position, then that is up to them. 'Inclusivity' has become a major value in modern democracies, and this should be, above all, true of the Christian church. But this can never be an undiscriminating inclusivity that simply accepts anything. The churches exist to propagate the Christian faith as a way of believing and behaving. Of course, the invitation to enter this faith and way of life is open to all. Yet it involves for all of us conversion and submission to the Lordship of Christ. Otherwise, it becomes meaningless. For many of those who identify as LGBT, there is an understandable resistance to accept or to internalise attitudes that relegate them to a status that is 'less than' or of less worth than others. This is the impetus behind the 'Pride' celebrations and the insistence on equality. My attitude to this is akin to my understanding of religious or ideological liberty: I fully accept, and indeed insist, that those of differing religious convictions should have the inalienable right to live according to conscience without any fear of discrimination or persecution. These rights are protected in law and are codified in widely accepted statements about human rights. This does not mean, however, that everything is equal to everything else. Any such statement would be self-contradictory. A Christian cannot accept that other religious or non-religious claims can be 'equally' true as Christian claims, even if the right to hold them is 'equal'. In the political sphere, I don't think our society has yet negotiated its way around these distinctions. People are equally free to hold contradictory beliefs and to deny that other claims to truth can be equally true. This leads me to the conclusion that LGBT human and civil rights should be fully respected, albeit critically, while we are all free to make our own judgements as to whether they are equally true. In my judgement this means that heterosexual sexual activity is of greater significance than same-sex ones since the propagation of humankind depends on one, not the other. Immanuel Kant proposed that a test of morality is to universalise behaviours and to ask the question, what would be the case if everybody were to do a particular thing?: 'Act only on that maxim which you can at the same time will that it should become a universal law.' I have not the slightest doubt that if the Christian aspiration of fidelity within marriage and chastity outside of it were universally embraced, the world would be a better place. Powerful sexual energies would be directed in ways that make for a better world. If everybody engaged in same-sex sexual activity, humanity would cease to be.

People may not choose to be gay, but being sexually active certainly is a choice. I concede that the responsible gay Christian position does not by any means seek to legitimate all and any sexual activity. It stands against promiscuity and instead advocates the containment of sexual activity in relationships that are loving, exclusive and permanent. In this way, in parallel with historic Christian understandings of marriage, sex can become a way of expressing and fostering a loving and positive relationship. I have said enough above to indicate my difficulty in accepting this to be true of anal intercourse, which I have characterised as 'objectively disordered'. To my mind, it is objectively unloving, and I struggle to see how it can be part of a loving relationship. This is my point of fundamental disagreement. Whereas I find the thought of sexual activity short of this unattractive, mutual male masturbation, for instance, I concede that this is not harmful in the ways that may be true of penetration. I concede that gay people can claim the right to a sexual life just as do those who are straight. I certainly have no difficulty in agreeing that those who are gay have the right to loving relationships and partnerships. It is not good for the man or the woman to be alone, and the Prayer Book language of 'mutual society, help and comfort that the one ought to have of the other' is something I would not deny to anyone. At this point, the rhetoric about 'having the right to love whom you want to' strikes me as incoherent. Such a right did not come into existence with the legislation of civil partnerships or 'equal' marriage. To be sure, it may have been socially awkward and have lacked legal sanction; but the fact that very many straight people choose to cohabit outside of marriage and even to raise children surely indicates that the right to love someone does not depend on state legislation. When same-sex civil partnerships were introduced, this seemed to me unproblematic for several reasons: the first is that it supported gay people with the intention not to be promiscuous but to build committed and enduring relationships; in other words, it was legislation that endorsed the responsible end of the sexually active gay community in a way that was good for society. The second reason was that it did not, by definition, have to be a conjugal, that is, sexual, partnership. As I recall, when partnerships were introduced, certain assurances were given, probably to placate the religiously minded, that they would not lead to 'gay marriage'. As with other promises by our political masters, this has proved hollow.

To my mind, civil partnerships were the appropriate way to validate stable same-sex relations and to grant equal rights in the process. When the debate about 'gay' or 'equal' marriage then took place, all that was added to this was the legal right to use the word 'marriage', a choice that was open to people anyway. Equal rights had already been conceded, even while preserving the notion that there was a distinction between homosexual and heterosexual partnerships, most noticeably the begetting of the next generation. A deficiency in the debate as it was conducted was that it suggested the choice was between gay marriage and nothing, as though civil partnerships had never existed. To be clear, to my mind, those who are gay ought, if they wish to enter a permanent relationship, seek for a civil partnership or, since it now exists, a legal marriage. I can readily see how this can contribute to the common good and regard this as a strong argument. It is also hard to see who is harmed or disadvantaged by it. But my preference would have been to stick with the arrangements that pertained before the introduction of gay marriage as such.

The question revolves around the definition of marriage itself and what this might lead to. When it was defined in law as between a man and a woman in a way that accords with traditional biblical and Christian teaching, this was no breach in the principle of equality since all were equally subject to it. Once it was redefined as between two people irrespective of gender then the urge towards a new understanding of equality came into play. Meanwhile, there are those of us who persist with the older definition of marriage. We do not believe we have the authority to change the definition or to bless what God has not blessed. This does not mean that I regard gay marriage as wrong, simply that it is the wrong way to do the right thing, namely, to reward those who opt for stable and permanent relationships. Allegedly, we nonconformists are protected in our right to disagree; indeed, we have been told that there is a 'triple-lock' on any attempt to compromise this position. Whether this will be maintained will be an interesting test as to whether we really do live in a pluralist, liberal democracy or are sliding into something different, one that is sometimes called 'liberal intolerance'. Yet the problem with the claimed liberalism is that it is not liberal enough. It is unable to accommodate differences, which is what liberalism is supposed to do, on the basis that civilised people can agree to disagree and continue to co-exist. Because I am unsure whether this protection will continue, I advocate two courses of action: The first is to denationalise marriage. This means taking the state out of the marriage business and confining it to civil partnerships and the law. This runs counter to the trend to broaden the definition of marriage. 'Marriage' would then be left to religious or cultural preference while the law confined itself to the law. The second proposal is for churches to take themselves out of the business of legal registration of marriage and to adopt a more

Continental approach whereby the state does what it does, and the churches do what they do; in other words, a separation of church and state in the solemnising of marriage. Such a situation would obviate the possibility of the state coercing or penalising the churches for noncompliance. Churches would then be left free to act according to their own theologies, which might or might not include some liturgy for same-sex relations.

Having 'come out' as a dissenter from the current ideologies concerning same-sex practice, it still seems to me that abundant questions remain for those who share my assessment. I have indicated that my position is more calibrated than those of some others. The challenge is to maintain the more traditional response I believe to be correct while not allowing this to become an expression of hostility towards persons whose well-being and salvation the churches should earnestly be seeking. I believe this to be possible if a spirit of welcome and mutual acceptance is allowed to prevail. I am prepared to accept others and walk with them in the journey of faith as they discover how to live in the presence of God. The same should be true the other way round if acceptance is to be mutual. I would hope that others could walk with me and respect my own convictions and what a former generation might have described quaintly as 'scruples'.

Post Twenty-Three: The Holy Spirit and Charismatic Renewal

It surprises me that I have so far written next to nothing about the person and work of the Holy Spirit, especially given that involvement in various instantiations of the charismatic movement has been so much part of my life. This began when, very shortly after taking the step into a personal Christian faith, I went to hear David Wilkerson, author of *The Cross and the Switchblade*, a very impactful book in the 1960s, at the Bethshan Tabernacle very close to my Manchester home. I found the wild Pentecostalism rather frightening. However, I then went on to take part in milder forms of the movement, to engage in conversation with the 'Restoration' movement associated with the Dales Bible Week and the Bradford House Church, so-called, in the 1970s and 1980s and then even more extensively with the 'Third Wave' identified with John Wimber and the Vineyard movement of churches. All this intensity has now moderated and become integrated into the general church scene, but I cannot deny that these 'times of refreshing' were exciting, interesting, and cumulatively significant for my growing understanding. I endeavoured in those times to be more than a 'participant observer' but to be an active theological critic (in a positive sense) of what was taking place. Symbolic of this was my involvement as a writer and speaker with Tom Smail and Andrew Walker, a genuinely harmonious and ecumenical partnership. Tom was a Presbyterian-cum-Anglican, and Andrew a Pentecostal-cum-Russian Orthodox. I, of course, was a Baptist with Anabaptist tendencies. This was not the only productive ecumenical partnership I enjoyed. Previously, as I became charismatically involved, I met regularly with Father Ian Petit OSB (a monk of Ampleforth Abbey with a roving charismatic brief), Father Peter Dolan, a Catholic parish priest in Preston, Rev Cyril Ashton in Lancaster (who later became Bishop of Doncaster and at whose consecration in York Minster I was privileged to preach), and Dr Michael B. Smith, an enterprising and distinctly independent Pentecostal minister in Fleetwood. We possessed an amazingly strong bond of affection. We found very little to disagree about, and we all valued our own traditions without holding any illusions about them. Neither did we harbour illusions about the charismatic movement that we had in common but retained our denominational roots and general level-headedness.

It is an equal surprise to me, therefore that I don't have a huge amount to write about at this point, perhaps because I have exhausted my insights elsewhere. The charismatic movement now feels a though it is something that has passed. This ought not to surprise. The image of a 'wave' implies both something coming in and something going out. There have been many waves of spiritual intensity in the history of the church, and one of the features is that however long they persist, they do not go on for ever. Viewed constructively, each one contributes something to the ongoing life of the church, but none of them, however much is initially claimed, prove to be a final chapter in a long story. Though I feel I have little to add to what I have previously written, there is nonetheless little I would choose to retract. There are positive gains and some losses. On the positive side of the ledger the most important I can identify is the rediscovery, if that is what it is, of the person of the Holy Spirit. The Spirit has never been absent – this would be an impossibility – but theological awareness of the Spirit's presence may indeed be lacking. If balance is to be achieved in Christian theology, worship, and lifestyle it must have a trinitarian shape, a due recognition of God as Father, Son and Spirit. Sometimes, this has been portrayed, not unhelpfully, in terms of ages: the age of the Father is followed by the age of the Son, which in turn is fulfilled in the age of the Spirt and then in the fullness of time, the whole of existence is consummated by being wholly enclosed within the communion of the divine Trinity, Father, Son and Spirit. Yet there are certainly reasons why, in this narrative, the Spirit of God has been the neglected member of the Trinity, and this has, to a degree, been rectified both in renewed reflection on the life of the church as the temple of the Holy Spirit as well as the Body of Christ and the people of God. The Spirit is God at God's closest to us and in the world, the one who breathes through all creation. Charles Taylor, some time ago, drew a distinction between two forms of religion: the first emphasises objectivity, the fact that there is an ontological reality over against human beings, a moral order to which we are called to be subject. This would be a view shared by Orthodox Jews, Muslims, and others, as well as Christians. The second is subjective, sometimes called 'post-confessional' (or pejoratively 'do-it-yourself' religion) and emphasises the need for inner and emotional fulfilment in a way that captures the 'expressionist' mood of the present world and of the 'New Age'. In the doctrine of the Spirit and its hinterland in the doctrine of the Trinity, we have a way of responding to both these imperatives, and this helps to explain why, in an age of religious decline, Pentecostalism and charismatic movements have proven more resilient. A faith that acknowledges Jesus as Lord cannot escape the fact that there is the objective dimension that is not, or should not be, subject to human manipulation – it is a given, though perceptions of it may develop. On the other hand, the Christian faith is also a testimony to 'realised communion' with the divine and abounds with a sense of the forgiveness of sins, of acceptance by God, of assurance of salvation, and the gracious power of God unleashed into personal lives and the communal reality of the church. This is where much of the impact of the various charismatic movements has been felt – a heightened awareness of God, a renewal of the intensity out of which the Christian faith was born, an intensity that is renewed from time to time and which, at its most powerful results in 'revival'. In the early days of charismatic renewal, much argument was expended around the term 'baptism of the Spirit, which certainly belongs to this category of heightened experience. There were theological objections to the term in that it could imply that there were two dimensions of the Christian life, the first of which was being in Christ and the second was being in the Spirit, with the second being an advance on the first. This was theologically objectionable in that there can be no advance beyond being 'in Christ'. The construct also suggested a distinction between Christians along the lines of those who had passed their 'O-levels' and those who had their 'A-levels' (to refer to a now-defunct system!), to those who were 'in' the circle and those who were 'out'. This was, without doubt, pastorally and spiritually unhelpful. My own resolution to this was to affirm that the fullness of God is available to us in Christ and that it takes a lifetime, and an eternity beyond it, to plumb the depths of an inexhaustible God. There are and ought to be spiritual experiences aplenty that belong to the witness of the Spirit within and the sense of assurance that comes with this. Through conversion, we are baptised into Christ by the Spirit and so stand on level ground; but along the way of the Christian life, there are intensifications of what it means to be 'in Christ', and I have no hesitation in seeing these as 'baptisms' in the Spirit, not one 'second blessing' but multiple blessings and moments of assurance that blessedly come our way. I find the Pentecostal doctrine that the 'second blessing' is evidenced uniquely by the gift of speaking in tongues neither consistent with scripture nor with experience. This doctrine is rather the elevation of some people's experience into a general rule that makes it a straitjacket for all and a constriction on the Spirit, yet another attempt to turn grace into law. On the other hand, there is no reason to deny the reality or the value of this gift and of those others mentioned, for instance, in 1 Corinthians 12 and 14. The insistence of some that such manifestations have ceased with the end of the apostolic age or the completion of the canon appears to me a convenient way of rationalising our lack of experience. A cardinal principle I value as a Protestant and a Christian of free church conviction is that the New Testament is normative and not 'abnormal' on this point as on others. To then say that this is not true about spiritual gifts is, in effect, to place the authority of tradition above that of scripture: the nonexperience of spiritual gifts we experience now trumps the fact that they were a ready part of the New Testament church. This won't do, however much of an uncomfortable challenge it might leave us with. Where I might differ from those who prefer to see these gifts as 'supernatural', that is, intervening in our experience from above and otherwise inexplicable, is in understanding them as inspirations within our natural human experience once renewed in the Spirit. This requires some explanation.

If I have learnt anything from the charismatic movements in which I have been involved, it has been as much about the nature of human religious experience as about God's own self. As I see it, these movements have largely been about the more conscious incorporation of the intuitive and mystical or psychical aspects of human beings into the experiential reality of faith. I would argue that both in the doctrinal traditions of Protestantism and in the materialist and reductionist assumptions of modern patterns of thought, some aspects of human experience have come to be regarded with suspicion. Some suspicion is justified in that religious nonsense is as nonsensical as any other form of nonsense; but this should not lead us to dismiss what is an essential aspect of being human. The heart has reasons that reason does not know (Pascal), and in the imperative to be reasonable, it is possible to downgrade the fact that we are also emotional, or in my preferred language intuitive, beings. We are not so much logical as psychological. Much that shapes us remains hidden in the unconscious, and, as I have previously hinted, there is a corporate dimension to the unconscious that also shapes what we experience. This does not excuse us from employing our analytical and rational capacities, nor ought the intuitive to be hostile to reason. Yet 'reason' does well to take other dimensions of our created being into account and only so can it be properly reasonable. In some Pentecostal assumptions, the work of the Spirit is spoken of as though it overrides the merely human; so, the more supernatural the use of spiritual gifts is thought to be, the less our humanity is involved in their expression through premeditation or preparation, the more likely they are to be of God. This, then, is the discussion as to whether the Spirit of God is thought to abolish or to perfect human nature. My perspective is that the Spirit works with the grain of human nature and both sanctifies and uses all dimensions of our being, both rational and intuitive. So, Paul encourages us to value both dimensions to pray with both the mind and with the spirit (1 Corinthians 14).

A good example of this is glossolalia, or speaking in tongues. Some may want to understand this phenomenon as intersecting our humanity from above, so to speak, and so being properly supernatural. It may come as a disappointment to know that it is a human capacity, rooted in the brain as all such capacities, and consequently can be found in other religions and even in the non-religious. What renders a human capacity 'spiritual' is that it is inspired by the Spirit who 'plays' upon our human nature and transforms it into prayer and worship of God. Although it is often assumed that 'tongues' is a recognisable human language ('if I speak in the tongues of mortals and of angels' – 1 Corinthians 13), I suspect Paul is speaking here hypothetically. Several times I have heard the claim that certain persons in meetings were speaking a known language they had never learnt. I have never found proof of this other than hearsay, and the claims fall to my mind in the category of anecdote or urban myth. Such things are not unknown in charismatic circles, and I suspect they are a product of the will-to-believe. Reference is also made to Acts 2 and the fact that the Pentecostal pilgrims to Jerusalem heard the apostles speaking in their own languages. The question here is whether this was a miracle of speaking or of hearing. I am inclined to the latter view. Whereas it is entirely possible that the phenomenon of tongues is several things and not one and that Acts 2 is not the same phenomenon as 1

Corinthians 12-14, to my mind, it comes into the category of inspired 'pre-conceptual speech' rather than an unlearnt natural language as such. It is no less valuable if we take the point that both the intellectual and the intuitive dimensions have their place in holistic encounters with God.

The point of my analysis is that there is no such thing as a non-human human experience of God. To respond to God, there must be a corresponding brain or physiological activity through which it is mediated to us. By incidental extension from this, there can be no human knowledge of anything in the universe without its being registered in the brain, and since human brains are limited rather than unlimited in capacity, there must be that in the universe, not just that we do not know but that we are never capable of knowing. This is a call to continuing human enquiry and pushing the boundaries, but also to profound humility and to a form of reverent agnosticism. Philosophical atheism (as distinct from methodological atheism) is, therefore, a form of faith, not knowledge, since we cannot exclude the reality of God in those realms beyond our knowledge.

Conversely, God may make God's own self known by entering our experience from realms beyond us. The assertion of the very human nature of the experience of God may help us in other ways: it helps us to recognise that religious experience, as all other forms of experience, is subject to distortion. The charismatic and renewal movements of history have undoubtedly benefitted humankind in warming hearts towards God, enriching lives and communities, and inspiring good works. Equally, they have been paralleled by movements of 'enthusiasm' that were illusory and mistaken. They may have been felt to be 'of God' but proved not to be. The injunction to test all things and to hold fast to the good must apply to all aspects of such movements. Self-awareness and self-criticism are appropriate. On another scale, the fact that apparent religious experiences can be induced through, for instance, hypnotism or drugs does not mean that any claim to knowledge of God must, therefore, be invalid. One presumes that the illusion of any human experiences (listening to music, taking part in discussion, reliving past experiences) can be produced through the appropriate stimulation of the brain; but this does not of necessity mean that such real experiences do not exist.

Engaging the intuitive (can one also say 'psychic' and 'mystical'?) dimensions also illuminates to my mind the ways in which other charismatic phenomena work. 'Prophecy' consists in an intuitive sense of how God's being bears upon a particular people at a particular time. 'Interpretation of tongues' is not a translation of what is said by one who speaks but a 'picking up the mood' and putting it into words, either as prayer to God or a word to the people. 'Discernment of spirits' or 'words of knowledge or wisdom' may be sudden intuitive insights into persons or situations. 'Healing' fits less well into the framework indicated, but the urge to pray for it may do so. All these expressions only prove to be 'edifying' if they are exercised in a context of trust, mutual love and spiritual bondedness. This can be high-octane, exciting stuff requiring careful handling, which is no doubt why some prefer to avoid it and settle for safe and programmed forms of life and worship instead. Alternatively, like the Quakers, they might transmute what was originally a powerful movement of waiting on God into a preference for silence. The area where I have been most uncomfortable is precisely that of healing. There are encouragements in scripture, not least the ministry of Jesus and of the apostles, that prize the ability to heal as a sign of God's kingdom. Yet when this is attempted, and even worse promised, by those whose 'power to heal' is nowhere like that of Jesus, the danger of spiritual fall-out is considerable. When the Third Wave associated with Vineyard Ministries and John Wimber in the 1980s was at its exciting heights, a primary message was that the power of God, including healing, was available to all God's people. In context, this was a criticism of big-name, platform-based healing ministries that elevated certain star performers. It attempted, by contrast, to empower and democratise the people of God in a way seemingly quite consistent with scripture but which, in many ways, was unwise in the hands of inexperienced people. One aspect of this was the inclination to place the needs of the persons who prayed above those of those prayed for, in other words, the urge to have verification of the power to heal superseded the highly sensitive needs of the sick person, leaving them worse off. Putting such supposed power in the hands of those who lacked the pastoral and spiritual sensitivity that should go with it and who were never trained to do this is not a good idea. If healing is promised in a way that no human has the warrant to do, or then suggesting that lack of healing is the product of a person's lack of faith and is, therefore, their fault, is a way of treading the vulnerable underfoot and, as such, is shameful.

I have drawn several conclusions from all this. The first is that big-meeting, platform ministries tend to corrupt and have no basis in scripture. The healing spectacle that has grown up in revivalist movements has to justify itself and so tends in an atmosphere of excitement to claim healings that subsequently prove not to be so. The drive within them is to win financial support, to enhance their reputations and to be always coming up with new insights to justify their continuation. They are best avoided. The second is that healing is a gift of God and cannot be produced by human effort. We may promise to pray for the sick yet cannot determine what the outcome of that prayer might be and so should never promise what we cannot bring to pass. One piece of wisdom that John Wimber passed on was that when someone is prayed for, it should be the most loving experience they have ever had. Where this is the case, it is highly unlikely that they will regret the experience, whatever the outcome. A third conclusion is that prayer for healing should certainly be part of a church's ministry but is best exercised on an intimate, pastoral, and personal scale as part of a loving community of faith by people who know what they are doing. The 'showmanship' approach conflicts with this.

The intersection of Christology and pneumatology is a further area where I would register a charismatic gain. To describe this as a 'Spirit-Christology' is good but insufficient, and so needs to be developed into a 'Trinitarian-Christology'. The former term foregrounds the work of the Spirit in the ministry of Jesus but is liable to an adoptionist misinterpretation that portrays Jesus as a human being embued with the Spirit to a greater extent than others rather than as the Word made flesh. Yet an incarnational Christology could risk neglecting the role of the Spirit in the gift of God's Son. To be truly Trinitarian, we need to reckon with the Spirit as the one through whom Christ is conceived in the womb of Mary, by whom he grows in wisdom and stature, through whom he is anointed for his ministry and engages in acts of power and healing, by whom he offers himself as an atoning sacrifice and by whom he is raised from death to risen life. The Spirit is, in all respects, the Giver of Jesus. All of this is so explicit in the biblical text that it is hard to see how it has been overlooked. Christologies 'from above' tended to reduce the Spirit and blur the continuity been Christ's humanity and our own. At their worst, these resulted in 'heavenly flesh' Christologies or assumptions that Christ assumed an 'unfallen', supposedly 'Adamic' human nature.

At one time it was problematic to claim that Christ assumed human nature in its fallen condition, but this must surely have been the case if there is to be a true redemption. Christ came seeking the lost, and this means he came to us in our present, fallen condition to restore and exalt us. Because this could be thought to mean he was implicated in human sin, former Christian thinkers have been reluctant to say this; but it is precisely in intersecting human nature in its fallen condition and then regenerating, redeeming, and sanctifying it so that he was without sin that we have the hope that a 'new creation' may be formed in us. We are being conformed to his image, being progressively transformed into his likeness, and herein is the nature of the Christian life and the ground of our hope. The distinction between Christ and ourselves is not found in the fact that he bears a different kind of humanity but that he embraces ours and then becomes the Pioneer of our salvation. I enjoy the image I once read of an Alpine guide who first had to find his own way across the mountains with all their dangers and difficulties before he was qualified to lead others along the same routes. Christ did (and does) this for us in the pilgrimage of life. Crucially, it is in dependence on God's Spirit that he did so. It is not that because of his divine nature, he was 'bomb-proof' against the temptations and trials of life but that, through God's Spirit in and by whom he lived, he was kept for God. So, if we, as we should, give thanks to Christ for giving us God's Spirit, we should equally and always give thanks to the Spirit for giving us the Christ, the anointed One. And if we are to live the Christian life, it must be according to the pattern that we see in Christ himself: Christ is the One in whom the very image of God is realised, and through him, as our Mediator and by the Spirit this new kind of humanity can be realised in us through regeneration, sanctification, empowering, self-offering, and final glorification – all by the Spirit of Christ.

It is clearer to me than ever that Christian theology must be resolutely Trinitarian in form. I owe much to Tom Smail in the way I have developed theologically and am mindful of the nature of his own theological writing. What I have just written shows the hallmarks of three of his books: the first was *Reflected Glory*, in which he developed a Spirit-empowered Christology and its implications. From this, he moved to *The Forgotten Father*, which sought to restore a balance he believed to be lacking. He then moved on to *The Giving Gift*, in which he, as a proponent of charismatic renewal, developed our understanding of the Spirit. Together, these books represent a wholesome and balanced theological approach that holds us in good stead, though it must be said that in theology, in worship and in personal devotion, there is a constant tendency towards some form of unitarianism. In much charismatic worship, this tends to be a unitarianism of the Son rather than the Spirit. For all that we should be Christ-centred, and for all that the ministry of the Spirit is to highlight the glory of the Son, a failure to be truly trinitarian inevitably leads to spiritual impoverishment, and that should be the last thing that charismatic renewal is about.

I said that through the various iterations of charismatic renewal I have learnt something about God but considerably more about human beings. Over the years, I have taken a passing interest in psychic studies mainly because that field of experimental endeavour, much maligned by more materialist approaches, is an exploration of what it means to be human. Being human involves various 'subterranean' dimensions that may be likened (perhaps with a variation of metaphor) to the proverbial iceberg, nine-tenths of which are below the surface. Our conscious selves are a small part of our total existence, and therefore, there is the hidden 'natural' depth-component to all our experiences, including experience of the divine. If, according to the charismatic perspective there is a diversity to the manifestations of the Spirit in accordance with 1 Corinthians 12, this is as much to do with the configuration of our conscious and unconscious selves as with 'what God is doing'. Some more readily respond to spiritual stimuli than others. Some find it easier to speak in tongues; the gift never comes to some others. We are past the stage where any great significance is attached to this. Some 'tremble' in the manifest presence of God, and others never do. I recall John Wimber saying that even though he was much used to mediate 'signs and wonders', the kinds of phenomena that are historically associated with 'revivalism' and so are not as unusual as they initially appear, he had never himself been the subject (or object?) of these phenomena. It is reasonably clear to me that this is more to do with our varied 'psychic' make-ups than with our level of personal devotion. Their actual spiritual value is also a question: people respond differently, and how they respond is no direct guide to their spirituality or maturity. It intrigues me that in the Old Testament, the person who most manifests the quaking and trembling phenomenon is King Saul, who, however well he began, ended tragically. He is a fascinating psychological study, astonishing in such ancient literature. I am almost inclined to say that he showed a kind of 'vulnerability' to the divine, collapsing under the power of the Spirit and showing no lasting benefit because of it.

Added to all of this is my speculation as to the degree to which we are in the 'subterranean' dimensions shaped and configured by the communities to which we adhere. That this happens on the level of the family is undeniable – how we are brought up determines much about us. But the same must be true on the societal level. If there is indeed a 'sociology of knowledge' that shapes our 'plausibility structures', things that seem eminently believable in some social contexts, such as seems to be the case in Islamic or African contexts, are deemed implausible in others. There can also be a contagion or infection about religious and spiritual experiences. Some might call this 'hysteria', and if the term is used non-pejoratively, I don't see the need to deny it. We catch things from each other. Behind the Third Wave associated with the Vineyard movement were certain people who acted as catalysts. We might think of them as 'super-spreaders'. They, in turn, catalysed others, usually by their physical proximity (though sometimes in more mysterious ways), and so a movement was born, the effect of which inevitably died down with time. I have wondered whether there was significance in the fact that John Wimber, before pioneering with the Vineyard movement, belonged to the Quakers in one of their more evangelical North American expressions. Could it be that there is something that is passed down through a community's culture that then shapes later generations? I don't know the answer, but I can't escape the question. However, uncovering the 'natural' dimension helps to recognise how it is that all such spiritual movements require a proper discipline and sometimes pruning to remove the less helpful elements, and this can be done without feeling we are disrespecting the Spirit's work. It also makes us aware of the temptations that potentially confront those who emerge as catalysts or 'stars' at such times. They do well to imitate John the Baptist: 'I must decrease, and Christ must increase'. There is only one Celebrity for those who are in Christ Jesus.

Post Twenty-Four: Returning to Holy Scripture

I return as promised to understanding the nature of scripture and its interpretation. Of the two exercises, the latter is more challenging. Without the scriptural tradition, there would be no Christian faith. Following what is summarised in John 20:30-31, we can make certain lapidary statements. In the divine providence, we have things that are written, that is, scriptures or writings, that capture what was once spoken. This applies to the whole scripture, Old and New Testaments, which can be characterised above all as 'prophetic', even when they deal with history or belong to the 'wisdom' strand. As merely spoken words, they would have been lost in the mists of time or distorted in the process of transmission. As it is, we have what was once spoken preserved in stable and permanent form, which means that they record what belongs to the past (subject to the vagaries of copying, translation, and onward transmission). As records, the scriptures are available for everybody for ever, and through them, their message can be communicated to the ends of the earth. This is an astonishing but indisputable fact and accounts in part for the global spread of the faith. In addition, these given scriptures now regulate what the content of that faith is deemed to be. This is not to say that they cannot be interpreted in varied and sometimes contradictory ways. As writings that are 'out there', they assume a life of their own and come into the possession of an abundance of people with a multiplicity of worldviews. Once inserted into human cultures, the horizons of scripture and those worldviews merge, and the results of the process can be creative and productive or distorting. One reason why the gospel should be preached to the ends of the earth is so that the full significance of scripture might be realised in the encounter with multiple worldviews. It should not be disguised, however, that this is an immensely risky process as people everywhere impose their own culturally derived meanings and then trumpet their own imaginings as the very Word of God. The scriptures themselves give rise to this fact by reason of their diversity and differing perspectives. They don't always speak with one voice, and discerning the primary Voice is a considerable task. Despite this, the canonical writings regulate what can be believed and claimed in their name. There are those things which they cannot be taken to mean, a limit to what is possible in their interpretation. Following Martin Luther, it can be claimed that there is a basic perspicuity to scripture: the central message can reasonably be agreed upon even if the subsidiaries are often a matter of debate.

Charles Spurgeon famously declared that it is foolish to try to defend the Bible. Like a lion, it should be allowed to defend itself. Despite his wise challenge, I find myself wanting to speak for scripture when it is depreciated. I would describe myself as holding to moderate 'higher-critical' views when it comes to the human (if inspired) product that we call the Bible. I find a magnificence in the fact that God has chosen to speak through limited and finite human beings in a way that is subject to scrutiny. I see an analogy here with the incarnation; the Word made flesh and communicated to us through the medium of one very particular human identity, Jesus of Nazareth. I do not take this to mean that Jesus was an authority on all subjects, that he had an inerrant understanding of cosmology, of history, of mathematics or of psychology. He was, rather, a Jewish male situated in the context of the first century and of second Temple Judaism, a man of his time, albeit one equipped by God's Spirit to fulfil his mission. This, to my mind, is not a diminution of his significance or glory but quite the reverse, a celebration of the divine humility and compassion. None of this wholehearted embrace of human nature compromises the central mission of the Christ as the True Witness and Word of God who unlocks for us the greatest mysteries of life, God and creation in the way proclaimed by John 1. Indeed, it makes this possible. By analogy, the scriptures are thoroughly human writings, but they are breathed out and into by the Spirit of God in order that we may know and encounter the Living God and be brought into the reality of God's own being. We look to them for this and bring them into conversation with our God-endowed abilities to interpret the world in all other ways.

The fact that the scriptures are human, historical artefacts means that our understanding of them has progressed as we have come to understand other areas of life more fully. None of the biblical authors could have understood the sheer size not only of the world they inhabited but of a universe in which there are an estimated 125 billion galaxies in which ours on its own may contain 100 billion stars – such a thing is scarcely imaginable even to modern people. The ancients are not to be blamed for this. They spoke and speak out of their own contexts and worldviews. This does not mean that the wisdom with which they spoke can or should be discounted. Arguably, in the progression of human knowledge, we have lost as well as gained. It is understandable that as knowledge increased, our predecessors in faith struggled to square what they found in the Bible with what they were learning through modern endeavour. It should also be remembered that many of those who were pioneering new scientific understandings, for instance, were themselves people of faith, and the resistance to their ideas was as much from fellow-scientists as from the religious. It takes time to assimilate new ideas and to sift through what is to be modified and retained of the old as paradigms shift. Nobody is entitled to claim that we have reached 'the end of civilisation'. We do not know what is yet to be discovered and what its impact might be. Arguably, the world is becoming more mysterious rather than less. There will always be a choice whether we interpret the universe within a theistic framework or not, and I emphasise the word 'choice'.

One level of critique of the Bible consists in historiography: is it historically reliable? The Bible concerns itself with history, specifically with the history of a people, Israel, and the religious faith that emerged from that people. This culminated, for the

Christian, in the emergence of Christ and the church that grew out of the resurrection. Historical scrutiny of the Bible is, therefore, inevitable. Yet 'history' means different things. At the basic level it refers to things that actually happened, to events. At a more advanced level, it refers to the brand of scholarly enquiry that attempts to recover and reconstruct those events. At this point, the enquiry becomes subject to assumptions and ideologies that may distort the process. Good historians are aware of this, expose their own assumptions and prejudices to scrutiny and acknowledge that there are limitations to their discipline, areas into which they are unwise to trespass. What can a historian as a historian say about God, for instance, or the meaning of the crucifixion? To recognise the Bible as a historical document surely means to take seriously that those who contributed to it were using the assumptions and conventions of their own day and age and knew little of historiography as practised post-Enlightenment. Yet from within their world, a changing one, they had something to say. I oppose, therefore, both the fundamentalist claim that scripture is at all levels historically accurate by modern standards and the sceptic's dismissal of it as having limited historical value. Instead, the Bible, particularly the Hebrew scriptures, is an example of social or cultural memory in which a people, Israel, recalls and rehearses its own self-understanding. I advance the idea that at its core are events, realities and agents, which are then wrapped around with interpretations of their significance in the ongoing history of the people. The core of events is sometimes difficult to uncover; it is, for instance, clearer to modern historians at the time of the Exile than at that of the Exodus, not least because of the availability of parallel sources. The Bible has its own rules. Discernible history (as we understand it, and with the above qualifications) begins with Abraham. What comes before that in narratives such as the Garden of Eden, the Tower of Babel, and Noah's Ark has, to my mind, the character of 'myth' (a category I use in a non-prejudicial way). My guess is that these accounts were learnt by Israel by the time of the exile and were pressed into service to communicate Israel's distinct understanding of God's character and purpose. It is impossible to understand Noah's Ark as literally true when the details are analysed, but as a shared myth across several civilisations, it is likely that there is a genuine memory within it. The ideas that the flood was universal and that two of each species (of which there are millions) were gathered into the Ark reflects the more limited worldview of that age and exceeds reasonable belief. We should respect it for what it says in its own terms rather than try to accommodate it to our own criteria. When so taken, it can still speak to us, but in the category of 'theology in pictures'. So, with the other events of pre-history. Yet with the coming of Abraham we emerge from the undatable events of pre-history to roughly datable history that we can recognise.

If we assume that before what is contained in the Old Testament existed in written form (and there were certainly older writings on which it drew), it circulated largely in oral form, we gain new insights into it. One aspect of this was the device of hyperbole, exaggeration for the sake of good storytelling. Precision is a virtue of writing, but oral communication benefits from drama. A comparison here: observing paintings of Scottish landscapes, there is a marked tendency to exaggerate the landscapes, to make the valleys deeper, the hills steeper and the cataracts wilder than they are in real life. It makes for impressive art and cannot be characterised as deceptive, just interpretative. Still, the actual landscapes prove, by and large, to be more modest. Numbers in the Old Testament are particularly subject to exaggeration, although this may sometimes be for scribal reasons. What I say here may seem impious when describing a sacred text, but some of what is there has significant entertainment value with a didactic purpose. The Jacob and Joseph cycles in Genesis easily come into our category of 'soap opera', which helps to explain the elements of tension and repetition. The same can be said of the Samson narratives: their preoccupations with sex and violence appear to have limited theological value. The accounts of Saul, David and Solomon have been pronounced narrative genius, astonishing for the times in which they were written, especially because of their psychological perception. Overall, then, how we handle this as 'history' needs to allow that we are also dealing with literature, and literature has its own power and energy. The Bible is designed to be read as literature not just history, and the narratives were written down sometimes long after they happened. It should not surprise us that there is a blending of record and folklore. As it is said: 'The past is another country – they do things differently there'. For me, as with Professor James Barr, the status of the Bible is one of sufficiency rather than perfection. If it is 'infallible', it is so in relation to the primary purposes for which it has been given, namely that we may come to know the true and living God, supremely in the person of God's Son. It does not need to be 'inerrant' to be effective, and many years of careful and honest Bible study have convinced me of this.

It would be tedious and unhelpful to my purpose to demonstrate the truth of my last sentence in detail. However, I can refer to the points made years ago in the dialogue between David Edwards and John Stott in their jointly authored book *Essentials: A liberal-evangelical dialogue*.[51] Neither of them doubts the other's sincere and genuine faith, but it is clear enough that Edwards suspects that beneath Stott's urbane, conservative evangelical exterior, there lurks a concealed fundamentalist. Stott is unwilling to concede the category of 'error' and, truth to tell would have suffered great reputational damage among those more conservative had he done so, even greater than his admission that he has doubts about the category of everlasting torment. In Edwards' chapter on the authority of scripture (pp. 41-82), I find myself more sympathetic to his argument in which, among other things, he draws attention to a

---

[51] (Sevenoaks: Hodder and Stoughton, 1988).

catalogue of scriptural discrepancies than to Stott's response. What he writes bears out Barr's comment, as stated above, that in the process of inspiring and teaching faith and the way of living that goes with it, scripture does not need to be inerrant, just sufficient. Particularly noteworthy is Edwards' comment that, unlike Stott and Edwards themselves, neither Jesus nor the biblical writers had access to the kind of extensive library that would enable 'inerrant' precision to be attained. I am happy to maintain and teach the belief that the scriptures are of their time, not ours, and yet they reliably bear witness to what is needed for us to know, love, and serve God. Since they are given to us by God for our benefit, we should receive them as they are rather than impose upon them a set of assumptions as to what they must be to satisfy our prior criteria. While we should engage with them critically and bring their contents into dialogue with present knowledge, I strongly resist the notion that we should feel ourselves superior to them in any measure. Humility should accompany our approach, and whichever part of the scriptures we are studying, the over-riding concern should be, 'What am I to learn from this, and how does it shape my life?

What, then, about the moral status of the biblical tradition? I return here to the statement cited above from Diarmaid MacCulloch that there is much about which the Bible is simply 'wrong'. In this regard, he cites both 'the plain anti-Semitism which runs through so many sections of the text of the New Testament' and its 'clear acceptance of slavery as a normal part of social structure' (pp. 705-

7). As it happens, I think MacCulloch and others who make similar claims on these topics are simply wrong on the first of these issues and unjust on the second. Both Jesus himself and nearly all of those who wrote the New Testament were themselves ethnically Jewish. *Anti-Semitism* is a construct concerned with race and ethnicity and is to be distinguished from *anti-Judaism*. Two things should be clear: as Christianity progressively distinguished itself from first-century Judaism, there was a degree of hostility between the two, and this is indeed evident in the New Testament, but it was a disagreement over belief, not race, and so is not anti-Semitism. Also, it originated in particular occasions of estrangement and bad feelings rather than being in-principle hostility, though it may later have become this. Several contemporary Jewish scholars acknowledge this. This is not to say that anti-Judaism is not regrettable in a way that all 'anti' positions might be, nor that the 'parting of the ways' was not unfortunate. But arguably, the original faults lie on both sides of the divide; and some fault can be identified in the continuing reluctance of Judaism to recognise a valid way of being Jewish in contemporary messianic Judaism. The second point is that it is beyond doubt that the anti-Judaic texts in the New Testament have, in later Christian history, been at times been used for anti-Semitic purposes. This does not make them anti-Semitic in themselves. On the point about endorsing slavery, I shall make some points below.

The Bible might be judged wrong if, for instance, we take the view that it 'teaches' a certain kind of cosmology. I deny this to be true for the reasons already set out. There is a difference between teaching things a certain way and simply speaking or writing from within a cultural and intellectual context governed by shared assumptions we no longer hold, particularly when there is no easy way of questioning those assumptions. Inevitably, the Copernican revolution, by which the earth was understood to revolve around the sun and not vice versa, has led to a new way of reading the Bible. In that way, it could be claimed that biblical assumptions about cosmology were simply 'wrong'. But the biblical witnesses had no way of knowing this scientifically and were operating with common sense assumptions according to which the earth remains stable and the sun rises and sets. These perceptions are true to experience if not to science. We who know otherwise, for instance, that the earth is tearing through space and at the same time revolves, continue to use the old language because it remains true to our experience and, in that sense, is not 'wrong'. 'Flat-earthers' or 'young-earthers' who, out of a misguided form of loyalty to the Bible, cling to an old cosmology are indeed mistaken and act as a warning to us to engage in appropriate interpretation. What we learn from non-biblical sources legitimately shapes how we approach scripture, and something similar applies to all other ancient texts. We read them with sophistication.

So, how does this impact upon interpretation of biblical moral prescriptions? For one thing, it brings cultural context into the calculation. Every generation of God's people must negotiate how the will or command of God applies to its social context, usually one they do not have the power, or perhaps imagination, to change. An example of this is the practice of 'levirate marriage' in Israel. This was the custom by which if a husband were to die leaving his wife without children, the man's brother had an obligation to take her as a wife, probably in addition to existing wives, and beget children by her. This today would be regarded as bigamous and so immoral and illegal yet was seen of old as a moral duty. The cultural assumptions that determined this included the fact that without a man to provide for her, the woman might become destitute and that her now-dead husband needed a posterity in which his name could be remembered. What to us might seem immoral took on the form of moral duty in a different context. We might retrospectively consider that the woman here is being treated as a possession rather than a partner, and this would be a fair point, one which could be adduced at other points of the biblical text. My point, however, is that the advice was *the best that could be given in the circumstances*, a guiding principle to which I shall return. It is worth pointing out here that the basis on which much Old Testament law proceeds is that of case law. The presumption is that the laws of Israel are interpreted and applied to specific cases by 'the elders at the gate' who administer public justice.

It is unfair to approach the Bible, or for that matter other ancient texts, with a 'presentist' mindset to judge it according to present-day standards without regard to its varied contexts. Much of what we take for granted was inconceivable to previous generations. Present-day assumptions are formed by an awareness of human rights codified between the eighteenth and the twentieth centuries with a long pre-history and period of gestation. It is appropriate to see the prescriptions of the Old Testament as an early catalyst in this process, one which is surprisingly advanced when set against the background from which it emerged. The moral guidance of both testaments needs to be understood first as modifications or ameliorations of the world as it then was, not achieving everything at once yet moving in the right direction. The effect was to make the world better than it would otherwise have been while leaving room for further movement. It is wrong, therefore, to read the Bible as though it were a 'flat' book, equally valid at all points. Biblical revelation gathers pace. For a Christian who interprets the Bible, this forward movement culminates in the coming of Christ as the very Word of God, and so what is revealed through the Hebrew scriptures is to be read retrospectively in the light of Christ. It is as though light appears in the developing revelations of the Hebrew narratives but then shines in its fullness in the face of Christ. There is no difficulty in principle, therefore, in saying that parts of the Old Testament no longer apply in Christ. But this is not to say that nothing is to be learnt from them: there is always something to learn because what goes before foreshadows what is to come. Crucial here is that the Old Testament scriptures are to be interpreted not in the light of *external,* present-day moral prescriptions, and so rendered palatable (the 'modernist' tendency) but *internally* in the light of Christ, who has come as the definitive revelation of God and of God's will. A primary principle in biblical interpretation, therefore, is that of 'sublation', which needs some explanation.

Karl Barth used to speak about the 'abolition' of religion. The German word he used was *Aufhebung,* which has a nuanced meaning. On the one hand, it means that something is done away with and passes away, and on the other, that elements of what is abolished are taken up into something new. 'Sublation' is an appropriate translation of *Aufhebung.* A relatively uncontroversial example of this is the way in which animal sacrifices are deemed no longer to be necessary or efficacious in the light of Christ's atoning sacrifice. He is the Lamb of God who takes away the sin of the world, and so the shedding of the blood of animals is no longer required. To be accurate, animal sacrifice is already being relativised in the Old Testament when contrasted with heartfelt contrition and personal devotion. In Christ the need for such sacrifices is abolished altogether since what those sacrifices foreshadowed is realised definitively in Christ. Yet our understanding of the vicarious sacrifice in Christ is shaped and formed by what has gone before, perhaps most visibly in the rituals of the Day of Atonement on which the sins of the people of Israel were expiated and carried away from them. Now Christ is both High Priest and sacrifice and bears away the sins not only of Israel but of the whole world. Much is to be learnt, therefore, by studying the sacrificial 'system' of the Jewish law and temple, but the learning has a Christological form. We can be grateful that animal sacrifices have been abolished, but their meaning has been 'taken up' into our appreciation of the atonement. It should be noted that a similar movement has taken place within Judaism as morning and evening sacrifices are of necessity (given the destruction of the temple) transformed into the daily rhythm of prayer, and the Day of Atonement has come to focus on contrition and repentance, not sacrifice. The principle of sublation might be seen to apply to other themes: so, the circumcision that matters is not that in the flesh but in the heart; the sabbath becomes the principle of rest in God rather than confined to Saturdays; Israel's purity and food laws are broadened out to refer to the living of distinctive lives of thanksgiving. How to navigate 'sublation' was clearly an issue for the New Testament church as Gentiles became believers and the Jewish originators of the faith had to accommodate their influx. The compromise arrived at was that Jews would continue to practise their laws but should not require the same of Gentiles. But it is not surprising that while the moral demands of the law were maintained, its ritual requirements were relativised. What we might discern in all of this is the matter of continuity and discontinuity: without doubt, the Christian faith grows out of the faith of Israel and the

Judaism of the Second Temple and is incomprehensible without this background. With equal certainty, in Christ there is that which is New and transcends these roots in a way that is faithful to them and yet grows out of them. Jesus was truly and faithfully Jewish in that he understood with divine wisdom the direction in which the revelation of God was tending and needed to go. He came not to destroy but to fulfil. The 'new covenant' written on the heart and envisaged by the prophets is realised in him and brought to completion and applies to all the nations, not Israel alone.

Whereas for contemporary Jewish believers, the Torah continues to be the embodiment of God's will for God's people, for the Christian, that will is embodied, literally, in the man Jesus of Nazareth, now exalted to be the Christ of God and Lord of all. What we read in the Torah (the 'Law') continues to enlighten us and helps to illuminate the righteous demand of God made upon us in Christ, the call to holy lives. But at the same time, it is 'sublated', rendered obsolete in one form in order that it may be re-established in another. There is continuity and discontinuity; and if this seems problematic to Jewish believers, then the same is true for them; the Temple system no longer exists and so must take a new form in Jewish practice. Contemporary Judaisms are, therefore, supersessionist in their own ways. Judaism and Christianity are both descended from the same original biblical roots and each makes its claim to fidelity – one to the Word written in the Torah, and the other to the Word as embodied in the Christ. But there is more here than sublime repetition: there is interpretation and application in new contexts. Despite Judaism's general inability to recognise Jesus of Nazareth as the Messiah, I hold open, as did Paul, the hope that this day may come, a hope I entertain for all the nations. Because of the promises of God to the patriarchs and their descendants I hope confidently for those who are still to be considered 'the people of God'. Messianic Judaism is a pointer in this direction, a downpayment, so to speak.

The concept of sublation is essential for the sometimes-complex task of interpreting scripture. I say 'complex' because it is evident that many varying interpretations both of doctrine and ethics exist among and between those who hold to the authority of those scriptures. We are left, therefore, with traditions of interpretation. This is even, and perhaps particularly, the case when it comes to the very point at which Christians should be united around the table of the Lord. One might hope that we could eat and drink together while holding to differing understandings of what happens to the bread and wine in the process, but sadly, not even this is acceptable to all. Overall, however, I have tried to set out the discipline of reading scripture in the light of God's fullest revelation in Christ and that means to be conscious of development throughout the biblical narratives. Whereas a Christian approach to interpretation might require us to learn from the whole scripture and to appreciate its didactic power, we are not bound to all the prescriptions of the Hebrew scriptures, nor to regard all the examples set there as appropriately followed. The Bible is not a flat book in which all its parts are of equal weight wherever they occur. Sublation points to a forward movement in which some things are left behind, as already illustrated. We might consider as a pointer the record of Jesus dealing with the woman taken in adultery in John 8 (though misplaced in that context). Whatever the motives of those who wished to stone her (whether concealed guilt or misogyny or both), they were taking their clue as to what to do from the Law. Jesus exposed their hypocrisy and, by contrast, refused to condemn the woman, prizing mercy above punishment. He did this without condoning her alleged adultery. Since the Hebrew scriptures lay down several harsh penalties for actions that were deemed to undermine the community and the forms of behaviour that sustain it, we find them problematic. I must recall that the past is a foreign country. Resources that are available in modern societies, such as prisons and forms of rehabilitation, were not available in early Israelite culture. I return to my theme that often, the laws that were laid down and the judgements made were the best that were available *in the circumstances*. Set against the background of their own day, these scriptures tended to moderate the exercise of civil and criminal justice. They move incrementally in more humane directions, and it is the trajectory of the increment that counts for us as we apply the principle of sublation.

Although the books of the Torah certainly lay down penalties and punishments, it is difficult at this distance to know how much of what was prescribed was carried out. Law codes do not necessarily give a rounded picture of how societies behaved. My suspicion is that they skew the picture, as they would if we observed our own culture mainly through its statute books. I suspect that, for instance, the Book of Leviticus, like much else in scripture, has a primarily didactic rather than judicial purpose. It intends to make statements about behaviours deemed unacceptable, reserving the most severe penalties for the most serious misdemeanours. In other words, it is 'making statements' about how crimes and misdemeanours should be weighted. Those who studied it with the responsibility of administering justice would form mentalities, which would then be applied to specific instances.

I am really trying to show how the Old Testament leans in humane directions and, in the context of its times, moves incrementally towards justice tempered by mercy. To illustrate this and to show how things can be misrepresented, I choose to take what is probably the most misunderstood prescription of all, Leviticus 24:19-21: 'Anyone who maims another shall suffer the same injury in return: fracture for fracture, eye for eye, tooth for tooth; the injury inflicted is the injury to be suffered' (also Exodus 21:22-26). These verses are often cited as a recipe for a cycle of recrimination with the result that 'the whole world would be blind'. In fact, it is the precise opposite. It sets out a principle of justice that requires punishment equal in weight to the offence committed and by no means greater than it (as was frequently the case in ancient times). Although clearly a statement of retribution, the retribution is to be proportionate. This is a principle that guides the administration of public justice and holds good even today. What is imposed by a court is unjust if it proves too lenient and fails to recognise the gravity of the wrong that has been done. Equally, if it exceeds it, a wrong has been committed in reverse. It is a principle of proportion to guide the court, not a requirement to be fulfilled by the offended party in a vendetta. The distinction here is that between vengeance and revenge: courts avenge the wrong done to others; revenge is what I take in hand to 'get my own back'. It is not necessary to conclude the literal intention was to maim wrongdoers in return for their actions. Probably the concern was to find a way of measuring the degree of compensation that would need to be made. If the trajectory here is away from unbridled revenge and towards the limitation of punishment to what is proportionate, this may help us understand the way in which Jesus was later to teach, 'You have heard that it was said, "An eye for an eye and a tooth for a tooth", But I say to you, Do not resist an evildoer. But if anyone strikes you on the right cheek, turn the other also' (Matthew 5:38-9). This is a very important teaching as part of what should be considered quintessential Christian behaviour, behaviour that Jesus himself demonstrated. I doubt here that Jesus was revoking the principle of proportion for the exercise of civil justice. He was saying that that correct principle should not be used as a pretext in personal behaviour for retaliation. Instead, he was extending the trajectory of the limitation of retribution to the point where destructive behaviour is overcome by not seeking 'evil for evil'. He was interrupting the vicious cycle of recrimination so that bad situations were not made worse.

A similar text that is often misunderstood or misrepresented is the crucially important one that runs like a thread through the Old Testament to the extent that it can be seen as a major theme. It first appears in Exodus 34:6-7: 'The LORD, the LORD, a God merciful and gracious, slow to anger, and abounding in steadfast love and faithfulness, keeping steadfast love for the thousandth generation, forgiving iniquity and transgression and sin, yet by no means clearing the guilty, but visiting the iniquity of the parents upon the children, and the children's children, to the third and fourth generation'. What is immediately noticeable about these verses is the contrast made between the divine love and the divine wrath: the latter is inconsiderable by contrast with the former. God is slow to anger and abounds in love. God's wrath in holding the guilty to account is for the fourth generation but God's steadfast love is for a thousand generations. There is no comparison and no false equivalence. This does not prevent the modern mind from worrying more about God's refusal to 'clear the guilty' and so questioning God's justice. These verses need to be read in the light of their clarification in Ezekiel, which denies that guilt is inherited (Ezekiel 18, esp. vv14-20). There is a necessary truth here in that to say 'God does not clear the guilty' governs what is to follow, and so if the later generations are not guilty of the sins of their parents, there is nothing to fear, but if they persist in the same guilty behaviour, they are indeed accountable. In context, therefore, the warning runs like this: God is abundantly loving, forgiving, merciful and gracious – all of this, but do not make the mistake of believing that you can trade upon God's goodness and get away with it. Instead, be informed that God persists in resisting and punishing wrongdoing will not overlook what should not be overlooked. There is also the truth here that sin has intergenerational effects; it unlocks consequences for our posterity that have little to do with their choices but a great deal with our own. This is the concealed truth once the necessary qualifications have been made.

It is a major challenge to the moral authority of scripture that it apparently does not advocate for the abolition of slavery. More than once, I have heard politicians seek to disqualify scripture for this reason. My response in defence is that whereas there is no outright and general demand to this effect, the seeds were sown that would lead to humanising the practice of slavery, and that would, in time, subvert it. Again, it is the trajectory to which scripture points and the direction in which it is moving that guides our moral vision. The enslavement of any human being for the profit and benefit of others is always and everywhere reprehensible and not to be justified. But it is a mistake to imagine that slavery is always and everywhere the same. Our imagination tells us that slavery consistently resembles that of enslaved Africans in the eighteenth century and that of the southern states of the USA in the nineteenth. But slavery is a consistent phenomenon of the ancient world, not least of Roman society, and was not questioned by anybody, least of all by the philosophers to whom we look back with admiration. Roman society was built upon slavery. Its elites were dependent upon the work of slaves, who frequently were the literate, educated and managerial sustainers of society. It was also utilitarian in an age which did not have the institutional resources we take for granted today, such as prisons or probation. Prisoners of war and the indebted would be integrated into the work force but treated as slaves. The experience of slavery, though most of the time dehumanising, tended to depend on to whom you were enslaved. It was known that for some to sell themselves into slavery was a good career move. Slaves could inherit from their owners or could be granted their freedom by them. I suggest that in the Old Testament, we may trace a humanising process in which slavery became for many a form of indentured labour which issued in ultimate freedom, and this represented the best available application in the circumstances. In the Christian movement, the status of believing slaves was transformed into one of spiritual equality.

Both within and beyond the churches, it is almost a sporting activity to find fault with the apostle Paul and to regard him as a dubious genius and reactionary. A clearer understanding of the context in which he worked and preached refutes this decisively. In the context of his day, he was a reformer with a universal and liberating moral vision, one which is expressed with authority in

Galatians 3:28, 'There is no longer Jew or Greek, there is no longer slave or free, there is no longer male and female, for all of you are one in Christ Jesus'. In Christ, a new and transformed social reality was coming into being. Yet this reality needed to be translated into practical counsel in a world in which the nascent churches were fragile and threatened. To criticise Paul for not leading a slave revolt in the style of Spartacus, one which would similarly have been destined for bloody failure, is simply off-the-wall. Paul's shortest letter, that to Philemon is an example of this approach. It concerns a runaway slave, Onesimus, who has left his 'master' Philemon to team up with Paul in his apostolic ministry. There is the suggestion that he had even stolen money (v.18). Both Philemon and Onesimus are Christians. Onesimus has opened himself to severe penalty according to Roman law, not excluding crucifixion, as a runaway. Paul appeals to Philemon in the most tender terms and uses considerable emotional pressure to take Onesimus back and to see him restored without punishment to his previous status. It might be considered, therefore, that Paul was colluding with an unjust institutional structure when he failed to call it into question. My contrary point is that Paul was taking the best possible course of action in the circumstances. He points out that Onesimus should be treated 'no longer as a slave but as more than a slave, a beloved brother' (v.16). This is subversion. Moreover, the only person who could set Onesimus free was Philemon himself, and Paul writes, 'knowing that you will do even more than I say' (v.21). Ignatius of

Antioch in the second century was to refer to a bishop of Ephesus in the last years of the first century whose name was Onesimus. Because Ephesus was close to where Philemon lived it is entirely likely that he was one and the same with the former slave for whose forgiveness and freedom Paul appealed, thus vindicating his strategy in so doing. Both the Old and New Testaments should be read fairly and contextually according to what was possible for its authors, not what might be possible for those who live in very different circumstances. The revelatory trend in holy scripture is towards the subversion of the institution of slavery, and this would lead in time to its abolition (although bearing in mind that some forms of slavery continue to exist even where these are now considered illegal). It is beyond doubt that no responsible Christian voice would regards these texts as anything other than limited to their day and age and no longer applicable. The fact that certain conditions and behaviours, such as slavery, are found in the scriptures does not mean that they are thereby given approval.

This latter principle needs also to be applied to the frequent appearance of violence in the scriptures, particularly in the history of Israel. I confess this to be, for me, the most problematic of the moral issues raised by the biblical story. Part of me wishes this aspect of the Bible did not exist. The problem is not that violence is described. Violence and warfare are constants of human history, and were they not to be found in the story, we would conclude that the scriptures are divorced from hard reality. The problem resides in such texts as Deuteronomy 7:1-2 which concern Israel's entry into the land of Canaan and the dispossession of the tribes already occupying that land: 'When the LORD your God brings you into the land that you are about to enter and occupy . . . and when the LORD your God gives them over to you and you defeat them, then you must utterly destroy them. Make no covenant with them and show them no mercy'. Other texts issue the same or similar commandments. That many Christians find such requirements morally abhorrent is, to me, less surprising than the capacity of others to take them in their stride. It is beyond doubt that no responsible Christian voice would regard these texts as being limited to their day and age and no longer applicable. They do not constitute a moral norm. How does such lack of mercy cohere with a God who is known to be merciful? Most of all, how can they be set alongside belief in the compassion, kindness and mercy that is exemplified in Christ and is believed to be a manifestation of the true nature of God? Colliding texts and cognitive dissonance prevail.

I hope to give a perspective on this, but I am not persuaded that what I say fully satisfies myself, let alone others. One approach would be to say that there is a difference between what the authors of the biblical tradition believed to be the case and what properly was the will of God. So, those who framed the biblical accounts and interpreted slaughter as God's will were reflecting a primitive stage in their understanding, which was later to be eclipsed with fuller revelation. In other words, the writers of this material were simply wrong. This even though the Deuteronomic theologians were amongst the most advanced of the Hebrew scriptures. Others who would justify the slaughter might argue that the destruction of corrupt nations was like a surgical operation intended to cut out a cancer-like element, regrettable but necessary. After all, when a surgeon wields the knife to remover a malignant growth and save a life, this is morally entirely different from using one to murder. Furthermore, the argument goes, the judgement on the Canaanites had been long delayed by God until the point when the corruption had reached a point at which it could no longer be ignored. So, Genesis 15:16, 'And they (Israel) shall come back here in the fourth generation, for the iniquity of the Amorites is not yet complete'. Indeed, the Canaanites brought their fate upon themselves by 'hardening their hearts' (Joshua 11:20). This sounds suspiciously like victim blaming and has a defensive, self-justifying flavour to it. The existence of these texts indicates that there was considerable unease among the biblical authors and that the actions taken needed to be justified. What is portrayed was exceptional, a departure from the general tenor of those scriptures to be kind to strangers and do them no harm. 'The alien who resides with you shall be to you as the citizen among you; you shall love the alien as yourself, for you were aliens in the land of Egypt: I am the LORD your God' (Leviticus 19:33-34). And later when referring to 'the aliens who reside among you and have begotten children among you', it prescribes, 'they shall be to you as citizens of Israel; with you they shall be allotted and inheritance among the tribes of Israel' (Ezekiel 47:21-23). In this sense, action in the conquest against the Canaanites was 'sealed', not something to be repeated, a one-off that in no sense sets a precedent for further generations. It is portrayed as a specific command of God for a situation that would not otherwise be remedied. In other words, it was essential to God's purpose that the land of Canaan should be occupied by the tribes of Israel and in such a way that they could avoid the contamination of pagan practices and enticements to fulfil their vocation as a paradigm people.

Whatever the truth of these approaches, my own is either different from them or complementary. It is hard to accept that the Canaanites function as tropes and that their humanity is denied. The biblical portrayal of what happened in occupying the land fits into the pattern prevalent in the ancient world of both boasting of success in war and of exaggerating the achievement. It is astonishing that the Book of Joshua, in particular, presents within its own borders two very divergent accounts of the same events. One picture offers a picture of total victory: 'So Joshua took the whole land, according to all that the LORD had spoken to Moses...And the land had rest from war' (11:23). '(N)ot one of all their enemies had withstood them, for the LORD had given all their enemies into their hands' (21:43-45). By contrast, and juxtaposed with this in the very same book, is the frank admission that the conquest was only partially successful and that the Israelites were unable to conquer significant parts of the land. Where this was the case, the Canaanites were 'a snare and a trap for you, a scourge on your sides, and thorns in your eyes' (23:13 also Numbers 33:55). The conclusion lies at hand that we have two separate perspectives at work here, brought together by an editor. One account is the propaganda version, which, in a triumphalist way, seeks to exalt Israel and Israel's God. The other is the acknowledgement of reality: the Canaanites were not fully overcome (Joshua 13:13, then also Judges 1:19, 21, etc). A retrospective explanation of this is given in Exodus 23:29-30, 'I will not drive them out before you in one year, or the land would become desolate, and the wild animals would multiply against you. Little by little, I will drive them out before you until you have increased and possess the land'. At least we can give the editors credit for not smoothing out the narratives but letting them stand together with their conundrums intact. This is not the only place where this happens, and it bespeaks a respect for the sources. But once more, it leaves us with cognitive dissonance. That allows an entrée into my own proposal, one that will not be satisfactory to those who take a stricter view of biblical accuracy but one that is content to give scripture greater latitude.

I am concerned to see scripture in didactic terms: what are we meant to learn from it? True enough, I have also suggested that there are parts that are probably there for our amusement, but we can still learn from them. When I first became a Bible reader, and being wholly ignorant of what was there, I started to read the text from the beginning and quickly was confronted by battles, conflict, and war. Strangely enough, I initially found no great moral problem with this. I was reading the text 'non-inferentially', without giving thought to the human cost involved. Armies like those of Pharoah were tropes or figures, symbols of hostility towards God rather than real persons. The same might be considered in relation to another seemingly violent text, the Book of Revelation. It was only later that I began to worry, say, about the hosts drowned in the waters of the Reed Sea and to ask myself the moral questions. I was reading the Bible devotionally. When it came to the Amalekites, the Amorites, and their various kin, these were representative of those parts of my own life that needed to be overcome and eradicated, the parts that had not been dealt with. I was doing the typical evangelical thing: reading the text in a highly individualised, spiritualised form and seeking to learn what it might mean *for me*. As a more educated Bible reader I began to question this and to ask larger questions about the purposes of God in history and their social embodiment in Israel and church. However, in a further turn I have come to see that my first readings, though needing qualification, were not entirely misguided: there is the challenge to be a holy person amid a holy community. And there is a place for metaphor.

There is no doubt that the biblical accounts of Israel's wars in the early chapters of the Old Testament come to us in a highly edited form. To state the obvious, whereas the events of the conquest of Canaan took place somewhere in the region of 1200 BC, the accounts as we have them derive in all probability from the seventh century BC. Caution is required since the traditions will all have had a pre-history in oral or recorded form before being finally edited. In the reign of King Josiah (r.640-609BC), one of the few godly and reforming kings Israel produced, part of his reforms involved the 'Deuteronomic reform' by which crucial Hebrew scriptures were compiled and edited. Even the historical books of the Old Testament were regarded as 'prophetic' in nature – they had, and have, an overriding concern to warn, teach and guide the people of Israel. Josiah's intent was to restore religious purity to Israel and to rid it of the contamination derived from the surrounding nations that had never been fully converted or overcome and exercised a corrupting influence on Israel's religious practice. We typically interpret the past with concern for the realities of the present. We might consider here how approaches to Britain's colonial and imperial history have shifted from the laudatory to the condemnatory within a short period of time. Similarly, when we read the Gospel of John, it seems clear that it was written with an awareness of the opposition the nascent Christian church experienced some of the time and in some places by established Jewish communities. The 'Jews' are presented in a poor, decidedly hostile and possibly unfair light; but 'unfair' in whose eyes? This is not to say that opposition to Jesus and his movement in his lifetime was an invention; but the writer (or writers) of John's Gospel had reason to record it and highlight it in the light of his (or their) own community's experience. I am proposing the conquest of Canaan was recounted some 500 years afterwards from the perspective of another agenda, that of radical reform by which the enduring influence of Canaanite religion was to be rooted out. As so often, Israel's experience is being made sense of retrospectively in the light of its belief in a sovereign God. By the time this history was being written, the nations to be eradicated had long ceased to exist either because they were absorbed into Israel (such as Uriah the Hittite, for instance) or had lost their identity. They no longer existed to be eradicated and, therefore, could safely be incorporated into the narrative, knowing that the action advocated could not, in fact, be carried out! But radical action in rooting out false religion from Israel's life was profoundly needed. It was necessary because Israel would shortly face the crisis of the Exile in Babylon in which they could either lose or establish their identity. It was through the crucible of that experience that Judaism, as we came to know it and as Jesus inherited it, received decisive formation. Whether this would have happened without Josiah's reforms and the new scriptural impetus is a matter of speculation.

I am not saying that the conquest of Canaan happened without violence. I am, however, saying that the way the conquest is scripturally portrayed as by God's command a root and branch destruction of a people, or peoples, is a religiously motivated reading of history intended to call the people of Israel to a radical return to faithfulness in eliminating the contamination of false religion. Here is its didactic value, for then and for now. It is not entirely different from the later challenge of Jesus, 'And if your right-hand causes you to sin, cut it off and throw it away; it is better for you to lose one of your members than for your whole body to go into hell (Gehenna)' (Mathew 5:30). Jesus surely did not intend this to be taken literally, and very few Christians have ever taken it so. But he did intend radical action in overcoming sin. My proposal offers a way of retrieving problematic scriptures and giving them devotional value. It does not remove all offence since even using the language employed is risky, especially when we are aware of genocide. But the same is true of what Jesus taught in that, even if self-mutilation is never what he intended, it could be taken that way by the foolish and unwise reader.

Archaeology, both relating to biblical times and British history, is far from fully reliable. But it is worth pointing out that archaeological deposits for the time of the conquest are not suggestive of wholesale slaughter and destruction but rather of a gradual process of settlement in the land. This is rather akin to more recent readings of the Saxon settlement of England which tend to qualify the idea of violent seizing of the land with that of a gradual process of co-existence. This does not make for such a good story to tell in developing the national 'myth'. Perhaps the same was true for Israel. It is tempting to speculate that the triumphalist account of the conquest in Joshua was the 'propaganda' version or even the historian's retrospective account of 'what should have happened' in the light of subsequent syncretism, whereas the more measured alternative was the honest recognition of what did happen. There are ideological readings of the past at work here, but that always happens in writing history. Objectivity is hard to achieve. What I have set out here will no doubt be thought either idiosyncratic or just plain wrong by both sceptics who find Israel's history morally compromised and believers who are more inclined to take it at face value. I do not conceal the fact that it requires a more complex attitude to scripture than inerrantists, for example, could tolerate. Wrestling with the Bible was never intended to be straightforward. Even so, I hold by my principles of refusing to consider myself superior to scripture, of always wishing to learn humbly from even the problematic parts, and of believing that moderate-higher criticism can enable rather than obstruct our capacity to hear what the Word of God happens to be. The biblical call is to the purity of life and wholehearted adherence to the God of Israel, who is also the Father of our Lord Jesus Christ.

For all that the Christian church has played its major part in preserving, transmitting, and interpreting scripture so that the memory of Jesus Christ remains luminous from generation to generation, it is wrong to imagine that the church 'possesses' those scriptures. The Bible belongs to the world, and it comes as a surprise when Christians encounter those outside its circles who derive inspiration and wisdom from it. For Jewish believers, the Bible is what Christians call the Old Testament, a designation that emphasises its ancient origins, not its lack of importance. The Old lives in the New. Jewish critics fault the Christian use of the Old as taking texts out of context and finding references to Christ where they are not intended. It must be agreed that Christian use of the Old Testament is not straightforward. It proceeds along the lines of believers in Jesus finding multiple echoes of him, his work and his destiny within the texts they knew. Sometimes, the reasoning is difficult to follow as, for instance, in Paul's arguments in Galatians or the exegesis around Melchizedek in Hebrews. Yet the methods used do resemble characteristic Jewish and rabbinic forms of argument and make sense in that context. I am left agreeing with the conclusions without always being fully convinced about the ways of getting there!

It is accurate to say that the New Testament is saturated by the Old, with some 283 direct quotations and thousands of indirect allusions. The ways in which Christians and Jews variously order their Bibles indicates how the two communities diverge in its interpretation. For Jews, that order is Torah (Law or Teaching}, Nevi'im (Prophets), and Ketuvim (Writings) designated in the word 'Tanakh', and the divisions differ in importance. For divine revelation, Jews traditionally emphasise the Torah in their liturgical readings while also giving place to reading the prophets. They look to the Writings as 'revelatory insight' rather than primary revelation. Significantly, when so ordered, the last book of the Tanakh is 2 Chronicles whose final chapter anticipates the return from exile under Cyrus. For Jews, therefore, the return to Zion, going home to one's roots, where they may live lives ordered by God, is the heart of their religion. By contrast, Christians order the Old Testament so that its final book is Malachi. This book looks forward to the Lord who was to come and who would take the story further. The Old Testament needed to be fulfilled by a coming messenger of God, and for Christians, that fulfilment was perceived in Christ and his church. The Old Testament is, therefore, interpreted in this light through a schema of creation, fall, election, redemption, extension, and the expectation of consummation. There is certainly a parting of the ways here, even while there is much that is shared. Jewish critics are right to point out that traditional Christian readings of scripture do not always sit easily with the Old Testament texts. Inspiration is not as linear as Christians imagine. If they happen to believe that all parts of the Bible fit together coherently and present a systematically neat understanding of God at work, they will be disillusioned. Progress in Biblical revelation is given in narratives interspersed with statements about the God of Israel such that a picture emerges of who this God must be. God's name, YHWH, 'I Am Who I AM' or 'I Will Be Who I Will Be', suggests that who God is will be known through God's unfolding actions. There are multiple images and they do not always easily slot together. The narratives are dialectical as well as didactical and require responsible interpretation. Christians do this in the belief that the light shines brightest in the face of Jesus Christ, the Son of the Father known in the Holy Spirit. From the beginning they have been concerned to root their understanding in what has gone before, to yield insights and apply them to Christ in creative ways, and at the same time to lend them legitimation. The Old Testament has prepared the way for

Christ and leant the categories by which he may be understood. Christians borrow them to illuminate him. He 'sublates' them, and they become incorporated into the Christian theological understanding. At this point, Jews and Christians certainly diverge but hopefully agree to do so.

Some significant principles to guide our work of biblical interpretation and to avoid abuse should be understood. The Bible is complex and needs to be indwelt patiently and humbly. We should never use its contents as a weapon against other people. It is to be interpreted in love. Its primary function is to bring our own lives under judgement, to correct us and teach us how we should live (2 Timothy 3:16). Its authority consists in its capacity to shape our understanding and behaviour, to bring us into meaningful encounters with God. It is wisdom literature that imparts the mind of Christ to the humble. This means we should interpret the Bible with a hermeneutic of trust. Howsoever we should question it, and it allows us to do that abundantly, we are persuaded that beyond the much-vaunted 'hermeneutic of suspicion,' the voice of God is to be trusted - only we need to hear it clearly. To trust, we add the virtue of love, and only so will we hear that voice correctly. The outcome of our study is love for God, love for friends and neighbours, love for 'others' and even love for enemies. Without these qualities, we are unable to do justice to holy scripture. 'And now faith, hope, and love abide these three; and the greatest of these is love' (1 Corinthians 13:13).

Postlude

Thinking back on what I have written, there are topics I have not covered. I have focussed instead on subjects that have been of concern to me at this stage of my life, and they are at the centre of the living evangelical faith I embrace. To bring my thoughts to a conclusion, I choose to summarise that faith and the generous and orthodox theology that undergirds it by reproducing the hymn *I cannot tell*. I find its every word meaningful. I love the Irish traditional melody, *Londonderry Air,* to which it is normally sung. I have great admiration for its author, William Young Fullerton (1857-1932), Irish evangelist and Baptist minister, former President of the Baptist Union of Great Britain and Home Secretary of the Baptist Missionary Society. And the hymn's Christ-centred, universally hopeful, evangelically humanist, and passionate spirituality accord, I think, with my own. In addition, Fullerton was a graduate of Spurgeon's College, a friend and mentee of Spurgeon himself, and one of his later biographers. All these things connect with me very positively. I offer it as a last word to all that has gone before.

How My Mind Has Changed (or not) - A Theological Memoir

I cannot tell why he, whom angels worship,

should set his love upon the sons of men,

or why, as shepherd, he should seek the wanderers,

to bring them back, they know not how or when.

But this I know, that he was born of Mary,

when Bethlehem's manger was his only home,

and that he lived at Nazareth and laboured,

and so the Saviour, Saviour of the world, is come.

I cannot tell how silently he suffered,

as with his peace he graced this place of tears,

or how his heart upon the cross was broken,

the crown of pain to three and thirty years.

But this I know, he heals the broken-hearted,

and stays our sin, and calms our lurking fear,

and lifts the burden from the heavy-laden,

for yet the Saviour, Saviour of the world, is here.

Nigel G. Wright

I cannot tell how he will win the nations,
how he will claim his earthly heritage,
how satisfy the needs and aspirations
of east and west, of sinner and of sage.
But this I know, all flesh shall see his glory,
and he will reap the harvest he has sown,
and some glad day his sun shall shine in splendour
when he the Saviour, Saviour of the world, is known.

I cannot tell how all the lands shall worship.
when at his bidding, every storm is stilled,
or who can say how great the jubilation
when every human heart with love is filled.
But this I know, the skies will thrill with rapture,
and myriad, myriad human voices sing,
and earth to heaven, and heaven to earth, will answer,
at last the Saviour, Saviour of the world, is King!

(Baptist Praise and Worship, No. 381)

Publications

- *You are my God: A Study Guide to the Passover Psalms* (London: Bible Society, 1982).

- *Moving On: The Church* (London: Scripture Union, 1983) (also published in Arabic and in Latvian as *Draudze* [Latvia: 1984]).

- *The Radical Kingdom: Restoration in Theory and Practice* (Eastbourne: Kingsway, 1986).

- *The Fair Face of Evil: Putting the Power of Darkness in its Place* (Basingstoke: Marshall-Pickering, 1988).

- *The Satan Syndrome: Putting the Power of Darkness in its Place* (Grand Rapids: Zondervan, 1990). Also published in Korean by Seoul Theological University Press, Seoul, 2012.

- *A Theology of Mission* (Didcot: Baptist Union, 1990).

- *Mission i Morgens-dagens Menighed* (Copenhagen: Baptist Union of Denmark, 1992).

- *Lord and Giver of Life: An Introduction to the Person and Work of the Holy Spirit* (Didcot: Baptist Union, 1990).

- *Challenge to Change: A Radical Agenda for Baptists* (Eastbourne: Kingsway, 1991).

- *Charismatic Renewal: The Search for a Theology* (London: SPCK, 1993) [first edition with T. A. Smail and Andrew Walker]

- *The Love of Power and the Power of Love* (Minneapolis: Bethany House, 1994) [with T. A. Smail and Andrew Walker]

- *Makt och Lärjungskap: En frikyrklig teologi om förhallandet fösamling-samhälle* (Orebro: Orebro Missionskolas Skriftserie Nr 8, 1993).

- *Charismatic Renewal: The Search for a Theology* (London: SPCK, 1995) [second, enlarged edition with T. A. Smail and Andrew Walker].

- *The Radical Evangelical: Seeking a Place to Stand* (London: SPCK, 1996).

- *Power and Discipleship: Towards a Baptist Theology of the State* (Oxford: Whitley Publications, 1996).

- *Disavowing Constantine: Mission, Church and the Social Order in the Theologies of John Howard Yoder and Jürgen Moltmann* Biblical and Theological Monograph Series (Carlisle: Paternoster Press, 2000).

- *New Baptists, New Agenda* (Carlisle: Paternoster, 2002).

- *A Theology of the Dark Side: Putting the Power of Evil in its Place* (Carlisle: Paternoster, 2003).

- *A Theology of the Dark Side: Putting the Power of Evil in its Place* (Downers Grove, Il.: IVP, 2003).

- *Free Church, Free State: The Positive Baptist Vision* (Carlisle: Paternoster, 2005).

- *God on the Inside: The Holy Spirit in Holy Scripture* (Oxford: Bible Reading Fellowship, 2006).

- *Disavowing Constantine: Mission, Church and the Social Order in the Theologies of John Howard Yoder and Jürgen Moltmann* Biblical and Theological Monograph Series (Reprint: Eugene, Oregon: Wipf and Stock, 2006).

- *Participating without Possessing: The Public and the Private in Christian Discipleship* (Horley: Industrial Christian Fellowship, 2007).

- *Baptist Basics* (Didcot: Baptist Union of Great Britain, 2009).

- *The Real Godsend: Preaching the Birth Narratives in Matthew and Luke* (Oxford: BRF, 2009).

- *Jesus Christ – the Alpha and the Omega* (Oxford: BRF, 2010).

- *A Theology of the Dark Side: Putting the Power of Evil in its Place* (Reprint: Eugene, Or.: Wipf and Stock, 2010).

- *Free Church, Free State: The Positive Baptist Vision* (Reprint: Eugene, Or.: Wipf and Stock, 2012.)

- Editor: *Truth that Never Dies: The Dr G. R. Beasley-Murray Memorial Lectures 2002-2012* (Eugene, Or.: Wipf and Stock, 2014).

- Editor: *Truth that Never Dies: The Dr G. R. Beasley-Murray Memorial Lectures 2002-2012* (Edinburgh: James Clarke, 2015).

- *Vital Truth: The Convictions of the Christian Community* (Eugene, Or.: Cascade, 2015).

- *Vital Truth: Convictions of the Christian Community* (Cambridge: Lutterworth Press, 2016)

- *The Radical Evangelical: Seeking a Place to Stand* (Reprint: Eugene, Or.: Wipf and Stock, 2016).

- *How to be a Church Minister* (Oxford: BRF, 2018)

- *Sut Mae Bod Yn Weinidog Eglwys* (Cyhoeddwyd Gair: Presbyterian Church of Wales, 2019).

Articles and Contributions to Books:

- 'Worship: The Baptist Experience', *Liturgy,* Vol 4 No 2 (1980).

- 'Ansdell Baptist Church: A Profile', *Mainstream Newsletter*, No 6 (January, 1981).

- 'Gleanings from the North West', *Mainstream Newsletter*, No 9 (January, 1982).

- 'Who's Radical Now? A Review Article', *Mainstream Newsletter*, No 9 (January, 1982).

- 'Leadership in the Believers' Church', in Keith Hodson, ed., *The Believers' Church: An introduction to Radical Discipleship Themes* (Heywod: Heywood Bible College Publications, 1983)

- 'Doctrines, Principles and Values', *Mainstream Newsletter*, No 15 (January, 1984).

- 'Church Membership Re-evaluated', *Mainstream Newsletter*, No 20 (September, 1985).

- 'Church Planting - One Church's Experience', *Church Growth Digest* (Autumn 1986).

- 'The Baptist Way of Being the Church' in G. R. Beasley-Murray, ed., *A Perspective on Baptist Identity* (Mainstream, 1987).

- 'Weighing up Wimber', *Renewal* (January, 1989).

- 'Asking the Forbidden Questions', *Renewal* (February, 1989).

- 'The Case for Wimber Revisionism', *Renewal* (March,1989) (The above three articles were also printed in Edward England, ed., *Living in the Light of Pentecost* (Crowborough: Highland, 1990).

- Monthly column in Renewal January-December 1990.

- 'An Agenda for Baptist Christians', *Mainstream Newsletter*, No 35 (January, 1990).

- 'Born Again for Labour Victory', *The Guardian* (May 21, 1990).

- 'Time to Disestablish', *The Guardian* (October 8, 1990).

- 'Restorationism and the "house church" movement', *Themelios* Vol 16 No 2 (January/February 1991).

- Monthly column *Baptist Times* 1991-1993.

- 'Mission, the Shape of the Church and Ecumenism', in Paul Beasley-Murray, ed., *Mission to the World: Essays to celebrate the 50th anniversary of the Ordination of George Raymond Beasley-Murray to the Christian Ministry* (London: Baptist Historical Society, 1991).

- 'The Kansas City Prophets: An Assessment', *Themelios* Vol 17 No 1 1992.

- 'Evangelism and Religious Liberty', *Planting Papers* (Summer/Autumn 1992).

- 'Catching the Bellrope', *Anabaptism Today*, Issue 1 (November, 1992).

- 'Radical Dissent' in D. J. Tidball, ed., *The Baptist Basics Series* (Didcot: Baptist Union of Great Britain 1993).

- '"Revelation Knowledge" and Knowledge of Revelation: The Faith Movement and the Question of Heresy', *Journal of Pentecostal Studies* Vol 5 (1994) [with T. A. Smail and Andrew Walker].

- '"Koinonia" and Baptist Ecclesiology: Self-Critical Reflections from Historical and Systematic Perspectives', *Baptist Quarterly* Vol 35 No 8 (October, 1994).

- 'The Church and "God's Servant" The State', *Anabaptism Today* (Issue 7, October, 1994).

- 'The Powers and God's Providential Rule', *Anabaptism Today* (Issue 8, February, 1995).

- 'Respectful and Subversive: Christians in the Political Realm', *Anabaptism Today* (Issue 9, June, 1995).

- 'The Theology of Religious Liberty', *Baptist Ministers' Journal* Vol 249 (January, 1995).

- 'The Influence of the Charismatic Movement on European Baptist Life and Mission', *Journal of the European Pentecostal Theological Association*, Vol 13 (1995).

- 'Disestablishment: A Contemporary View from the Free Churches', *Anvil,* Vol 12 No 2 (1995).

- '"The Sword": An Example of Anabaptist Diversity', *Baptist Quarterly* Vol 36 No. 6 (April, 1996).

- 'Baptist and Anabaptist Attitudes to the State', *Baptist Quarterly*, Vol 36 No. 7 (July, 1996).

- Chapter 4 in John Gunstone, ed., *Meeting John Wimber* (Crowborough: Monarch, 1996).

- 'The Charismatic Theology of Thomas A. Smail', *Journal of the European Pentecostal Theological Association*, Vol 16 (1996).

- 'Charismatic Interpretations of the Demonic', in A. N. S. Lane, ed., *The Unseen World: Christian Reflections on Angels, Demons and the Heavenly Realm* (Carlisle: Paternoster, 1996).

- 'On Disentangling Inderjit Bhogal: A Response Article', *Joppa Bulletin*, February 1997.

- 'Suffering', in Ernest Lucas, ed., *Christian Healing: What Can We Believe?* (London: Lynx, 1997) [with Sheila Smith].

- 'The State We're In', *Christianity* (May, 1997)

- 'Re-imagining Evangelicalism', in Graham Cray et al, *The Post-Evangelical Debate* (London: Triangle, 1997).

- 'The Nature and Variety of the "House Church Movement"', in Stephen Hunt, Malcolm Hamilton and Tony Walter, eds, *Charismatic Christianity: Sociological Perspectives* (London: Macmillan, 1997).

- 'A Baptist Perspective', in David Pytches, ed., *John Wimber: His Influence and Legacy* (Guildford: Eagle, 1998).

- 'Signs and Wonders', *Chrism: The St Raphael Quarterly* Vol. 36 No 2 (Summer, 1999).

- 'Public Truth or Private Option? Gospel and Religious Liberty in a Multi-faith Society in the Light of the Resurrection', *Joppa Occasional Paper* (September, 1999).

- 'Preaching on Holy War', *Preaching Today* Volume 43, No 2 (Summer, 2000).

- 'Inclusive Representation: Towards a Doctrine of Christian Ministry', *Baptist Quarterly*, Vol 39 No. 4 (October, 2001).

- 'Covenant and Covenanting', *The Baptist Quarterly*, Vol 39 No 6 (April, 2002).

- 'Still a Case for Baptist Bishops', in *Talk: The Mainstream Magazine* (Autumn, 2002)

- 'A point where the shoe might pinch?', in *Talk: The Mainstream Magazine* (Spring, 2003)

- "Does Revival Deaden or Quicken the Church?', in Andrew Walker and Kristin Aune, eds., *On Revival: Lessons for Today's Church* (Carlisle: Paternoster, 2003).

- 'Religious Abuse: The precarious potential of religious believing', in *Journal of European Baptist Studies,* Vol. 3 No. 2 (January, 2003).

- 'Re-inventing Christendom', *Anabaptism Today* 33 (June, 2003).

- 'Baptists and Academic Freedom', *Baptist History and Heritage*, Vol 39 No 1 (Winter, 2004).

- 'To tolerate is not to approve', *Talk: The Mainstream Magazine* (Spring, 2004)

- 'Disestablishment: Loss for the Church or for the Country?': The Liddon Lecture for 2003, *Journal of European Baptist Studies*, Vol 4 No 3 (May, 2004).

- 'The Case for Translocal Ministry', in Stuart Murray Williams, ed., *Translocal Ministry: Equipping the Churches for Mission* (Didcot: Baptist Union of Great Britain, 2004).

- 'Looking for a Right Wing', *Talk: The Mainstream Magazine* Vol 4 Issue 2 (Autumn, 2004).

- 'The Petrine Ministry: Baptist Reflections', *Pro Ecclesia: A Journal of Catholic and Evangelical Theology'*, Vol XIII No 4 (Fall, 2004).

- 'On Returning to a Theme', *Talk: The Mainstream Magazine* Vol 4 Issue 2 (Spring, 2005)

- 'A Dissenting Perspective on Establishment', in *Crucible* (April/June, 2005)

- Review article, John Howard Yoder, *The Jewish-Christian Schism Revisited*, eds, Michael G. Cartwright and Peter Ochs (London: SCM Press, 2003) in *Ecclesiology* Vol 2 No 3 (2006).

- 'A View from One of the Free Churches', in R. M. Morris, ed., *Church and State: Some Reflections on Church Establishment in England* (London: University College, 2008).

- 'Two Versions of the Reality and Origin of Evil', in *The Bible in Transmission*, Summer, 2008.

- 'Spirituality as Discipleship: the Anabaptist Heritage', in Paul S. Fiddes, ed., *Under the Rule of Christ: Dimensions of Baptist Spirituality* (Macon, Ga.: Smyth and Helwys, 2008).

- 'Jumala riik ja kogudus' in Toivo Pilli, ed., *Jumala Riik Ja Gogudus* (Tartu: Kõrgem Usuteaduslik Seminar, 2008)

- 'Sind Baptistgemeinden autonom?', in *Theologishes Gespräch: Freikirchliche Beiträge zur Theologie*, 2009 Beiheft 10

- Articles on 'Apostles', 'Charismatics', 'Fruits/Gifts of the Spirit', 'Glossolalia', 'Pneumatology', 'National Churches', 'Pentecost', 'Prophecy', 'Prosperity Theology' in John H. Y. Briggs, ed., *A Dictionary of Baptist Life and Thought'* (Carlisle: Paternoster, 2009)

- 'Government as an Ambiguous Power' in Nick Spencer and Jonathan Chaplin, eds, *God and Government* (London: SPCK/Theos, 2009).

- Review of Steven R. Harmon, *Towards Baptist Catholicity: Essays on Tradition and the Baptist Vision* (Carlisle: Paternoster, 2006) in *Ecclesiology* Vol 5 No 3 (2009).

- Review of Brian Haymes, Ruth Gouldbourne and Anthony R. Cross, *On Being the Chuch: Revisioning Baptist Identity: Studies in Baptist History and Thought* Volume 21 (Carlisle: Paternoster, 2008) in *Baptist Quarterly* Volume 43 October 2009.

- 'Baptist Christians: Repentant and Unrepentant', in David J. Cohen and Michael Parsons, eds, *Beyond 400: Exploring Baptist Futures* (Eugene, Oregon: Pickwick Publications, 2010).

- 'Humane Religion: Evangelical Faith, Baptist Identity and Secular Liberalism' in David J. Cohen and Michael Parsons, eds, *Beyond 400: Exploring Baptist Futures* (Eugene, Oregon: Pickwick Publications, 2010).

- With Brian Harris, 'Summary Reflections on Beyond 400', in David J. Cohen and Michael Parsons, eds., *Beyond 400: Exploring Baptist Futures* (Eugene, Oregon: Pickwick Publications, 2010).

- 'Bearer of our Sins: Atonement Theology after Steve Chalke', in Anthony R. Cross and Ruth Gouldbourne, eds., *Questions of Identity: Studies in Honour of Brian Haymes* (Oxford: Regent's Park College, 2011).

- 'The Goodness, Wisdom and Patience of the Living God', *Faith and Thought* (April, 2011) No 50.

- 'Deliverance and Exorcism in Theological Perspective 1: Is there any substance to evil?', in William K. Kay and Robin Parry, eds, *Exorcism and Deliverance: Multi-Disciplinary Studies* (Milton Keynes: Paternoster, 2011).

- 'Predestination and Perseverance in the early theology of Jürgen Moltmann', *Evangelical Quarterly*, Vol. LXXXIII No 4 (October 2011).

- 'Church and State in the UK from a Free Church perspective' in *Journal of the Royal Army Chaplains' Department*, Volume 50 (2011).

- 'Universalism in the theology of Jürgen Moltmann', *Evangelical Quarterly*, Vol. LXXXIV, No 1 (January 2012).

- 'Election and Predestination in Baptist Confessions of the Seventeenth Century' in Pieter J. Lalleman, Peter J. Morden and Anthony R. Cross (eds), *Grounded in Grace: Essays to Honour Ian M. Randall* (London: Spurgeon's College, 2013).

- *BRF Guidelines: Bible study for today's ministry and mission* (September-December 2013): Matthew 1-2.

- 'A Kinder, Gentler Damnation?' in Christopher M. Date, Gregory G. Stump, Joshua W. Anderson, (eds), *Rethinking Hell: Readings in Evangelical Conditionalism* (Eugene, Or.: Wipf and Stock, 2014).

- *BRF Guidelines: Bible study for today's ministry and mission* (January-April 2014): Matthew 3-6.

- *BRF Guidelines: Bible study for today's ministry and mission* (May-August 2014): Matthew 7-10.

- *BRF Guidelines: Bible study for today's ministry and mission* (September-December 2014): Matthew 11-14

- Foreword to Stephen Jonathan, *Grace Beyond the Grave: Is Salvation Possible in the Afterlife?* (Eugene, Or.: Wipf and Stock, 2014).

- 'Sustaining Evangelical Identity: Faithfulness and Freedom in Denominational Life', in Nigel G. Wright, ed., *Truth that Never Dies: The Dr G. R. Beasley-Murray Memorial Lectures 2002-2012* (Eugene, Or.: Wipf and Stock, 2014).

- 'The "Three-fold Order" in a Radical Protestant Perspective', in Anthony Clarke, ed., *For the Sake of the Church: Essays in Honour of Paul S. Fiddes* (Oxford: Regent's Park College, 2014).

- 'Encounters with the Son of Man: Luke 17:11-20:19', in *Encounter with God* (Bletchley: Scripture Union, 2015).

- 'Christianity and Secularism: Prospects and Possibilities', FORB Consultation European Baptist Federation, 27-28 September 2015, Sofia, Bulgaria. www.ebf.org/.../Wright_Christianity%20and%20Secularism_FORBsep2015_Sofia.pdf.

- Articles 'Exorcism' and 'Devils and Demons', in Martin Davie et al, eds., *New Dictionary of Theology: Historical and Systematic* (London: Inter-Varsity Press, 2016).

- 'Biblical Perspectives on Nationhood', *Mission Catalyst: Intelligent comment on faith and culture*, Issue 3 2016.

- Foreword to Michael J. Hooton, *The Extended Family: Why are there so many different Churches?* (Eugene, Or.: Resource Publications, 2016)

- *BRF Guidelines: Bible study for today's ministry and mission* (January-April 2017): Matthew 15-18.

- 'Baptists and Leadership', *Baptists Together* (Spring, 2017)

- '"The Ground on which we dare to build"': Putting Calvinism to work', in Myra Blyth and Andy Goodliff, eds, *Gathering Disciples: Essays in honor of Christopher J. Ellis* (Eugene, Or.: Pickwick Publications, 2017).

- 'Living the Transformed Life: Romans 12-16' in *Encounter with God* (Bletchley: Scripture Union, 2017).

- 'Preaching on Genocide: Reflections on some "alien" texts', in *Ministry Today UK,* Edition 70 (Summer 2017).

- *BRF Guidelines: Bible study for today's ministry and mission* (September-December 2017): Matthew 24-28.

- Foreword to Daniel Kirkpatrick, *Monergism or Synergism: Is salvation cooperative or the work of God alone* (Eugene, Or.: Pickwick Publications, 2018).

- Foreword to Ian M. Randall, A *Christian Peace Experiment: The Bruderhof Community in Britain 1933-1942* (Eugene, Or.: Cascade, 2018).

- 'Chiese Battiste in Europa: Identità in movimento: Relazione presentata sabato 7 aprile 2018 al convegno"Identità Battista in movimento"', Roma. *https://www.ucebi.it/identita-battista-in-movimento.html.*

- *'Preaching the Birth Narratives in Matthew and Luke', Word and Worship: Quarterly Publication of New Zealand Lay Preachers, Series 17:1 (Summer, 2018/2019).*

- 'Easter: Constructing Resurrection Narratives', in Andy Goodliff and Paul Goodliff, eds. *Rhythms of Faithfulness: Essays in Honor of John E. Colwell*, (Eugene, Or.: Pickwick Publications, 2018).

- 'The Cost of Discipleship: Luke 9:18 – 13:9', in *Encounter with God* (Bletchley: Scripture Union, 2019).

- 'Fellowship: Bible Readings and Reflections', in Andrew Roberts, ed., *Holy Habits: Fellowship* (BRF: Abingdon: 2019).

- *BRF Guidelines: Bible study for today's ministry and mission* (January-April 2020): 'Jesus and the Way to the Cross'.

- 'Are Baptist Churches Autonomous?', *American Baptist Quarterly*, Volume XXXVIII (Spring 2020) Number 1.

- 'Christianity and Secularism: Prospects and Possibilities', *Journal of European Baptist Studies*, No 01 Spring 2020

- 'A History of Salvation: Romans 1-8', *Encounter with God*, January-March 2021. (Bletchley: Scripture Union, 2021).

- *BRF Guidelines: Bible study for today's ministry and mission* (May-August 2021): '1 Corinthians'.

- 'Kirigad ja ühiskondlik kord: baptislik vaatenuurk', in *Usuteaduslik Ajakiri: Akadeemilise Teoloogia Seltsi väljaanne* 1/2021 (79) [*Estonian Journal of Theology*]

- '2 Corinthians' Psalms 49, 50, 51' in *Encounter with God* April-June 2022 (Bletchley: Scripture Union, 2022).

- *BRF Guidelines: Bible study for today's ministry and mission* (May-Aug 2022), 'The Holy Trinity'.

- 'Theology and Ministerial Formation in the Bristol and Baptist Traditions, *Journal of Baptist Theology in Context*, Issue 5 (2022), (jbtc.org.uk)

- Afterword to Seidel Abel Boanerges and John Woods, editors, *Well Done, Good and Faithful Servant: Essays in Honour of Stephen I. Wright, Reflections on Effective Christian Ministry* (2024).

www.ingramcontent.com/pod-product-compliance
Lightning Source LLC
Chambersburg PA
CBHW070455120526
44590CB00013B/655